Port Security and Preman Organizations
in Indonesia

The **ISEAS – Yusof Ishak Institute** (formerly Institute of Southeast Asian Studies) is an autonomous organization established in 1968. It is a regional centre dedicated to the study of sociopolitical, security, and economic trends and developments in Southeast Asia and its wider geostrategic and economic environment. The Institute's research programmes are grouped under Regional Economic Studies (RES), Regional Strategic and Political Studies (RSPS), and Regional Social and Cultural Studies (RSCS). The Institute is also home to the ASEAN Studies Centre (ASC), the Singapore APEC Study Centre, and the Temasek History Research Centre (THRC).

ISEAS Publishing, an established academic press, has issued more than 2,000 books and journals. It is the largest scholarly publisher of research about Southeast Asia from within the region. ISEAS Publishing works with many other academic and trade publishers and distributors to disseminate important research and analyses from and about Southeast Asia to the rest of the world.

SENIA FEBRICA

Port Security and Preman Organizations in Indonesia

First published in Singapore in 2023 by
ISEAS Publishing
30 Heng Mui Keng Terrace
Singapore 119614

Email: publish@iseas.edu.sg
Website: bookshop.iseas.edu.sg

All rights reserved. No part of this publication may be reproduced, stored in a retrieval system, or transmitted in any form or by any means, electronic, mechanical, photocopying, recording or otherwise, without the prior permission of the ISEAS – Yusof Ishak Institute.

© 2023 ISEAS – Yusof Ishak Institute, Singapore

The responsibility for facts and opinions in this publication rests exclusively with the author and his interpretations do not necessarily reflect the views or the policy of the publisher or its supporters.

ISEAS Library Cataloguing-in-Publication Data

Name(s): Febrica, Senia, author.
Title: Port security and preman organizations in Indonesia / Senia Febrica, author.
Description: Singapore : ISEAS-Yusof Ishak Institute, 2023. | Includes bibliographical references and index.
Identifiers: ISBN 9789815011883 (paperback) | ISBN 9789815011890 (PDF) | ISBN 9789815104516 (epub)
Subjects: LCSH: Private security services—Indonesia. | Ports—Security measures—Indonesia. | Security sector—Indonesia. | Gangsters—Indonesia.
Classification: LCC HV8291 I5F28

Cover design by Refine Define Pte Ltd
Index compiled by Raffaie Bin Nahar
Typeset by Stephen Logan
Printed in Singapore by Mainland Press Pte Ltd

To Robert

Contents

List of Figures and Table	vii
Foreword	xi
Acknowledgements	xiii
List of Abbreviations	xv
Introduction	1
1. International and Domestic Politics	21
2. Jakarta: *Preman* Organizations and Port Security in the Capital City	49
3. *Preman* Organizations in North Sulawesi: To Guard *Tanah Toar Lumimuut*	77
4. Riau Islands: *Preman* Organizations in the Cross-Border Region	106
Conclusion	134
Index	168
About the Author	176

Figures and Table

Figures

1.	Map of Indonesia	2
2.	Indonesian Maritime Security Agency Budget, 2005–23 (million USD)	25
3.	Indonesian Ministry of Defence Expenditure for Maritime Security (percentage of total Ministry of Defence budget)	26
4.	Indonesian Anti-Terrorism Agency's Expenditure, 2013–23 (million USD)	37
5.	Locations of FBR Posts and the Secretariat Office around Tanjung Priok Port, Marunda Port and Surrounding Areas	66
6.	Convoy of Front Pembela Islam Members Heading to Central Jakarta to Take Part in Protests against Basuki Tjahja Purnama on 14 October 2016	70
7.	Locations of FBR Guard Posts around Muara Baru Port, Samudera Fishing Port	71
8.	Brigade Manguni	81
9.	Location of Brigade Manguni Secretariat Office near Bitung Container Port and Bitung Passenger Port	86

10. Small Ports in Batam and Tanjung Pinang — 107
11. Locations of Pemuda Pancasila and Ikatan Pemuda Karya Posts and Headquarters near Batu Ampar Port, Batam — 108
12. *Preman* and Youth Organizations in Batam — 109
13. Locations of *Preman* and Youth Organizations Posts around Tanjung Pinang Port and Tanjung Unggat Port — 110
14. Location of Pemuda Pancasila Office near Bulang Linggi Speed Boat Port and Roro Tanjung Uban Port, Tanjung Pinang — 111

Table

1. Provincial Government Grants and Social Assistance to Civil Society Organizations — 64

Foreword

As a scholar who has conducted over four decades of research in Indonesian politics, I can attest that the *preman* organizations are still part of the country's political and security fabric. In the run up to the next Indonesian presidential elections in 2024, blaring sirens and convoys of *preman* organization members in camouflage attire, out in support of certain candidates, will continue to be a constant reminder of the presence of these organizations in Indonesian politics.

The need for this book is obvious: to provide much needed insight on the use of non-state security providers by a developing non-Western democracy such as Indonesia. It sheds new light on the uncivil components of civil society that have been overlooked by most scholars of politics and international relations, activists, and diplomats who are not trained in the specificity of Indonesian political dynamics.

In the midst of the complexity of civilian-military relations in Indonesia, Dr Senia Febrica has written a book that explores the niche area of the involvement of *preman* organizations in Indonesian security. The book has mapped comprehensively the participation of *preman* organizations in securing ports, particularly small ports, which are important points of societal interaction and nodes of transportation that are often forgotten. It covers areas that border the three key sea lanes of communications in Southeast Asia that overlap with Indonesia's waters, including the Sunda Strait, the Strait of Malacca and the Sulawesi Sea. By doing so, it provides a new and novel way to understand the complexity of the involvement of *preman* organizations in port and border security in Indonesia. This book effectively combines observation, document and newspaper analysis, and interviews with various stakeholders, including those who are leaders and active members of *preman* organizations.

Fundamentally, what I really like about this book is its ability to tell the stories that address the implications of the involvement of *preman* organizations in Indonesia's political and security sectors, which are certainly not trouble free. The book describes how "incidental" conflicts between *preman* organizations with government authorities such as the police or societal groups such as fishermen represent just a fraction of the price the Indonesian government and society pay for the involvement of *preman* organizations in the country's politics and security. As Indonesian democracy is maturing, this book has helped us to identify fruitful lines for further inquiry, including what role *preman* organizations have in exacerbating electoral violence, or the role of these organizations in port security in other parts of Indonesia. Recognizing the implications of the use of *preman* organizations is needed to enable Indonesia to transition to a fully functioning democracy.

Suzie Sudarman
Senior Lecturer, Department of International Relations,
and Director of American Studies, Universitas Indonesia
Interim Director, Indonesian Institute of Advanced International Studies

Acknowledgements

I have received enormous support from various people and institutions to complete this book. I am deeply indebted to Mba Suzie Sudarman for guidance and advice.

I thank the American Studies Center, Universitas Indonesia, for facilitating and hosting my fieldwork.

The Gerda Henkel Stiftung provided the post-doctoral scholarship as well as fieldwork and conference funding that made the completion of this book possible.

During my field trips in Jakarta, North Sulawesi and the Riau Islands, academics, government officials and various resource persons were willing to share their time, ideas and knowledge with me. I thank them for their invaluable cooperation and insights.

A special thanks to Om Edy and Pak Buang for their help during my field research in Manado and Bitung. I thank Sayed Fauzan for his tremendous support during my research in Tanjung Pinang. I thank my friends and colleagues in Indonesia and Scotland for your warm friendship.

My most profound debt is to my parents, Julien and Santje; my brother, Michael; and his wife, Nia. Thank you for your generous support, encouragement and delicious sustenance. I also thank Michael for his assistance in designing maps for this book.

Most of all, I thank my husband, Daniel, for his understanding and assistance in reading an early draft of this book, cooking, baking, organizing holidays, and doing most of the school runs to give me time to write. Thank you, Robert, for giving me joy and a welcome distraction. I am grateful for Judith and Phil for their helping hand with childcare-related matters and organizing family outings.

Abbreviations

AMJ	Aliansi Masyarakat Jakarta
ASEAN	Association of Southeast Asian Nations
BIMP-EAGA	Brunei–Indonesia–Malaysia–the Philippines East ASEAN Growth Area
BIN	Badan Intelijen Negara
BNPT	Badan Nasional Penanggulangan Terorisme
BP BATAM	Badan Pengusahaan Batam
BULOG	Badan Urusan Logistik
CSO	civil society organization
FBR	Forum Betawi Rempug
FKDM	Forum Kewaspadaan Dini Masyarakat
FKPPI	Forum Komunikasi Putra Putri Purnawirawan dan Putra Putri TNI Polri
FORKABI	Forum Komunikasi Anak Betawi
FPI	Front Pembela Islam
GMF	Global Maritime Fulcrum
IPK	Ikatan Pemuda Karya
ISIS	Islamic State of Iraq and Syria

ISPS	International Ship and Port Facility Security
IUU	illegal, unreported and unregulated
KODIM	Komando Distrik Militer
KOPASSUS	Komando Pasukan Khusus
KOTI	Komando Inti
MABES POLRI	Markas Besar Kepolisian Republik Indonesia
MABES TNI	Markas Besar Tentara Nasional Indonesia
MCS	monitoring, controlling and surveillance
MITA	Mitra Utama
MKGR	Musyawarah Kekeluargaan Gotong Royong
OKP	Organisasi Kepemudaan
OPM	Organisasi Papua Merdeka
PDIP	Partai Demokrasi Indonesia Perjuangan
PEMDA	Pemerintah Daerah
PERPAT	Persatuan Pemuda Tempatan
PKB	Partai Kebangkitan Bangsa
PKPI	Partai Keadilan dan Persatuan Indonesia
PMC	private military company
PP	Pemuda Pancasila
PPM	Pemuda Panca Marga
PPP	Partai Persatuan Pembangunan
PSA	port security advisory
RUU	Rancangan Undang-Undang
SATPOL PP	Satuan Polisi Pamong Praja
SIJORI	Singapore-Johor-Riau
SLOC	sea lanes of communications
TNI	Tentara Nasional Indonesia
UPC	urban poor community
UU	Undang-Undang

Introduction

Indonesia is the largest archipelagic state in the world, comprising 17,480 islands and with a maritime territory measuring close to six million square kilometres (Indonesian Ministry of Defence 2008, p. 145). Cross-border maritime activities have long shaped Indonesia's economic, social and political development. As an archipelagic country with 95,181 kilometres of coastline, Indonesia's national borders are primarily located at sea (Sekretariat Jenderal Departemen Kelautan dan Perikanan 2006, p. 58; Ford and Lyons 2013, p. 215). This book focuses on the importance of the notion of ports as borders (Sciascia 2013, pp. 164, 171). Ports signify a state's boundary where people and goods can exit or enter a country legally (Sciascia 2013, pp. 163–87).

Over ninety per cent of Indonesia's national and international trade is conducted across the country's vast maritime borders. It has a total of 141 international ports across the archipelago, which connect the country to the world economy. Despite the importance of port security for Indonesia, for a long time ports have been characterized as permeable and undefended areas. This situation changed after 9/11. Following the terrorist attacks on the United States in 2001, and the Bali bombings in 2002, which claimed the lives of 202 people, including 88 Australians, the Indonesian authorities began to reassess the security of its seaports and coastal areas (*Jakarta Post*, 7 August 2003).

FIGURE 1
Map of Indonesia

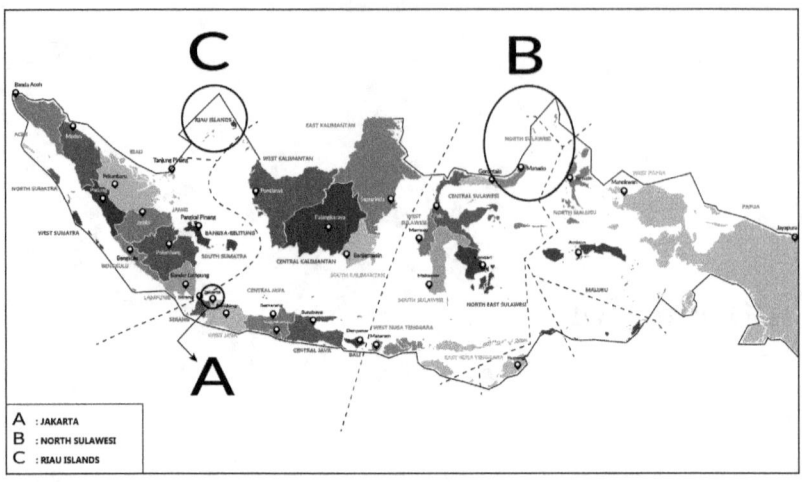

In the wake of the 9/11 attacks, Indonesia also faced mounting international pressure to improve the security of its ports. The security of Indonesian waters and ports is crucial for the international community because of their strategic geographical positions. Indonesia is located at the crossroads of busy maritime traffic between Europe and the Far East, between Australia and Asia, and between the Persian Gulf and Japan (Coutrier 1988, p 186). Three major sea lanes in Southeast Asia—the Straits of Malacca and Singapore, the Lombok Strait and the Sunda Strait—overlap with Indonesia's maritime jurisdiction (Djalal 2009, p. 63). In February 2008, the US Coast Guard issued port security advisories (PSAs) to Indonesian ports in view of unsatisfactory and inconsistent procedures for security checks prior to entering port facilities; an easily manipulated identity card system; low compliance in providing International Ship and Port Facility Security Code (ISPS) training, drills and exercises at port facilities; and insufficient knowledge of related parties regarding their tasks and function in the implementation of the ISPS Code (Direktorat Jenderal Perhubungan Laut 2010, p. 2). The issuance of PSAs meant that any vessels calling at one of the affected Indonesian ports would be obliged to go through extensive security procedures before being granted permission to enter US ports.

In a bid to improve port security in the archipelago, outsourcing border control to *preman* organizations has become one of the main features of Indonesian government policy. There are around thirty organized paramilitary groups, with an estimated membership of

700,000 people. Most of them are identified as modernist Islamic groups (Nordholt 2002, p. 51, cited in Sindre 2005, p. 69). Some of these groups are attached to political parties, like Gerakan Pemuda Kabah, which is loosely affiliated with Partai Persatuan Pembangunan (United Development Party) (Hadiz 2003, p. 603). Others are linked to religious organizations; for instance, Pemuda Ansor is affiliated with Nahdatul Ulama. A small number of these groups are characterized as independent gangster organizations (commonly referred to in Indonesia as *preman* organizations) that in the past gained support during Suharto's New Order regime, such as Pemuda Pancasila and Ikatan Pemuda Karya (Hadiz 2003, p. 603).

This book will examine the contradictions and implications of the use of *preman* organizations in Indonesia's efforts to establish a truly democratic civil society. The use of *preman* organizations is not trouble free. Several concerns have been raised regarding conflicts between different *preman* organizations and between these organizations and the state's security apparatus. In recent years, acts of destruction and attacks have been carried out by *preman* organizations against other groups and against the state's security forces, and these organizations have also been involved in smuggling activities. Such activities have created an increasingly insecure environment and in some instances have halted export-import activities at Indonesian ports (*Berita Sore*, 12 August 2011; *Sumut Pos*, 13 April 2013; Sciascia 2013, pp. 164–71). This book will draw attention to this unresolved tension within Indonesian society that could hinder the country's transition into a fully functioning democracy. Against this backdrop, the book aims to answer the following questions: Does the use of *preman* organizations represent a change of direction or a continuation in Indonesia's security practices? And what are the tensions between state and non-state organizations in securing the country's maritime borders?

Understanding the involvement of *preman* organizations in Indonesia's port security is important for two reasons. First, efforts to improve port security in the archipelago is not only a matter of national security for Indonesia. The security of Indonesian ports is important to the international community because the country occupies an important position in global maritime transportation. Situated between the Indian and Pacific Oceans, and with maritime areas covering the three sea lanes of communications (SLOC) of the Straits of Malacca and Singapore, the Strait of Lombok and the Sunda Strait, Indonesia exercises responsibility for a large percentage of the world's shipping trade. Almost half of the world's traded goods and oil passes through these three key Indonesian straits (Carana 2004, p 14; US Department of Homeland Security, 20 September 2005). In one year, it is estimated that over three million ships pass through Indonesian waters.[1] This makes Indonesia's role in securing maritime borders of great significance.

Second, understanding ongoing processes and challenges of democracy in Indonesia is deemed important to ensure the sustainability of the democratic system in this emerging economy. Indonesia is the largest Muslim-majority country in the world, with a total population of over 220 million people, and it is strategically located at the crossroads of busy maritime traffic between Europe and East Asia, between Australia and Asia, and between the Middle East and East Asia. For twenty-four years, Indonesia has been in transition from an authoritarian regime to a more democratic political system and society. But despite more than two decades of democratization, and the security-sector reform that accompanied it, *preman* organizations continue to play an important role in providing security alongside the state's security forces. Organizations with Islamic platforms, such as Pemuda Alawiyah, Pemuda Muhammadiyah, Ikatan Pemuda Nahdatul Ulama, Pemuda Muslimin and Gerakan Pemuda Ansor, and those with a nationalist outlook, such as Pemuda Pancasila and Angkatan Muda Pembaharuan, are actively involved in securing vital sites and major political events, including national legislative and presidential elections and local government elections.

This book compares the involvement of *preman* organizations in securing Indonesian ports situated in the three key sea lanes of communication. These include ports in Jakarta (close to the Sunda Strait), North Sulawesi (near the Lombok Strait and the Sulu-Sulawesi Sea) and the Riau Islands (adjacent to the Strait of Malacca).

Jakarta, North Sulawesi and the Riau Islands host ports that are assigned as the country's international gateways and several smaller ports. Jakarta is serviced by the largest port in Indonesia, Tanjung Priok Port, and the two smaller ports of Marunda and Muara Baru. Tanjung Priok Port alone is responsible for managing over 27 per cent of Indonesia's exports, worth around US$46.9 billion, and over 39 per cent of the country's imports, with a total value of US$56.1 billion (Badan Pusat Statistik 2020a; 2020b, pp. 36–39).

North Sulawesi is home to the major container port of Bitung and at least fifteen smaller ports, including Bitung Ferry Port, Manado Port and twelve new ports: Amurang Port in South Minahasa, nine ports in Sangihe regency (Tahuna, Petta, Bukide, Kalama, Lipang, Kahakitang, Kawaluso, Matutuang and Kawio) and two ports in Sitaro regency (Sawang and Buhias). Bitung Port is a key gateway for the eastern part of Indonesia and a designated port for the Brunei-Indonesia-Malaysia- Philippines East ASEAN Growth Area (BIMP-EAGA). Transport of people and goods through ports in North Sulawesi is crucial not only to support Indonesia's economy but also to improve regional maritime linkages and accelerate economic development in one of Southeast Asia's poorest sub-regions.

The cities of Batam and Tanjung Pinang in the Riau Islands are strategically located close to the Straits of Singapore and Malacca. Both cities have a substantial number of ports. Batam is serviced by a large international cargo port, Batu Ampar, and eight smaller ports, including Batam International Ferry Terminal, Batu Ampar Ferry Terminal, Harbour Bay Ferry Terminal, Kabil Marine and Oil Base Port, Telaga Punggur Domestic Port, Nongsa Pura Ferry Port, Sekupang Ferry Terminal, and Waterfront City Teluk Senimba Ferry Terminal. Batu Ampar Port plays an important role in the distribution and consolidation of cargo in the Indonesia-Malaysia-Singapore sub-regional growth triangle (Singapore-Johor-Riau, or SIJORI) (Sutomo and Alisyahbana 2013, p. 796). It manages a large quantity of domestic and international ocean freight (Sutomo and Alisyahbana 2013, p. 796). Tanjung Pinang, the capital city of the Riau Islands, is home to six ports: Sri Bintan, Sripayung Batu, Dompak, Pelantar Dua, Tanjung Merbau and Sungai Jang.[2]

Locating Indonesia in the Literature on Non-state Security Providers

This book offers a comprehensive account of the involvement of non-state security providers in securing ports and coastal areas in Indonesia. Traditionally, the state is perceived as the source of legitimate security authority. This traditional notion of authority derives from a Weberian conception of the state. To quote Weber, "A State is a human community that (successfully) claims the monopoly of the legitimate use of physical force within a given territory" (Avant 2005, p. 1). The end of the twentieth century saw a growing number of challenges to this traditional locus of authority. Hall and Biersteker argue that because of globalization, and various forms of international governance, numerous non-state actors have increasingly taken authoritative roles in the international system.

These non-state actors exercise their influence over important areas, including markets, morals and illicit activities (Hall and Biersteker 2002, p. 4). These developments have intensified the involvement of private actors in providing security and controlling the instruments of violence (ibid.).

Scholars from the global society school of thought argue that the process of globalization has challenged the authority of states. These authors argue that market integration and the development of finance, communication and technology have transformed state frontiers (Baylis 2008, p. 236; Friedman and Kaplan 2002, p. 64). Kaplan points out that greater interconnection brought about by globalization raises instability, particularly in underdeveloped states that cannot cope with the growing instability (Friedman and Kaplan 2002, p. 65). Such a process may lead to the fragmentation of nation states. In the context of globalization, the growing involvement of non-state security providers in a "new war" has been seen as a prominent feature. Kaldor explains that globalization has changed the social relations between public and private authority. She argues that, in the "new war", the war is fought by state and non-state actors, including insurgent groups, criminal organizations, paramilitary forces and private security contractors (Kaldor 2007, pp. 158, 162, 166). The involvement of private authorities in the provision of security has undermined the state's monopoly of violence.

Neorealism takes a different view from scholars on globalization regarding the use of private authorities in security. For neorealists, globalization does pose a challenge to states; however, the authority of states has demonstrated a great deal of resilience towards globalization (Waltz 2000, p. 53). Waltz points out that private authorities do not push states away from the centre stage of international politics (Waltz 1986, p. 98). This is primarily because states tend to "respond efficiently to changing international conditions" (ibid., p. 331; Grieco 1988, pp. 487–88; Waltz 1979, p. 105; Elman 1996, p. 43). States can transform their capacity and adapt to changes. More importantly, Waltz argues that the authority of states does not wither and fade away, because they also protect themselves in various ways (Waltz 2000, p. 51). The distinct institutions and traditions of different states may feed into different strategies that they choose to protect themselves and promote their interests (ibid.).

In contrast to both proponents of the global society and the neorealist argument regarding the privatization of security, this book argues that, although the state remains an important actor in the realm of security, the challenges posed by globalization and the emergence of private authority have affected the way a state delivers its security functions. The manner in which a state conducts its security and military tasks in response to a major challenge to globalization such as global terrorism is shaped by institutionalized local practice and domestic political dynamics within that state. Strategies that states use to protect and promote their interests sometimes cannot be seen as the result of a single decision by the head of state or a senior official but should be seen as a continual mode of action where the decision has been made by bureaucratic machinery and functionaries (Walker 2006; see also Doty 2007). The inclusion of private authorities as part of strategies to protect state interests is not trouble free, because it poses a direct challenge for the government to exercise its effective monopoly on the legitimate use of physical force.

In examining domestic sources of the privatization of security strategies, it will be useful to incorporate some insights from Gourevitch's work on domestic and international interactions. According to Gourevitch, the study of domestic and international political interaction suggests that ideas, understanding and discourse all have a political sociology of understanding, referring to groups who advocate or oppose them, institutions that support or obstruct them, or cultural commitments that promote or block their adoption (Gourevitch 2002, pp. 318–19). Discussion of a state policy, therefore, would "require considerable research into the actions of individuals and groups within society and their dialogue with counterparts elsewhere" (ibid., p. 318). For Gourevitch, regime type and coalition pattern are the properties of a political system most frequently used in explaining government policy (Gourevitch 1978, pp. 900–905). Regime type reveals the institutional structure and the machinery as well as the process and procedures of decision making (ibid., p. 883). Coalition pattern is defined as the type or combination of dominant elite (property owner, political elite, army or labour union) (ibid., pp. 900–905). The coalition pattern evokes the social forces and the political relationship among them. Awareness of domestic and international contexts is crucial in analysing the use of *preman* organizations for port security in Indonesia.

This book argues that institutionalized local practice and domestic political dynamics within the state are defining relations between state and private authorities in the provision of security. At the international level, the global war against terrorism has created pressure for Indonesia to improve its security measures in dealing with terrorism. Following the 9/11 attacks and the 2002 Bali bombings, Indonesia has improved the security of its major export and import ports and participated in various international measures to ensure its continuous participation in the international maritime trading system (Febrica 2017b). At the same time, in a bid to improve national counterterrorism efforts at small ports and in coastal areas located in remote or outlying islands, *preman* organizations began to play a greater role in security. The engagement of *preman* organizations in security became more apparent as they began to participate in providing intelligence information, to take part in anti-radicalization efforts and to help the government to guard ports and border regions. At the domestic level, security practices in developing countries such as Indonesia are different from those in democratic developed countries. Many poor developing countries have a tendency to be weak in terms of domestic, interdependent and Westphalian state capacity. These states are sovereign only in a legal sense (Paul, Ikenberry and Hall 2003, p. 354). Among those states that can be easily observed, it will be immediately evident that an erosion of state capacity is arguably the most defining characteristic produced by the process of political transition. In Indonesia, the combination of the decline of state capacity, the fact of there being many uninhabited outlying islands throughout the archipelago, and an underequipped law enforcement force contribute to undermining the capacity of the authorities to control the various networks of private authority that operate across the country's porous borders (see Ayoob 1984, p. 48). This situation renders Indonesia vulnerable to the problem of smuggling of goods, contraband and people. In the past twenty years, the sequence of violence in Indonesia has culminated in an intricate interconnection between the incapacity of the state to deliver some of its basic services and the involvement of *preman* organizations to fill the gap.

The burgeoning literature on the involvement of non-state security providers can be categorized into two groups. The first group tends to focus on the participation of private military companies (PMCs) in conflict areas in the Middle East and Africa. These works explain the historical development and international factors underpinning the privatization of conflict, the existing trend of the use of PMCs and the risks related to the use of PMCs (see Adams 2003; Shearer 1998; Davis 2000; Sullivan 2002). Works that touch upon maritime security explain the role of PMCs in counter-piracy operations in

East Africa and the Indian Ocean (Spearin 2010, pp. 56–71; Richard 2010, pp. 41–64; Hansen 2008, pp. 585–98; Liss 2008; Chalk 2012; Stevenson 2010, pp. 27–38; Møller 2009; Bueger, Stockbruegger and Werthes 2011, pp. 356–81; Ross and Ben-David 2009, pp. 55–70; Scheffler 2010; Bellamy 2011, pp. 78–83; Chapsos and Holtom 2015, pp, 1–4; Ono 2013, pp. 1–4; Buzatu and Buckland 2015, pp. 1–97; Brown 2012, pp. 1–23). Although Indonesia is one of the countries bordering the Indian Ocean, the literature pays little attention to the activities of non-state organizations in Indonesia.

The second group of literature examines the involvement of *preman* organizations in Indonesia's security sector. The specific literature on Indonesia is largely descriptive. It focuses on the political constellation of the country during and after the New Order era, which opened avenues for the engagement of non-state organizations in the country's security domain (Simpson 2013, pp. 10–13; Ryter 1998, pp. 45–73; Hadiz 2003, pp. 591–611; Freek and Lindblad 2002; Barker 1998, pp. 7–42; Sindre 2005; Anderson 2001; Van Klinken and Barker 2009; Headman 2008). The explanations suggested by the literature on Indonesia's outsourcing of security functions can be grouped into three categories: historical and cultural roots, the future relations between military organizations and civil society, and the political and security practices in post-reform Indonesia.

The argument for historical and cultural roots describes the presence of historical and cultural antecedents that have shaped Indonesia's policy to use *preman* organizations to secure its territory (Ryter 1998, pp. 45–73; Robinson 2001, pp. 271–318; Barker 1998, pp. 7–42; Simpson 2013, pp. 10–13; Roosa 2003, pp. 315–23; Collins 2002, pp. 582–604; Khanh and Indorf 1982, pp. 3–25; Silverstein 1982, pp. 278–91; Ahram 2011, pp. 531–56). Scholars that propose this argument explain that the origin of the growth of *preman* organizations in Indonesia can be traced to pre-colonial times, the long interactions with Portuguese and Dutch colonial authorities, the legacy of revolutions following the Japanese occupation of 1942–45, and Suharto's New Order security practices (Ahram 2011, pp. 533, 540; Silverstein 1982, p. 282; Simpson 2013, pp. 10–11; Robinson 2001, pp. 279–91; Ryter 1998, pp. 48–54; Barker 1998, p. 12).

Scholars arguing for the influence of Indonesia's pre-colonial cultural models cite ideas such as the sexual potency associated with the *jago*, the link between criminality and authority in the story of Ken Arok the robber king and the role of local enforcers in colonial Java as having shaped the persistent presence of *preman* organizations in modern Indonesia (Ryter 1998, p. 48; Robinson 2001, p. 313). Portuguese and Dutch colonial authorities throughout the eighteenth and nineteenth centuries and the occupying Japanese forces during World War II (1942–45) recruited local civilians to meet their security demands. This practice was sustained, particularly during the period of Suharto's New Order (1965–98). The Suharto regime directed *preman* organizations in 1965–66 to kill over half a million alleged supporters of the Indonesian Communist Party and mobilized such organizations between the 1970s and the 1990s for counter-insurgency operations in certain troubled regions, including East Timor, West Papua and Aceh (Ahram 2011, p. 541; Roosa 2003, pp. 317–18; Barker 1998, p. 12). Arguably, the use of semi-official forces had been deemed useful for the Portuguese, Dutch and Indonesian authorities as it was a cheaper option than maintaining a large standing army, and it could provide room for deniability for acts of violence that breached legal and moral norms (Robinson 2001, p. 315; Khanh and Indorf 1982, pp. 17–18; Ahram 2011, p. 532; Roosa 2003, p. 321; see also Collier 1999, p. 12). More importantly, scholarly works point out that the outsourcing of security functions to non-state actors helped to portray a situation whereby local citizens were fighting against each other and the state authorities served largely as neutral arbiters seeking to maintain peace and order (Robinson 2001, p. 315). The literature provides great detail on the use of *preman* organizations as a state instrument of violence from the colonial to the late Suharto era. Nevertheless, it falls short in explaining the continued practice of the use of *preman* organizations to enhance the country's maritime security.

The literature that focuses on civil-military relations draws attention to the process of security sector reform in developing countries, including Indonesia (Lee 2000, pp. 692–706; Smith 2001, pp. 5–20; Hendrickson and Karkoszka 2002, pp. 175–201; Collier 1999, pp. 1–23). This literature acknowledges that the narrow definition of the conventional Western security actors—such as armed forces and police—does not capture the diversity of non-state security actors in the developing world (Hendrickson and Karkoszka 2002, pp. 178–79). Lee, Smith, Collier, Hendrickson and Karkoszka explained that security sector elements in the non-developed world, including Indonesia, may include paramilitary forces, private bodyguard units, private security companies, and militias associated with political parties. The existing literature puts forward a liberal vision of security reform where reform agendas will be expected to succeed when civilian authority is ascendant and the military's role in politics is diminished (Lee 2000, pp. 695, 699–700, 703; Hendrickson and Karkoszka 2002, pp. 180, 182; Smith 2001, pp. 11–12). There is a general acceptance that civil society organizations as important agents for change can apply pressure and inform reform agendas (Hendrickson and Karkoszka 2002, p. 180; Lee 2000, pp. 701–2). The continued use of *preman* organizations in Indonesia to provide local defence at key sites such as ports, however, shows the opposite of a liberal vision of security reform. Concerned primarily with power relations between civil and military institutions, the existing works have overlooked that legal non-state organizations can continue to promote the status quo rather than reform security practices, and at the same time generate revenue for themselves.

The third line of argument found in the descriptive literature studies the continuity and change of political and security practice in post-reform Indonesia (Hadiz 2003, pp. 591–611; Sindre 2005, pp. 1–99; Sidel 2004, pp. 51–74; Hadiz 2004, pp. 615–36; Bertrand 2004, pp. 325–44; Brown and Wilson 2007, pp. 367–403; Barter 2013, pp. 75–92; Hadiz 2008, pp. 1–14; Jayasuriya and Rodan 2007, pp. 773–94; Aspinall 2013, p. 48; Kristiansen and Trijono 2005, pp. 236–54; Ufen 2006, pp. 1–35; Weatherbee 2004, pp. 179–91; Cribb 2000, pp. 183–202; Heryanto and Hadiz 2005, pp. 251–75). The burgeoning literature on post-authoritarian Indonesia argues that, despite the reconfiguration of politics in the archipelago after Suharto's authoritarian regime, fewer democratic forces are still largely at play at the national and local levels. They claim that paramilitary and gangster groups used as instruments in intra-elite struggles and often associated with political parties or mass organizations have flourished and have become increasingly important players in post-authoritarian Indonesia (Heryanto and Hadiz 2005, pp. 252, 256; Cribb 2000, p. 197; Weatherbee 2004, p. 190; Ufen 2006, pp. 26–27; Kristiansen and Trijono 2005, pp. 236, 247–48; Aspinall 2013, pp. 42, 48; Hadiz 2008, p. 8; Barter 2013, pp. 83, 88; Brown and Wilson 2007, pp. 375–76; Bertrand 2004, pp. 338–40; Wilson 2006, pp. 266–89; Hadiz 2004, p. 626; Sidel 2004, p. 64; Sindre 2005, pp. 1–2; Hadiz 2003, pp. 597–98).

These *preman* organizations on one hand offer "substitutes for many of the functions provided by the state", including in the security realm (Kaldor 2003, p 9, cited in Aspinall 2013, p 42). However, as Aspinall (2013, p. 48), Kristiansen and Trijono (2005, pp. 249–50), Brown and Wilson (2007, pp. 370, 386–88), and Sidel (2004, p. 64) point out, the activities of these organizations can increase insecurity in society because of competition among them over territory and resources.

Most of the scholarly works that discuss the activities of *preman* organizations in post-authoritarian Indonesia do not explicitly examine the role of these organizations in securing maritime borders. The work of Sciascia is an exception. Sciascia has examined a range of diverse for-profit actors such as private security firms and members of Pemuda Pancasila in providing security in the Port of Belawan, Medan. His work offers a detailed account of the relations between public and private security actors in Belawan Port. Sciascia, however, uses only one case study—the Port of Belawan—and focuses mainly on a single *preman* organization, Pemuda Pancasila. This limits the capacity to generalize his findings to other parts of Indonesia and constrains the ability to capture the complexity of interactions between various types of *preman* organizations—such as ethnic-based organization like Forum Betawi Rempug, nationalist organizations like Ikatan Pemuda Karya and religious organizations such as Pemuda Ansor—both between each other and with the government authorities.

This survey of existing works on *preman* organizations shows that the literature does not explain the underlying reasons for Indonesia's decision to involve *preman* organizations in port security, nor does it depict the dynamics and tensions between state and non-state security providers in securing the country's maritime borders. The existing literature is, nonetheless, a valuable resource for this book because it provides a detailed account of the development of *preman* organizations in Indonesia both before and after the political reform began in 1998. The existing literature on Indonesia's *preman* organizations therefore serves as a point of departure.

The Significance of Indonesia in the Study of Civil Society

The study of the participation of *preman* organizations in Indonesia's port security informs analytical and empirical debates for the study of civil society. In May 1998, the resignation of Indonesia's second president, Suharto, ended the state's authoritarian political system that had lasted for more than thirty years (Liddle 1999, p. 39). As a consequence, the years after 1998 witnessed a growing number of civil society organizations (CSOs), both in Jakarta and other parts of Indonesia. As of 2017, there were sixteen thousand CSOs registered with the Ministry of Home Affairs, a government ministry designated to register and supervise these organizations (McDonald and Wilson 2017, p. 248).

After 1998, CSOs have played a crucial role in informing Indonesia's security policies. A group of CSOs, which includes Kontras, Elsam, ProPatria and Lembaga Studi Pertahanan dan Studi Strategis Indonesia, has established the Civil Society Network for Security Sector Reform. These CSOs have been active in promoting a reform agenda in Indonesia's security sector, reformulating and proposing a range of legislation in the security sector, and encouraging transparency and monitoring of the implementation of state security policies (Maakarim 2009, cited in Bhakti 2009, p. iv). The success of the advocacy work of these CSOs could be seen in the array of new legislation passed by the House of Representatives and approved by the president within a few years of Indonesia beginning its reform process. These include Law No. 2/2002 on the Indonesian Police (Undang-Undang Kepolisian Negara Republik Indonesia), Law No. 3/2002 on State Defence (Undang-Undang Pertahanan Negara) and Law No. 34/2004 on the Indonesian Armed Forces (Undang-Undang Tentara Nasional Indonesia). CSOs have actively proposed several legislative drafts that are deemed important in improving the country's security policies, including in the area of counterterrorism. These include a draft of the State Intelligence Law (Rancangan Undang-Undang [RUU] Intelijen) and a draft of the Assistance of the Indonesian National Armed Forces Law (RUU Perbantuan Tentara Nasional Indonesia), designed to regulate how and when the armed forces could assist the police in dealing with terrorism (Bhakti 2009; *Tempo*, 25 July 2016). RUU Intelijen was ratified by the parliament in October 2011 (*Berita Satu*, 11 October 2011). But, despite pressure from civil society in Indonesia, RUU Perbantuan Tentara Nasional Indonesia has not been passed. In order to govern the involvement of the military in domestic security spheres, the Indonesian military (TNI) has signed at least forty-one memoranda of understanding (MoU) with various government agencies, such as the police (Perhimpunan Bantuan Hukum dan Hak Asasi Manusia Indonesia, 5 October 2020; *Kompas*, 2 February 2018). The Indonesian government is finalizing the draft of the Presidential Decree on the TNI's Tasks in Overcoming Terrorism (Rancangan Perpres Tugas TNI dalam Mengatasi Aksi Terorisme) (*Kompas*, 13 May 2020; Lembaga Ketahanan Nasional, 15 December 2021). These practices have been criticized by civil society as setbacks for

Indonesian military reform. Civil society deems that any military participation in counterterrorism should be governed by law rather than MoUs or presidential decrees (Bantuan Hukum, 3 August 2018; Perhimpunan Bantuan Hukum dan Hak Asasi Manusia Indonesia, 5 October 2020).

Given the rise of civil society influence in Indonesia's political and security affairs, the majority of works on CSOs in Indonesia tend to focus on the resurgence of CSOs and their role in the democratic transformation of the country (Ibrahim 2011; Hening 2014; Hefner 1993, pp. 1–35; Pohl 2006, pp. 389–409; Antlöv, Brinkerhoff and Rapp 2010, pp. 417–39; Nyman 2006). Others examine the transborder nature of CSOs and their role in the promotion of democracy and human rights not only in Indonesia but also in neighbouring Southeast Asian countries (Howell and Lind 2009, pp. 1279–96; Mietzner 2012, pp. 209–29; Bhakti 2009; Gomez and Ramcharan 2012, pp. 27–43; Gilson 2011; Rahim and Pietsch 2015, pp. 139–42; Gerard 2014, pp. 1–23; Chachavalpongpun 2012; Quayle 2012, pp. 199–222; Gerard 2013, pp. 1–16; Chong 2012, pp. 35–44; Acharya 2003, pp. 375–90; Allison and Taylor 2017, pp. 1–18). There is a small but growing body of scholarly work that focuses on the rise of un-civil organizations after 1998 (Beittinger-Lee 2009; Bakker 2016, pp. 249–77; Nugroho and Syarief 2012; Mudayat, Arif, Narendra and Irawanto 2009). These studies argue that not all CSOs in post-authoritarian Indonesia are characterized as tolerant and liberal (Beittinger-Lee 2009, p. 158; Bakker 2016, pp. 249–77; Nugroho and Syarief 2012; Mudayat, Arif, Narendra and Irawanto 2009). Their mode of operation does not echo the Western European civil society principles of the non-use of violence and being not for profit. Diamond defines these principles of civil society as

> the realm of organized social life that is voluntary, self-generating, (largely) self-supporting, autonomous from the state, and bound by a legal order or set of shared rules. It is distinct from "society" in general in that it involves citizens acting collectively in a public sphere.... Civil society is an intermediary entity, standing between the private sphere and the state. Thus, it excludes individual and family life, inward looking group activity..., the profit making enterprise of individual business firms, and political efforts to take control of the state... (Diamond 1996, p. 228, cited in Weiss 2008)

Democratization has encouraged the growth of "un-civil" elements within Indonesian society. Some of these CSOs are willing to use violence and intimidation to achieve their economic, social and political goals. These *preman* organizations gained access to government funding and on various occasions have collaborated closely with government authorities in the security sector. The existing works that touch upon the un-civil elements within Indonesian society, however, do not offer much insight on the involvement of CSOs in port security in Indonesia. By focusing on the involvement of *preman* organizations to secure Indonesian ports and outlying islands, this book provides a fresh perspective in studying state-civil society relations and the participation of non-governmental actors in the provision of security outside of the European/Western democratic setting.

Notes on Methods

My data gathering focused on the history and the engagement of militarized NGOs in securing ports and border areas. I relied on qualitative and quantitative types of information from primary and secondary sources.

As part of my data gathering, I conducted two periods of fieldwork in 2015 and 2016 in Jakarta, North Sulawesi and the Riau Islands to gather both quantitative and qualitative data related to Indonesia's outsourcing of port security. During these two periods of fieldwork, I carried out eighty-four interviews. Interviews were conducted with Indonesian officials, representatives of CSOs, industry representatives, national and local parliamentarians, academics and leaders as well as members of *preman* organizations based in Jakarta, Bitung, Manado, Batam and Tanjung Pinang.

I interviewed active duty and retired Indonesian officials who are well informed on the use of *preman* organizations in port and border security from the following government institutions: the navy; the Coordinating Ministry for Political, Legal and Security Affairs; the police; the National Defence Board; the Directorate General of Sea Transportation; the Port Authority; and representatives of local governments. I identified officials in these institutions through my previous research on Indonesian maritime security, their writings, newspaper articles, discussions with other interviewees and consultations with academics based in Jakarta, Manado and Tanjung Pinang.

During study in the field, in-depth interviews were conducted to seek the views of public and private stakeholders involved in the use of *preman* organizations in security. All the interviews that I carried out in Indonesia were arranged through the American Studies Center, Universitas Indonesia. As part of my data collection process, the host institution also sent letters of request to key Indonesian bureaucratic institutions in the field of port and border security. I did not use a strict sampling frame to select interviewees in Jakarta. In practice, to trace suitable interview subjects, a snowball sampling procedure was useful to help me to select further interviewees (Bryman 2004, p. 334). As I started the interview process, some of my interviewees put me in contact with other individuals, including officials, business representatives, security experts and representatives of *preman* organizations involved in the security field.

At the beginning of each interview, I provided a brief description of my research to the interviewee. Interview proceedings were recorded with a digital recorder if the interviewees deemed this was acceptable. Several interviewees asked not to be recorded and I respected their requests. To have proceeded to record the interviews would have entailed breaching their trust and could possibly have endangered my interview subjects and myself.

I am aware that there are three issues that could arise from the use of interview data for this research. First, not all interviewees can be assumed to be equally important (Dexter 1970, p. 6). Only a few interviewees were involved in the decision-making process or had access to closed meetings and therefore could explain how government decisions were formulated (ibid., pp. 6–7, 130). Most interviewees that provided insightful answers were either the current or former leaders of government agencies or the relevant leaders of *preman* organizations. One way to give weight to interviewee statements is to "place each item of material in light of the character structure and social position of the informant" (ibid., p. 148). Providing a detailed breakdown of each interviewee's professional position and role in relation to *preman* organizations would, however, breach ethical guidelines for reporting the data with anonymity, and in certain cases could endanger the career and safety of my interviewees (ibid., p. 148). Second, in numerous interviews I asked interviewees to recollect specific events, decisions or arrangements that happened in the past or "have developed over a long period of time" (ibid., p. 11). Under these circumstances, distortion of the interview report could take place if the interviewee could not recollect the precise details of what happened, and rather stated what they supposed had happened (ibid., p. 126). The data reported may also give a distorted account of what actually happened if interviewees unconsciously explained the situation to suit their own perspective or consciously modified the facts (ibid., p. 126). Third, I am aware that data from an interview is restricted to what the interviewee was willing to share with me at that particular moment (ibid., p. 120). Under other circumstances, what the interviewee might have stated to me could be different (ibid., p. 120).

I used triangulation techniques in data collection to address concerns about validity and bias (see Arksey and Knight 1999, pp. 22–23). Interviews with officials, representatives of civil society, and leaders and members of *preman* organizations were cross-checked against each other (Dexter 1970, p. 15; Arksey and Knight 1999, p. 27). I compared statements made by an interviewee with the account provided by other interviewees (Dexter 1970, p. 127). I talked to officials and members of *preman* organizations from different ranks. Talking to officials from different government agencies at different stages of their careers has proved useful (Arksey and Knight 1999, p. 27). Senior government officials or former officials were able to explain the extent of conflict or cooperation between government agencies and *preman* organizations because they were consulted or involved in the decision-making process to recruit or halt the activities of these groups. Their statements could be corroborated with mid-career officials involved in arranging meetings, conducting joint security operations in the field and assessing registered militarized NGOs. I asked for further clarification through re-interviewing informants in person or by phone when there were discrepancies found in the cross-examination of interviewees' accounts (Dexter 1970, p. 128).

In order to validate interview data, I also combined interviews with document analysis to learn about the involvement of *preman* organizations in port security. The documents I gathered during fieldwork were helpful as sources of information and for cross-checking interview data (Arksey and Knight 1999, p. 17). I collected over fifty primary documents related to outsourcing border security. The government documents include transcripts of official speeches, annual ministry accountability reports, defence white papers, meeting reports, development blueprints, intra-departmental correspondence, political and security surveys, analysis of provincial economic potential, and parliamentary newsletters. Most of these materials are only available in the Indonesian language.

I also used statistics on defence expenditure, the expenditure of Indonesia's maritime agencies, government counterterrorism spending, government allocation of funding to CSOs and the number of registered CSOs published by the national and local government. Some of these documents can be accessed online, while others are available from the Indonesian Coordinating Ministry for Political, Legal and Security Affairs and local government authorities. For documents that are not publicly available, this report has benefited from the generosity of some of my interviewees in granting me access.

The archives of newspapers, including the *Jakarta Post*, *Kompas*, *Tribun Manado*, *Manado Post*, *Tribun Batam* and *Batam Post*, were also valuable sources for this book. The analysis of newspaper articles has been useful to corroborate or contrast claims made by officials, parliamentarians and representatives of *preman* organizations.

Outline of the Book

Chapter 1 emphasizes the main question that this book seeks to address. It provides a detailed background for the chapters that follow. This chapter aims to achieve two objectives. First, this chapter explains the implications of the 9/11 attacks for Indonesia's port security. It shows how, despite Indonesia's long history and experience of terrorist incidents, only after 9/11 did governments around the world begin to highlight the possibility and significance of terrorist attacks in Indonesian waters and on maritime facilities. This chapter elaborates on Indonesia's efforts to improve the security of its ports and outlying islands following the 2002 Bali bombings and the 2008 issuance by the US Coast Guard of PSAs to most Indonesian ports. These include the involvement of *preman* organizations as one of the main features of Indonesian government policy in a bid to secure its ports and outlying islands in the archipelago. Second, this chapter intends to provide detailed background information on Indonesia's domestic political dynamics and the involvement of *preman* organizations in the process. It highlights the political practices that have changed and those that remain the same in post-authoritarian Indonesia. This chapter elaborates on the specifics of Indonesia's security and political practices that sustain the use of *preman* organizations in security. Drawing on documents and interview sources, this chapter identifies key actors and the institutional process of Indonesia's security policy-making.

Chapter 2 argues that although Pemuda Pancasila exercised a certain degree of control at ports in the past, at present, ethnic-based organizations play a more active role in port security in Jakarta. It shows that the involvement of CSOs in port security is not trouble free. *Preman* organizations have provided protection for smuggling activities and been involved in violent conflicts with the provincial government and private security companies in port areas. This chapter provides a comprehensive explanation of the involvement of CSOs in port security in Jakarta and the challenges that this practice has brought. First, this chapter maps key *preman* organizations that exist in Jakarta and their involvement in securing ports and in security in general. Second, it explores interactions—both in terms of cooperation and conflict—that have taken place between different *preman* organizations, between government authorities and *preman* organizations, and between *preman* organizations and other non-state security providers. The chapter also provides an assessment of the illicit activities at ports in Jakarta and of the involvement of *preman* organizations in seeking to curb or sustain such activities.

Chapter 3 addresses the participation of *preman* organizations in securing ports and outlying islands in North Sulawesi. To begin with, this chapter familiarizes readers with the geographical landscape of North Sulawesi—an Indonesian province that shares maritime border with the Philippines in the north—and the challenges that it poses. The next part of this chapter identifies *preman* organizations that participate in securing ports and the outlying islands of this province, their affiliations, and the major security and political events that underpinned their establishment. The chapter also explains the development of partnerships between state authorities and *preman* organizations in this province. It highlights the collaboration of government agencies with *preman* organizations and explains the lack of conflict that features in their relations. This chapter finishes by examining the role of *preman* organizations in combating transnational crime in North Sulawesi. Analysis of *preman* organizations in North Sulawesi shows that the participation of these organizations in port security is largely welcomed by government authorities. The local media, parliamentarians, the local government and the state security apparatus describe in positive terms the role of *preman* organizations in dealing with trans-border illicit activities, particularly terrorism and human trafficking, in North Sulawesi.

Chapter 4 explains the role of *preman* organizations in two port cities in the Riau Islands: Batam and Tanjung Pinang. The first part of this chapter accounts for the dominant *preman* organizations operating in Batam and Tanjung Pinang. It explains the similarities and differences of CSO characteristics in the two cities. The chapter then proceeds to explain various forms of cooperation between different government agencies and *preman* organizations to guard ports and outlying islands in areas surrounding Batam and Tanjung Pinang. It also analyses the reasons underpinning tensions and friction between *preman* organizations, the government and society. The final part of this chapter highlights the connection of *preman* organizations with illicit activities. The conclusion of this chapter points to the ambiguous role of *preman* organizations in port security. It argues that whilst *preman* organizations have played a role in securing ports and outlying islands, their involvement in illicit activities and their low-scale conflicts with government authorities and members of society has generated insecurity in port areas and beyond.

The concluding chapter brings together the threads of argument and the main findings presented in the core chapters. It reiterates the place this book has in the current literature and its contribution both to the literature on civil society and on non-state security providers. It then proceeds with a section for the identification of areas for future research.

Notes

1   This figure is an estimate generated from the data of vessels navigating Indonesian waters on 12 December 2013 at 08:30 GMT. As shown by the live marine traffic map (available at http://www.marinetraffic.com/en/), 1,735 vessels were plying Indonesian waters at this time. This number only includes ships that are fitted with Automatic Identification System (AIS) transponders. According to IMO regulations (Regulation 19 of SOLAS Chapter V), the AIS is only required to be fitted aboard ships of 300 gross tonnage and upwards engaged on international voyages. This figure, therefore, does not include vessels below 300 gross tonnage involved in international shipping.
2   Interview with a senior government official and his staff, Tanjung Pinang, February 2016.

Chapter 1

International and Domestic Politics

Any explanation for the use of non-state security providers by government authorities should not rely solely on the examination of international politics or the domestic structure. A government security policy is generated from the interface between interstate negotiations on the one hand and interaction within the domestic realm on the other—among individuals, social and interest groups, and the state (McSweeney 1999, p. 127; Gourevitch 2002, pp. 310, 316, 318). The interaction between international politics and the domestic structure may influence the use of *preman* organizations for port and coastal security in Indonesia. This proposition, however, has not been examined in the existing literature. This chapter will fill this gap.

This chapter consists of three parts. The first part will explain the implications of the 9/11 attacks for Indonesia's port security. It will examine why, despite Indonesia's long history and experience of terrorist incidents, it was only after 9/11 that governments around the world begin to highlight the possibility and significance of terrorist attacks in Indonesian waters and on Indonesian maritime facilities. It will also elaborate on Indonesia's efforts to improve the security of its ports and outlying islands following the 2002 Bali bombings and the issuance in 2008 of port security advisories (PSAs) to most Indonesian ports by the United States Coast Guard. These include the involvement of *preman* organizations as one of the main features of Indonesian government policy to secure its ports and outlying islands in the archipelago. The second part of the chapter will provide detailed background information on Indonesia's domestic political dynamics and the involvement of *preman* organizations in the process. It will highlight the political practices that have changed and those that remain the same in post-authoritarian Indonesia. It will elaborate on the specifics of Indonesia's security and political practices that sustain the use of *preman* organizations in security. And finally, the concluding part of the chapter will highlight that the use of *preman* organizations for port and coastal security in Indonesia is shaped by a combination of domestic political dynamics that compel the government to take low-key approaches to counterterrorism and institutionalized local practices and everyday politics that normalizes the use of *preman* organizations for the provision of security. The involvement of *preman* organizations for port and coastal security in Indonesia has been encouraged by various governmental and legislative actors following mounting international pressure after the 9/11 attacks and a growing perception that Indonesia has not done enough to secure its territory from terrorist threats in the aftermath of the 2002 Bali bombings. The participation of *preman* organizations in Indonesia, however, is not an exceptional measure taken by the government to deal with terrorism, as these non-state organizations have been involved in the country's security long before the 9/11 attacks. The involvement of *preman* organizations in port security needs to be understood merely as an expansion of the security role of *preman* organizations from their traditional "land-based" areas of work (e.g., securing parking lots, markets, buildings and local election) to include maritime frontiers (e.g., monitoring possible terrorist movements in a small port and helping guard passenger ports during religious holidays).

The 9/11 Attacks and International Pressure

Terrorism is not a new security issue for the Indonesian government.[1] In Indonesia, the Free Aceh Movement, as well as other armed separatist groups in Irian Jaya (Organisasi Papua Merdeka, or OPM) and East Timor (Fretelin/Falintil), have used terrorist modus operandi to gain greater autonomy from the central government (Chalk 1998, pp. 122–24). Several terrorist attacks have taken place in Indonesia since the hijacking of the Garuda Indonesian Airways flight from Jakarta to Bangkok in 1980. In the first decade after the resignation of Suharto in May 1998 there were at least thirty-four bomb attacks in Indonesia (Kementerian Koordinator Bidang Politik, Hukum dan Keamanan 2008, p. 40; Indonesian Ministry of Defence 2008, p. 19). LAB 45, a research institute based in Jakarta, reported that 522 acts of terrorism had taken place in Indonesia between 2000 and 2021 (*Kompas*, 30 March 2021). These include bombings (51 per cent), armed attacks (30 per cent), attacks on public facilities (8 per cent), murders (5 per cent), kidnappings (4 per cent) and unarmed attacks (1 per cent) carried out by Jamaah Islamiyah, Mujahidin Indonesia Timur, Jamaah Ansharut Daulah, Jamaah Ansharut Tauhid and Mujahidin Indonesia Barat (*Kompas*, 30 March 2021).

Despite Indonesia's long history and experience of terrorist incidents, it was only after 9/11 that governments around the world begin to highlight the possibility and significance of terrorist attacks on Indonesian land and in its waters. In February 2002, Singapore's senior minister Lee Kuan Yew labelled Indonesia "a terrorist nest" in an interview with CNN (Singapore Window, 9 February 2002). He claimed that Singapore would be at risk of terrorist attacks as long as leaders of regional extremist cells remained free in Indonesia, suggesting that Indonesia did not take any action against suspected terrorists (Emmers 2003, p. 429). Shortly after the 11 September attacks, US deputy secretary of defense Paul Wolfowitz made explicit connections between Al Qaeda and various other extremist groups operating in Indonesia:

> I said, "Look, there are some extremists in Indonesia ... but they are not international terrorists, and they are not tied to Al Qaeda." Well, I was wrong; ... every day we learn more about these connections. (US Department of Defense, 28 January 2003).

The United States began to express its concern that "Muslim extremists in Indonesia, Malaysia, the Philippines and Thailand" were a possible threat to world trade navigating through Southeast Asian waterways (Valencia 2006, p. 97). The international community has anticipated several worst-case scenarios of maritime terrorism incidents that could take place in Indonesian straits and ports. These include sea robbery and hostage taking carried out by terrorist groups to generate funding, terrorist hijackings, using a super tanker as a floating bomb to be directed at a port or blowing one up to block a key strait, the destruction of undersea pipelines and communication cables, and the spreading of sea mines in Indonesia's strategic waterways (Sondakh 2004, p. 7; Bakorkamla 2004, p. 5; 2010, p. 99; Richardson, 19 January 2004; US Energy Information Administration,

22 August 2012). A particular concern is the security and safety of the Straits of Malacca and Singapore, the world's busiest sea lane. Around 60 to 70 per cent of vessels plying the Straits of Malacca and Singapore are tankers carrying oil from the Middle East to East Asia (Dewan Maritim Indonesia 2007a, p. 25). A terrorist attack on a tanker navigating these waters would have a devastating impact, harming both Indonesia's inter-island and international trade.

International concern about terrorist attacks intensified after a series of attacks took place in Indonesia. This included two suicide bomb attacks in Bali, in 2002 and 2005; a bomb attack against the Marriott Hotel in Jakarta in 2003; a car bomb outside the Australian Embassy in Jakarta in 2004; simultaneous bomb attacks at the Marriott and the Ritz Carlton Hotels, Jakarta, in 2009; several assaults on police in 2010; and a series of bomb attacks in 2011 that targeted several public figures in Jakarta (*Jakarta Post*, 3 May 2011).

Indonesia, particularly after the 2002 Bali bombings, has adopted numerous counterterrorism measures. But, in the view of a senior government official, these have been "based on its own terms, not on the insistence of the United States or neighbouring countries, including Singapore" and "should not be directly aligned to the so-called war on terror" announced by President Bush.[2] After the Bali bombings, Jakarta promulgated a Presidential Emergency Decree on the Prevention of Terrorism and implemented a new anti-terrorism law. Although the legislation does not empower the Indonesian central government to the same degree as Singapore's Internal Security Act, it enables security personnel to detain suspected terrorists for twenty days, which can be extended for another six months based on preliminary evidence reported by intelligence services (Tan and Ramakrishna 2004, p. 96). The Indonesian government in 2008 issued an instruction to increase the security of government buildings and public facilities, including seaports, in a swift manner. Police, the state intelligence agency, immigration, customs and local governments were instructed to intensify their counterterrorism efforts to halt the mobility of terrorists. This was deemed important as "terrorist[s] could enter or travel through [an] airport or seaport" (Kementerian Koordinator Bidang Politik, Hukum dan Keamanan 2008, p. 7).

The Indonesian government implemented five measures to improve security in key ports in Indonesia. First, the government strengthened the Maritime Security Coordinating Board (Bakorkamla)—which later become the Maritime Security Agency (Bakamla)—to coordinate the country's maritime security policy. A senior government official responsible for determining the security budget claimed there has been a significant increase in government funding to deal with terrorism in ports since 9/11.[3] As Figure 2 shows, from 2005 to 2023, the allocation of resources for this institution increased by more than two hundred times.

As shown in Figure 3, in response to the 9/11 attacks and the 2002 bombings in Bali, the Indonesian Ministry of Defence also increased the percentage of the financial allocation to improve the security of ports and sea lines in Indonesia from 2002 to 2006. There was a sharp decline from 2007 to 2013, before the government started to increase spending for maritime security again gradually from 2014 to 2017.

Second, the government has been conducting counterterrorism training exercises in port areas to improve the capabilities of government agencies in responding to terrorist threats. The training exercises include intra-agency training and a combined exercise. The combined exercise involves several government agencies, including the marine police, the navy, customs, the Ministry of Transportation,

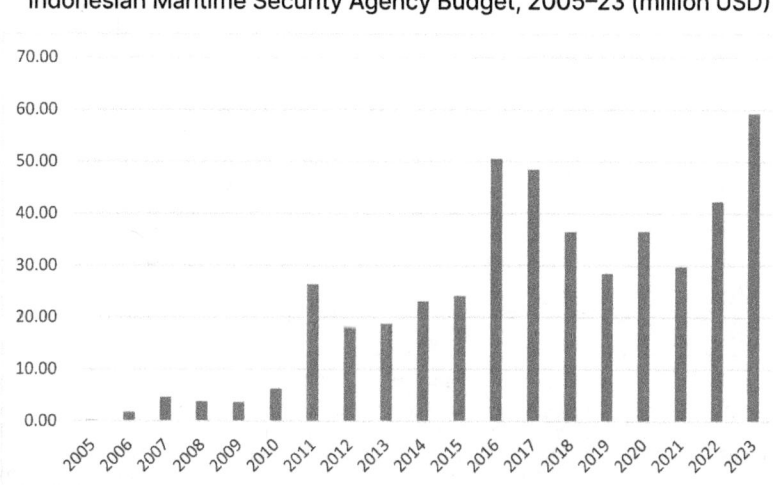

FIGURE 2
Indonesian Maritime Security Agency Budget, 2005–23 (million USD)

Source: Adapted from Badan Perencana Pembangunan Nasional (2005–2023).

Note: Budget for the Indonesian Maritime Security Agency from 2005 to 2015 was incorporated as part of the Coordinating Ministry for Political, Legal and Security Affairs budget. From 2016 to 2023, the budget of the Indonesian Maritime Security Agency was listed in the government funding allocation report separately from the Coordinating Ministry for Political, Legal and Security Affairs budget.

the national search and rescue agency, and the immigration agency (Supriyadi 2010, pp. 48–49).

Third, the government has introduced container security policies, including the harmonization of advance electronic cargo information and the adoption of a risk management approach. To achieve the harmonization of advance electronic cargo information, Indonesia has adopted the World Customs Organization Data Model for its customs clearance system (APEC Desk of the Indonesian Customs 2011, p. 19). Indonesia's advance electronic information programme requires all ships carrying import goods bound for an Indonesian port to provide manifest information twenty-four hours prior to their arrival (ibid., p. 27).

FIGURE 3
Indonesian Ministry of Defence Expenditure for Maritime Security (percentage of total Ministry of Defence budget)

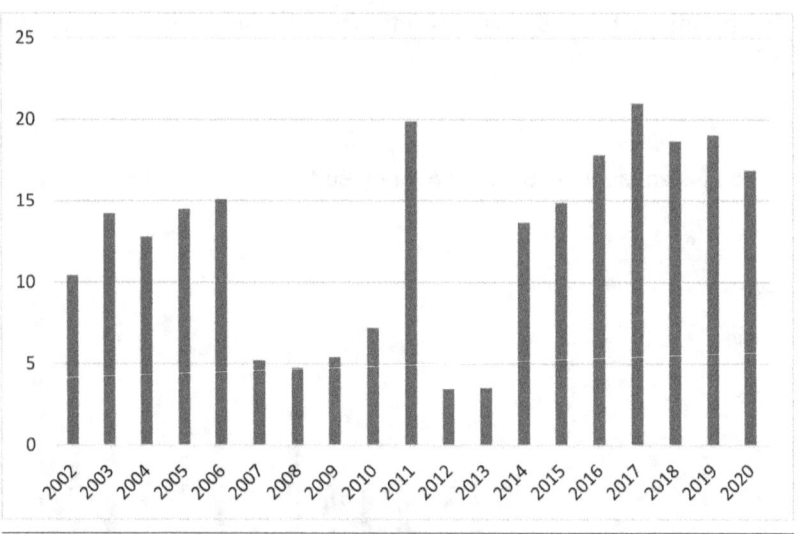

Source: Badan Perencanaan Pembangunan Nasional (2005–10; 2018, 2021; 2023)

Note: Data presented in Figure 3 is based on calculations from the Ministry of Defence total spending for the maritime preparedness support programme, the modernization programme for naval defence equipment and non-defence equipment and development of naval facilities and infrastructure, the naval personnel professionalism improvement programme, and the maritime service management and operations programme. The data presented also incorporates a third of the Ministry of Defence spending for the Ministry of Defence/TNI's education and training programme budget, the defence strategy programme, the defence industry and technology development programme, the defence potential programme, the defence force programme, the programme for the use of integrative defence forces, modernization programmes for defence equipment/non-defence equipment/integrative infrastructure, and the integrative soldier professionalism programme, which the author estimated to be allocated for maritime security purposes.

Fourth, Indonesia has developed a database of importers, exporters, customs brokers, criminal records and transport units as part of its risk management approach (APEC Desk of the Indonesian Customs 2011, p. 21). Indonesian Customs simplifies customs procedures for economic actors that have a good record of compliance with customs regulations. This approach is adopted by Indonesian Customs in the inspection of import and export cargo, packages delivered through mail services, passengers' goods, post clearance audits, and the inspection of ships and other vehicles (ibid., p. 20). In terms of risk-profiling system, the government issued the Decree of the Director General of Customs and Excise No:P-11/BC/2005 concerning Priority Line and the Decree of the Director General of Customs and Excise No:P-24/BC/2007 concerning MITA (*Mitra Utama*) to improve the security of maritime trade (Polner 2010, p. 33). The Priority Line and MITA risk-profiling systems are determined by the shippers' previous track record, the nature of the commodity, the nature of their business, and the Customs intelligence information.

Fifth, to complement these risk-profiling systems, Indonesia also uses non-intrusive cargo inspection devices, including Hi-Co, gamma and X-ray scanners in its major international ports. Non-intrusive devices such as X-ray scanners had been used in several major ports prior to 1990.[4] In 2009–10, Indonesia installed more advanced instruments to carry out inspection. These included several new gamma ray and Hi-Co scan devices. An Indonesian official claimed that Indonesia made an allocation from its national budget to purchase this equipment.[5] These devices are installed at three international ports: Tanjung Priok, Tanjung Emas and Tanjung Perak.[6] In comparison with other types of scanners, Hi-Co devices provide a more accurate scan result. Indonesia purchased four Hi-Co devices and operated them in Tanjung Priok and Tanjung Perak ports. These two ports are the main international gateways for Indonesia. Tanjung Priok Port alone is responsible for managing over 27 per cent of Indonesia's exports and more than 39 per cent of its import activities (Badan Pusat Statistik 2020a; 2020b, pp. 36–39). The X-ray devices are used to scan imported cargo. A gamma ray scanner, which is more accurate than an X-ray scanner, is used for export cargo inspection.

The various measures adopted by the Indonesian government to deal with terrorism focus primarily on major international ports, particularly the three largest ports in the archipelago: Tanjung Priok,

Jakarta; Tanjung Perak, Surabaya; and Tanjung Emas, Semarang. These three ports are located on the island of Java. The majority of training activities, maritime security exercises and scanning devices are located at these three ports. As of 2015, in Indonesia 294 ports were managed by the Indonesian Ports Cooperation and 901 ports were managed by the Indonesian government. There are also over 1,000 special terminals, which mainly serve mining and oil drilling companies involved in both domestic and export-import activities, and 247 ferry docks (Indonesian Ministry of Transport 2015, pp. 4, 42, 43; ASEAN 2009, p. 153). The security of most ports and ferry docks is not up to the same standards as those imposed at Tanjung Priok Port, Tanjung Perak Port or Tanjung Emas Port.

In February 2008, the US Coast Guard issued PSAs to most Indonesian ports, because of unsatisfactory security conditions. Sixteen port facilities, however, were exempted from these PSAs. These were as follows: PT Terminal Peti Kemas Surabaya, Banjarmasin Port, PT Pertamina Unit Pemasaran III, Pertamina Unit Pengolahan V Balikpapan, Senipah Terminal Total E&P Indonesia Balikpapan, Caltex Oil Terminal Dumai, Pelindo II Conventional Terminal Jakarta, Jakarta International Container Terminal, PT Pupuk Kaltim Bontang, PT Badak Bontang, PT Indominco Mandiri Bontang, Pertamina Unit Pengolahan II Dumai, PT Pelabuhan Indonesia I Cabang Dumai, Semarang International Container Terminal, Belawan Multi-Purpose Terminal and PT Multimas Nabati Asahan (US Embassy in Jakarta, 26 February 2008).

For port facilities, the issuance of a PSA means that all vessels stopping at these facilities will be subjected to additional security measures when calling at US ports. If, after the issuance of the PSA, the conditions at the port facility do not improve, the US Coast Guard will issue a maritime security directive or a commandant order, which will outline measures applied on vessels coming to the United States from the country of concern (US Coast Guard, 15 February 2005). These measures may include denying entry to US waters (ibid., 15 April 2004). Under the International Port Security Program, foreign vessels that arrive in the United States without a security certificate and a security plan will face a fine. The US Coast Guard can issue a US$10,000 fine for violators and oblige them to comply with the security requirements within thirty days or face additional fines of up to US$25,000 (Baldor, 25 March 2004). In just February and March 2004 alone, the Coast Guard issued US$66 million in such fines (ibid., 25 March 2004). As a consequence of the issuance of the PSAs, any vessels calling at Indonesian ports were obliged to go through extensive security procedures before being granted permission to enter US ports. An Indonesian government official explained that Koja, an important Indonesian port facility in Jakarta, for instance, lost millions of dollars when the US Coast Guard issued the PSA in 2008 because most of its major clients withdrew their contracts with the port facility.[7]

The Indonesian government increased the allocation of resources from the early 2000s to improve the compliance of Indonesian international ports with the International Ship and Port Facility Security Code, which has been used as a benchmark by the US Coast Guard to assess port security. The government has also allocated more resources to the maritime security agency (Badan Koordinasi Keamanan Laut, later changed to Badan Keamanan Laut) and the navy to improve their equipment and enhance maritime patrols. These increases, however, are dwarfed by the country's complex needs to secure vast maritime areas and coastlines. Underequipped Indonesian maritime institutions are struggling to secure the second-longest coastline in the world, measuring up to 99,093 kilometres, over 6 million square kilometres of waterways, and over 17,000 islands—most of which are uninhabited (Badan Informasi Geospasial, 16 September 2018).

Under increasing international concern over terrorism and a lack of resources to improve port security throughout the archipelago, the government has combined the use of relevant state institutions and *preman* organizations, which exist in most parts of Indonesia. The war against terrorism itself has provided justification for these organizations to expand their activities to the maritime domain.

The involvement of *preman* organizations to assist the government in addressing terrorism takes place in various parts of the country, including the capital city of Jakarta, border regions such as North Sulawesi, and major tourist destination such as Bali. In each province, the government has established several forums to encourage and monitor the participation of *preman* organizations in supporting government counterterrorism programmes. These include the Local Intelligence Committee (Komite Intelijen Daerah), the Coordination Forum for Terrorism Prevention (Forum Koordinasi Pencegahan Terorisme) and the Early Awareness Forum (Forum Kewaspadaan Dini).[8] In Jakarta, for example, the leader of Forum Betawi Rempug explained his organization's engagement in deradicalization and counterterrorism as follow:

Forum Betawi Rempug helps to counter terrorism.... We have assisted the arrest of terrorists in the south of Tangerang twice ... in 2008 and 2009. No matter how good intelligence officers are, sources of [their information] come from the community.⁹

In North Sulawesi, Brigade Manguni and other civil society organizations (CSO) such as Milisi Waraney have assisted the Indonesian police and armed forces to guard Bitung Port, the largest port in the province, and other vital sites during special events such as Eid, Christmas and New Year's Eve celebrations (see Viva News, 31 December 2012). In major tourist destination Bali, *preman* organizations such as Suka Duka Baladika Bali, Laskar Bali and Sanur Bersatu, to mention a few, "perform and enact security alongside the Indonesian state" to deal with terrorism (McDonald and Wilson 2017, p. 245). These groups regularly patrol the streets and coordinate security activities with the police and military advisory staff (Babinsa) (ibid., p. 251).

Domestic Sources of Privatization of Security: Democratization and Civil Society

In May 1998, the resignation of Indonesia's second president, Suharto, brought an end to the state's authoritarian political system that had lasted for more than thirty years (Liddle 1999, p. 39). Democratization opened the floodgates for various groups to organize themselves along the lines of ethnicity, religion, and economic and political lines. These organizations are known as CSOs (*organisasi kemasyarakatan/ormas*) (Bakker 2016, pp. 249–77). As a consequence, there was a growing number of CSOs both in Jakarta and other parts of Indonesia after 1998.

As suggested by Diamond, CSOs should display the key characteristics of voluntary organizations, not be motivated by profit or pursue political power, and be non-violent (Diamond 1996, p. 228, cited in Weiss 2008). Not all CSOs that developed and thrived in post-authoritarian Indonesia demonstrate these civil traits. Some of these CSOs are willing to use violence and intimidation to achieve economic, social and political goals.

Beittinger-Lee argues that in post-authoritarian Indonesia, "long suppressed aspirations, ideologies, religious dogmas and political agendas finally found ways to be expressed" through political parties and CSOs. Not all of them are characterized as tolerant and liberal (Beittinger-Lee 2009, p. 158). These uncivil elements of Indonesian civil society include "militant religious groups, violent vigilante groups, militant youth groups, violence-prone militias and racist/radical ethnonationalist groups" (ibid., p. 159). Beittinger-Lee (2009), Bakker (2016, pp. 249–77), Mudayat, Narendra and Irwanto (2009), and Nugroho and Syarief (2012) all point out the willingness of these uncivil society organizations to use violence against what they deem threats to their well-being.

A large number of *preman* organizations have sought and gained legal status as "legitimate" CSOs in Indonesia. They are formally registered with the Indonesian Ministry of Home Affairs and local governments at provincial and township levels. These organizations gained access to government funding for CSOs and on various occasions have collaborated closely with government authorities both in the security sector and beyond. In practice, however, their mode of operation does not echo the West European CSO principles of the avoidance of violence and of being not for profit.

The growth of *preman* organizations in post-authoritarian Indonesia has received a helping hand from encouragement by the Indonesian military for the formation of self-help civilian security forces (*pamswakarsa*) to deal with social upheaval and student demonstrations following Suharto's resignation (Brown and Wilson 2007, p. 375). These civilian security forces include Islamic vigilante groups, state-sponsored paramilitary groups—including Pemuda Pancasila and Pemuda Panca Marga—and other new organizations that are organized exclusively along ethnic and religious lines (ibid.). They see themselves as legitimate CSOs that are formally registered with the Indonesian Ministry of Home Affairs and the local government, an important agent that can connect the government and local communities, and a societal actor that can voice the concerns of marginalized groups. Leaders and members of *preman* organizations seek to distance their organizations from the image of gangs, thugs, privateers or "borderline-criminal youths" that is often associated with these organizations (Ryter 1998, p. 50)

The majority of *preman* organizations discussed in this research have met all the conditions stated in Ormas Law No. 17/2013 (Undang-Undang Republik Indonesia Nomor 17 tahun 2013 tentang Organisasi Kemasyarakatan). Law No. 17/2013 defined a civil society organization (*organisasi kemasyarakatan*) as an "organization that is established and formed voluntarily by a community that shares similar aspiration, willingness, need, interest, activities and purposes to participate in the development ... of the Republic of Indonesia"

(Article 1). The law stipulates that each organization must register with the Ministry of Home Affairs, the governor and mayor. CSOs are expected to work together with the central and local governments, private sector and other similar organizations (Article 20[f]). The law stipulates that financial resources of CSOs may come from members' contributions, donations from members of society or foreign donors, businesses carried out by these organizations, other legitimate businesses, or the central and/or local government budget (Article 37[1]). Only organizations that have formally registered with the Indonesian Ministry of Home Affairs and the local government can gain access to the state budget. CSOs are prohibited from using names, symbols, flags or attributes that are similar to those used by government agencies; from using violence, disturbing public order or damaging public facilities; and from carrying out activities that fall under the remit of the Indonesian law enforcement agencies (Article 59). Despite these prohibitions, the majority of community organizations that I studied in Jakarta, North Sulawesi and the Riau Islands are organized among semi-military lines; some of them wear uniforms similar to those of the Indonesian military; and they deliver security services (see Bakker 2016, p. 255).

The continuous participation of *preman* organizations in security in Indonesia is informed by the traditional Indonesian security doctrine of the Total People's Defence and Security System (Sistem Pertahanan Keamanan Rakyat Semesta). This Indonesian defence and security doctrine emphasizes the responsibility of civilians in the defence of the state. Civilians are at the heart of the development of Indonesia's national defence. In 1945, the Indonesian armed forces, Badan Keamanan Rakyat, was formed by militias established in various parts of Indonesia who had fought the Dutch forces for independence (Institute for Defence, Security and Peace Studies, Aliansi Jurnalis Independent and Frederich Ebert Stiftung 2008, p. 2). Following Indonesia's independence, from 1945 to 1949, various civilian organizations—including the Student Army (Tentara Pelajar), Village Guerrilla and Security Forces (Pasukan Gerilya Desa and Organisasi Keamanan Desa), the Peoples' Security Organization (Organisasi Keamanan Rakyat) and the Civil Defence (Pertahanan Sipil)—continued to fight alongside Indonesia's regular army to resist Dutch colonial rule (ibid.).

The Total People's Defence and Security System has been maintained "throughout the course of Indonesian history" and it continues to be seen to be "in line with the dynamics of national development" (Indonesian Ministry of Defence 2008, p. 86). It is viewed as "a system that was capable of fighting a colonial power and making Indonesia an independent and sovereign state" (ibid.). At present, the Total People's Defence and Security System is still considered a "suitable [doctrine] that needs to be maintained for the protection of the sovereignty of the Republic of Indonesia (*Negara Kesatuan Republik Indonesia*), the defence of the territorial integrity of the state and the safety of its people" (ibid.; Dewan Maritim Indonesia 2007b, pp. 60–61).

The Total People's Defence and Security System doctrine establishes the foundation of Indonesian maritime defence. The Indonesian Maritime Board highlights the central role of this doctrine in enhancing the archipelago's maritime security as follows:

> The orientation of the state defence is "archipelagic oriented". This means that state defence no longer focuses on land but instead on the sea because the largest threat will come from the sea.... [T]he Total People's Defence and Security System is placed within the format of a modern state through the state's political policies in order to raise awareness and provide responsibilities to society that defence of the state is not only the duty of the Indonesian Armed Forces (Tentara Nasional Indonesia, or TNI). Rather, it is an issue for the entire nation. In this regard, the integration of all [societal] elements ... becomes very relevant.... The responsibility to [maintain] maritime security is the responsibility of all components of the nation.... This is not difficult to materialize as long as there is strong willingness and determination to carry out sincere devotion to the nation and state. (Dewan Maritim Indonesia 2007b, pp. 60–61).

The Total People's Defence and Security System has provided the foundation and legitimacy for the participation of civilian organizations in Indonesia's security. The rest of this chapter will explain the dynamics of Indonesia's domestic politics after the 9/11 attacks that shaped the decision to use *preman* organizations for port security.

The idea to use civilian forces to secure Indonesia's maritime borders was first put forward by President Megawati in the aftermath of the 9/11 attacks. President Megawati's speech on the "Sunda Kelapa declaration" on 27 December 2001 emphasized the central role of civilians in maritime law enforcement, as she encouraged the Indonesian people to assist in developing the country's maritime strength. To quote her:

The Sunda Kelapa Declaration is proclaimed to be the foundation of Indonesian maritime policy that focuses on the following five areas: (1) to rebuild the Indonesian archipelagic vision; (2) to protect maritime sovereignty by (a) improving defence, security and law enforcement capabilities at sea; and (b) the participation of society… (Indonesian Ministry of Foreign Affairs 2005, p. 47)

In 2006, the Indonesian minister of defence, Juwono Sudarsono, announced the government policy to deploy civilian paramilitary forces to help the Indonesian military in patrolling and defending border areas across the country (*Jakarta Post*, 29 June 2006). These civilian patrols work in conjunction with the Indonesian police, army, navy and air force in securing Indonesia's maritime interests. Although Sudarsono's proposal was not met with any outpouring of public support from the president or other senior officials, the idea was not completely dismissed. This could be seen from the Indonesian Coordinating Ministry for Political, Legal and Security Affairs 2006 Work Plan under President Susilo Bambang Yudhoyono's administration. The work plan defined the phrase, "the enhancement of defence capabilities", as:

(a) a policy and strategy that illustrated the minimum essential force, (b) an improvement in the number and condition of the main instruments of the armed forces' defence system, (c) an increased use of domestically produced defence instruments, (d) an improvement in the professionalism of the armed forces, and (e) the utilization of the defence potential of civil society and of active participation in defence development. (Kemenkopolhukam 2006b, p. 40)

As part of the 2006 work plan, the ministry recommended the need to increase coordination in the use of "civil society elements" for state defence, and allocated Rp8,965,000,000 (US$626,546) to undertake research on this matter (Kemenkopolhukam 2006, pp. 40, 57).

At present, under the administration of President Joko Widodo (also known as Jokowi), *preman* organizations have continued to play an important role as an alternative to deter terrorists and criminals from Indonesian ports and borders. The use of *preman* organizations is in line with Indonesia's low-key counterterrorism policies and its focus on "soft" de-radicalization approaches. After the 9/11 attacks, Indonesia's weak as well as heterogeneous domestic coalition contributed to the seemingly slow and unaggressive government responses to terrorist threats (see Febrica 2010). The government's political support is drawn from various factions, such as the military,

Islamic parties, business interests and others (see Solingen 2005, p. 9, for a discussion of Indonesia's political coalition). Consequently, this heterogeneous coalition hinders the government from taking a strong stance in the "war on terror".

In the 2014 presidential election, Joko Widodo, who was endorsed by Partai Demokrasi Indonesia Perjuangan (PDIP), won 71 million votes, or 53.15 per cent of the total vote (*The Economist*, 26 July 2014). Support from a popular Islamic party, Partai Kebangkitan Bangsa (PKB), which is closely linked with Nahdlatul Ulama—one of the largest Islamic organizations in the country—was vital to ensuring victory for Joko Widodo and his vice-presidential running mate Jusuf Kalla (*The Economist*, 2 October 2014). In 2014, although Joko Widodo had won the presidential election, his "Indonesia Awesome Coalition" (Koalisi Indonesia Hebat)—which comprises four parties: PDIP (109 seats), NasDem (35 seats), PKB (47 seats) and Hanura (16 seats)—only won 207 seats, or 36.9 per cent of the total number of seats in the parliament (*Metro*, 26 August 2014). In 2016, Joko Widodo added two more parties to his presidential coalition. These were Golkar, a still powerful party that had taken the role of the main electoral machine during Suharto's authoritarian regime, and the conservative Islamic party Partai Persatuan Pembangunan (PPP). This move enabled Joko Widodo to turn a 37 per cent minority in the parliament when he first came to office in October 2014 into a 69 per cent majority by mid-2016 (Mietzner 2016, pp. 211, 215).

The coalitional approach also marked Joko Widodo's success in the 2019 election. Joko Widodo and his vice-presidential running mate Ma'ruf Amin won over 84 million votes, or 55.32 per cent of the total vote (Komisi Pemilihan Umum 2019). Support from five parties with a nationalist outlook (PDIP, Golkar, NasDem, Hanura and Partai Keadilan dan Persatuan Indonesia) and the two largest Islamic parties in Indonesia (PKB and PPP) was crucial in delivering this victory (CNBC Indonesia, 10 August 2018). In 2019 there was a significant increase in the total number of seats gained in the parliament by Joko Widodo's Indonesia Onward Coalition (Koalisi Indonesia Maju). The key parties supporting Joko Widodo's coalition—PDIP (128 seats), Golkar (85 seats), NasDem (59 seats), PKB (58 seats) and PPP (19 seats)—won a total of 349 seats in the parliament, or the equivalent of 60 per cent of total parliamentary seats (Detik, 1 October 2019).

This coalition formed of diverse elements compelled Joko Widodo to maintain a delicate balance among the various factions in dealing with the threats posed by terrorism during his first and second terms in office. The government needed to maintain a balance between cracking down on terror networks and in cooperating with foreign countries without going against the will of other members of the coalition (see also Febrica 2010).

At the domestic level, the Indonesian government's limited resources for maritime security and counterterrorism have also contributed to sustaining the use of *preman* organizations for port security for the country. Joko Widodo was inaugurated as the seventh president of Indonesia on 20 October 2014. Soon after taking office, Joko Widodo announced his plan to transform Indonesia into "the global maritime fulcrum (GMF), a locus of great civilization in the future" (*Tempo*, 22 July 2014). On 13 November 2015, at the East Asia Summit in Nay Pyi Taw, Myanmar, Joko Widodo announced his administration's plan to promote Indonesia as the maritime fulcrum of the world. The GMF plan is built upon five pillars (Indonesian Presidential Office, 13 November 2015). The first is the development of Indonesia's maritime culture. The second is a commitment to safeguard and manage marine resources, especially fishery resources. The third is a pledge to improve Indonesia's maritime infrastructure and connectivity by developing seaports, the shipping industry and maritime tourism. The fourth is to use diplomacy to encourage maritime cooperation between Indonesia and other countries. And the fifth is the development of Indonesia's maritime defence capacity. The need to develop maritime defence is underscored by the country's vast maritime area (5.8 million square kilometres) and a lack of equipment that has left Indonesia vulnerable to various maritime security concerns, including illegal, unreported and unregulated fishing; maritime terrorism; and armed robbery against ships. Despite one of the key pillars of the maritime fulcrum plan being a pledge to develop Indonesia's maritime defence, rather than exclusively relying on state security services or employing professional security companies, the government has continued the practice of involving *preman* organizations to monitor threats posed by terrorism and other criminal activities at small ports and on remote islands.

There is widespread disappointment among analysts that Indonesia's efforts to realize the GMF vision have dwindled (see Laksmana, 8 November 2019). Since his re-election in 2019, President Joko Widodo and senior officials in his administration have not made much reference to the GMF vision. The pledge to improve Indonesia's

FIGURE 4
Indonesian Anti-Terrorism Agency's Expenditure, 2013–23 (million USD)

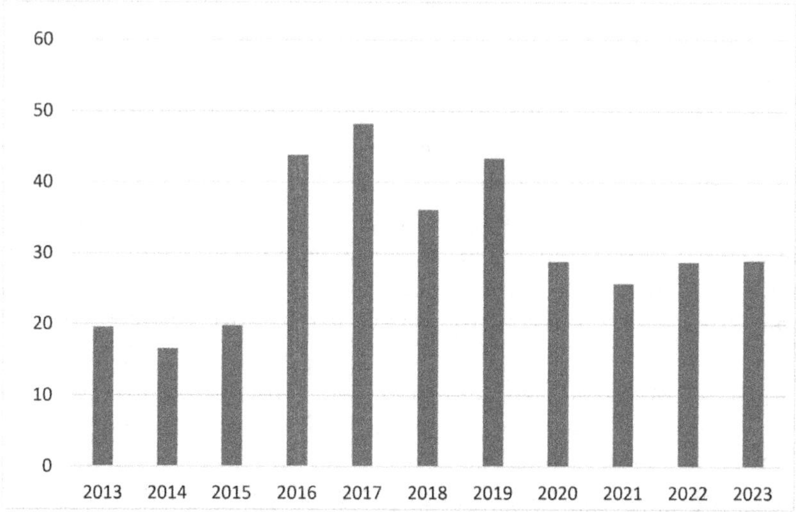

Source: Badan Perencanaan Pembangunan Nasional (2018; 2022; 2023).
Note: The 2013 to 2022 data is based on the Indonesian Anti-Terrorism Agency's spending, whereas the 2023 data is based on government allocation of funding rather than actual spending.

maritime infrastructure and connectivity has been the only goal of the GMF that the government has managed to consistently uphold throughout Jokowi's presidency (Laksmana, 8 November 2019).[10] In terms of maritime defence and security, as shown in Figure 3, when Joko Widodo came to power in 2014, expenditure by the Indonesian Ministry of Defence for maritime security increased by a factor of four, and the figure steadily increased from 2014 to 2017. But the percentage of the Ministry of Defence's maritime security spending began to decline towards the end of Joko Widodo's first presidential term. By 2020, maritime security spending accounted for less than 17 per cent of the Ministry of Defence's budget.

A limited government maritime security budget has direct implications for Indonesia's maritime defence and security. The Indonesian government targeted to attain a hundred per cent of its minimum essential force by 2024. For the Indonesian Navy, this means acquiring 182 warships (*kapal perang Republik Indonesia*, often shortened as KRI), 8 submarines, 100 aeroplanes and 978 marine combat vehicles (*kendaraan tempur*, or *ranpur*) (Indonesian Ministry of Defence, cited in Zhara and Rizky 2020, p. 4). By 2021, Indonesia, media reported that the government had achieved less than 65 per cent of its targeted minimum essential force (CNBC, 17 May 2021). It was reported that as of 5 October 2021, the Indonesian navy had acquired only 7 frigates, 24 corvettes, 5 submarines, 179 patrol boats and 10 minesweepers (Sindonews, 5 October 2021).

Under Joko Widodo, the government has used less than one per cent of the country's gross domestic product for security and defence purposes to allow for greater funding for programmes associated with the government's focus on improving people's welfare, such as infrastructure development across the archipelago, the implementation of nationwide health insurance (Badan Penyelenggara Jaminan Sosial Kesehatan) and a minimum allocation of the state budget of twenty per cent for education (Indonesia Baik 2022; *Kompas*, 9 August 2021).

Because of a lack of resources, the Indonesian government is not always able to meet its security needs. For example, in terms of national counterterrorism measures, the government needs to maintain sufficient funding to conduct counterterrorism operations in Poso, strengthen the Indonesian anti-terrorism agency (Badan Nasional Penanggulangan Terorisme, or BNPT), build adequate prisons to detain terrorist suspects and isolate them from criminals, and improve coordination between various law enforcement agencies, including the police, armed forces, immigration agency, customs and the maritime security agency (Badan Keamanan Laut, or Bakamla) to anticipate cross-border terrorist movements and the arrival of Indonesians who have joined Islamic State in the Middle East and the southern Philippines. In 2014, for instance, the Indonesian police only received Rp44 billion (approximately US$3 million) to support its counterterrorism operations (*Kompas*, 30 October 2014). This is less than half of the Rp100 billion (approximately US$7 million) that the former chief of the Indonesian police, Sutarman, claimed his institution critically needed (ibid.). As shown in Figure 4, resources allocated to the Indonesian anti-terrorism agency (BNPT) have also been in decline since 2018 (Riyono 2022, p. 8). The current domestic security focus to ensure the safety and success of the next presidential election, the purchase of new military equipment to meet Indonesia's defence-posture target, and the COVID-19 pandemic have contributed to the decline in the allocation of resources for counterterrorism (Riyono 2022, p. 8).

Shortages in resources, equipment and manpower capacity to secure Indonesia's ports and maritime domains are not problems unique to Joko Widodo's administration. These concerns have been raised by various government agencies involved in Indonesia's security sector before Joko Widodo was inaugurated as president in 2014.

In 2006, for example, the Indonesian Coordinating Ministry for Political, Legal and Security Affairs noted that,

> With vast areas, diverse social, economic and cultural conditions, as well as potential threats from within and outside of the country, the Indonesian Armed Forces are lacking personnel and having insufficient main weaponry systems.... The Navy's submarines, destroyers ... and patrol vessels and their supporting units are relatively old. (Kemenkopolhukam 2006a, p. 9).

In a separate document, the Coordinating Ministry highlighted several problems in securing borders and outlying islands, including "the insufficient infrastructure at the borders and outlying islands, [and] the [government's] limitation to conduct sea patrol" (Kemenkopolhukam 2008b).

The Indonesian maritime board identified similar weaknesses in Indonesia's maritime security governance, ranging from a lack of coordination between various maritime law enforcement agencies and insufficient budget, numbers of personnel and equipment (Dewan Maritim Indonesia 2007b, pp. 59, 62). As the Indonesian maritime board put it, "in terms of maritime security, there [are] limitations of the armada and an insufficient number of personnel" (Dewan Maritim Indonesia 2007, p. 62).

The lack of equipment and personnel, as articulated in the above-mentioned documents, has provided justification for the participation of non-state organizations in maritime security. Despite government documents not explicitly mentioning the names of *preman* organizations, non-state entities are seen as a key component in defending the country. The notion of civilian participation in security appears in government documents published by both defence and non-defence agencies (Dewan Maritim Indonesia 2007b, p. 59; 2007a, p. 52; Kemenkopolhukam 2006, pp. 29, 34–35; Marin 2005, p. 35; Suristiyono 2005, p. 49; Dewan Maritim Indonesia 2007c, pp. 4-8–4-9). This finding indicates how the decision to use *preman* organizations as a necessary measure to improve the monitoring of ports and guarding them from terrorist and other illicit activities is part of the norm and everyday politics in Indonesia. The decision to engage *preman* organization was not made at the executive level by Joko Widodo or his predecessors such as Presidents Megawati or Yudhoyono. Rather, the use of *preman* organizations for port security is a continual mode of action where the decision has been made by bureaucratic machinery and functionaries at national and local levels rather than by "grand sovereigns" (see Walker 2006, p. 80). The use of *preman* organizations has been widely dispersed and is not controlled or even initiated by the head of state or senior government officials (see Doty 2007, p. 116). It is part of the routine and norms of everyday politics at the national and local levels in various parts of Indonesia, such as Jakarta, North Sulawesi and the Riau Islands (see Williams 2003, p. 514).[11] The participation of *preman* organizations in port security is seen as a "normal" and desirable day-to-day security practice even for elected civilian leaders from the three case studies regions that the author interviewed. Some of these civilian leaders not only supported the involvement of *preman* organizations for monitoring and securing smaller goods and passengers ports, but also advocating their use by businesses as a form of corporate social responsibility towards the local community.[12]

In dealing with terrorism and other maritime security threats, the decision by the Indonesian government to use *preman* organizations should not be seen as a suspension of the normal rules and procedures in order to preserve political order, but instead should be seen as an attempt to "expand on the existing law" (see Doty 2007, p. 131). As explained earlier in this chapter, as part of the post-Suharto democratization process, the Indonesian government has issued an array of new defence-related legislation, including Law No. 3/2002 on state defence, Law No. 2/2002 on the Indonesian police, and Law No. 34/2004 on the Indonesian armed forces. These pieces of legislation point to the role of the Indonesian armed forces and police as the main institutions responsible for state defence (Law No. 34/2004, Article 17; Law No. 2/2002, Articles 13 and 14; and Law No. 3/2002, Article 1). Despite reforms, however, the new legislation continues to enable the Indonesian state to implement the Total People's Defence and Security System doctrine to address "military threats" that pose grave danger to state sovereignty, territorial integrity and the safety of the people (Law No. 3/2002, Articles 1, 7 and 8). This doctrine endorses the participation of civilians in defence of the state. Article 1(2) of Law No. 3/2002 defines the national defence system as

> a defence system with a universal nature that involves all citizens, regions and other national resources, and is prepared in advance by

the government and carried out in a total, integrated, directed and continual manner to uphold state sovereignty, territorial integrity and the safety of the whole nation from all threats.[13]

In facing a military threat, Article 7(2) of Law No. 3/2002 stresses that the national defence system "places the Indonesian armed forces as the main [defence] component (*komponen utama*)", which will be supported by the reserve (*komponen cadangan*) and supporting (*komponen pendukung*) components.[14] The reserve component here is defined as "citizens, natural resources, artificial resources, as well as national facilities, and infrastructure that have been prepared to be deployed ... to enlarge and strengthen the main components".[15] Supporting components are citizens, facilities and resources that "can directly or indirectly increase the strength and capability of the main and reserve components".[16]

The Total People's Defence and Security System is a legacy of Indonesia's postcolonial defence system that was used systematically throughout Suharto's authoritarian regime to put down insurgencies and student-led anti-government protests. This illiberal element of Indonesia's defence system has been maintained and has continued to guide the delivery of security provision in present-day Indonesia. This continuity in social and political life in Indonesia incorporates the deep-rooted and institutionalized local practice of the engagement of *preman* organizations in security. The institutionalization of the use of *preman* organizations in security is reflected in various assessments made by bureaucratic machinery and functionaries that called for the involvement of civilian groups to fill the gap in supply and demand for security in Indonesia.

A document published by the Indonesian Ministry of Maritime and Fisheries Affairs mentioned that

> The establishment of economic contacts between Indonesian society [living at the border] with the society of neighbouring countries has implications for the development of "national defence" at the borders.... It creates mutual dependence between the two societal entities.... This also opens opportunities for the development of emotional attachment between these societies that share cultural affinities.... [It is believed] this can influence the quality of Indonesian society's nationalism and lessen [the] attitude and awareness [of individuals] to defend the country. (Dewan Maritim Indonesia 2007a, p. 52)

The Indonesian Maritime Board identified that a lack of general public involvement in security has weakened government efforts to improve the country's maritime governance. As the Indonesian Maritime Board put it,

> the capability of Indonesian law enforcement agencies (navy, police, fishery monitoring unit) to enforce sovereignty and law at sea is still weak and the general public is not fully involved.... [M]aritime security needs to be dealt with in a more effective manner... (Dewan Maritim Indonesia 2007b, p. 59)

The above quotes point to the government's expectation for civilians, especially those living in border areas, to play an active part in defending the country from maritime security threats or perceived threats.

The role of civilians in defence and security is also echoed in work plans, accountability reports and survey results published by the Indonesian Coordinating Ministry for Political, Legal and Security Affairs. The ministry's nationwide survey on political, defence and security conditions in 2005 recommended that to maintain security in North Sulawesi certain steps are necessary. These steps mainly include various efforts to boost nationalism in society. The document pointed out that the concrete materialization of nationalism in the area of defence and security lies in the communities' "spirit to defend their country" (Kemenkopolhukam 2005). Civilian participation in security was also highlighted in the government's 2005 accountability report. According to the report, from 2005 to 2009, the Indonesian Coordinating Ministry of Political, Legal and Security Affairs established strategic targets for state defence and security that include

> better coordination to address criminal acts, including transnational crime; a reduction in security issues that intrude on the country's sovereignty at sea and air territory; and a decline of violations of law against marine and forest resources. In order to achieve these targets, the government has increased coordination between agencies in the utilization of society's potential in defending the state. (Kemenkopolhukam 2006, pp. 29, 34–35)

At the operational level, an expert staff of the Indonesian National Defence Institute (Lemhanas), Major General Djasri Marin, pointed out that societal actors are deemed the main defence and security potential that the government can use to address internal and external threats. Marin explained that societal involvement in security is part of the Total Defence System, and Lemhanas has continued to study ways to engage members of society in security both to defend the country from external threats and to deal with internal security issues (Marin 2005, p. 35). The main issue here, according to Marin, is to decide the engagement pattern for civilian forces. For instance, in dealing with a certain security problem, how many civilians should be involved relative to the ratio of state law enforcement personnel. As he put it, "do we need to hand everything to the state law enforcement authorities?... We are still using the Total Defence System; however, which patterns [of civilian engagement] shall we use? This is the issue that we continue to study" (ibid.).

The vice-director of the Indonesian marine police, Commissioner Suristiyono, explained that, as part of operational activities of the marine police to maintain security and order within society and to enforce the law, they have "cultivated coastal community participation to act as an early preventer against security disturbances and violations of law at the waterways; empower/encourage components of society to play an active role in creating Pam Swakarsa [voluntary security forces]" (Suristiyono 2005, p. 49). He further elaborated that the marine police "provides guidance and community coaching activities to members of society to enable them to carry out early prevention and address disturbances stemming from within or outside the country" (ibid.).

As part of the Indonesian government's grand maritime development strategy, it is developing a monitoring, controlling, and surveillance (MCS) system to protect the country's marine resources. The MCS system incorporates a community-based monitoring system (Pengawasan Berbasis Masyarakat/Siswasmas). The Siswasmas encourages members of society to carry out monitoring of illicit activities at sea or coastal areas and helps the government to optimize the security of borders and outlying islands (Dewan Maritim Indonesia 2007c, pp. 4-8–4-9).

Despite reform, the use of *preman* organizations continues to be seen by Indonesian decision-makers and parliamentarians as a beneficial instrument. There is a widespread perception among officials and legislators in Indonesia about the usefulness of these groups as an instrument to complement government security forces. As an official from the Indonesian National Defence Council (Dewan Ketahanan Nasional) put it,

> The involvement of these actors [*preman* organizations] has complicated the existing security system. We can deny the involvement of civilian organizations in security … however, at the practical level there is symbiotic mutualism between these

organizations and the state. As they [*preman* organizations] maintain security in some ports and border areas, the formal security guards would no longer be needed in large numbers there. The formal security authorities will view that as long as the presence of civilian organizations can secure the ports and border areas and no disturbance takes place then these organizations would be left alone. This is despite the system not allowing the participation of non-governmental organizations in port or border security. Even the system forbids the involvement of non-governmental organizations or units that are associated with political parties in port and border security.[17]

This view was echoed by an official from the Indonesian Coordinating Ministry for Political, Legal and Security Affairs. He claimed there is a need to regulate the use of *preman* organizations at ports and to design a plan of operation. According to him, "members of non-governmental organizations could be recruited to be security officers".[18] He argued that these non-governmental organizations must meet the requirements for security outsourcing. Thus, they need to train their members to secure the movement of goods and people—possibly under the guidance of the police force—and establish official security companies.[19]

The view of this government official on the use of *preman* organizations to improve port security is also shared among some members of the Indonesian parliament. Senators representing Jakarta and Riau are very supportive of the activities of groups such as Pemuda Pancasila, Forum Betawi Rempug and Musyawarah Kekeluargaan Gotong Royong (MKGR) in ports. A senator from the Riau Islands claimed that organizations such as MKGR are most useful in securing smaller ports in the Riau Islands.[20] In his opinion these organizations have helped in securing the loading and unloading of goods and have served as mediators when labour demonstrations take place. A senator from Jakarta went further to argue that the use of local non-governmental organizations by port operators should be seen as a form of corporate social responsibility of the port operator towards the local community.[21]

The positive perception of parliamentarians is shaped by their affiliation with these groups. Some parliamentarians are either respected members or leaders of *preman* organizations. After 1998, *preman* organizations have also become valuable sources of political support for politicians seeking election or re-election. Despite claiming neutrality, several *preman* organizations have provided support to their members who run for public office and to national and local politicians affiliated with their organizations. During the 2014 presidential election campaign, for example, Forum Komunikasi Anak Betawi (Forkabi) in Jakarta and Brigade Manguni in North Sulawesi pledged their support to presidential candidate Prabowo Subianto (*Berita Manado*, 10 March 2013; 12 June 2014; *Tribun Manado*, 9 March 2013; 27 August 2014). Subianto was the main challenger to Joko Widodo during the 2014 and 2019 presidential elections. Forkabi is a Betawi ethnic-based *preman* organization, and Brigade Manguni is the largest *preman* organization in North Sulawesi.

A similar situation emerged during regional elections. In Jakarta, this could be seen from the involvement of FBR in the 2017 election campaign for governor. The FBR had been reported making racist remarks about Basuki Tjahja Purnama, also known as Ahok (*Jakarta Post*, 8 September 2016). Lutfi Hakim, the FBR leader, called on his followers not to elect Purnama, a candidate who does not share their race or religion (ibid.). Following the FBR demonstration to reject Basuki Tjahja Purnama's decision to run for re-election, Purnama announced his decision to stop the annual allocation of funding worth Rp4–5 billion (over US$300,000) for the Betawi culture consultative body (Badan Musyawarah Betawi/Bamus Betawi), a Betawi ethnic group organization that oversees the FBR (*Jakarta Post*, 8 September 2016). Outside of Java, Jeffry Mentu, a mayoral candidate for Minahasa, a regency in North Sulawesi, claimed in a media statement that he was confident of winning the 2012 local election because he had support from society and various organizations, including a *preman* organization called Milisi Waraney. Mentu is one of the leaders (Panglima) of Milisi Waraney (*Tribun Manado*, 8 August 2012).

Conclusion

This chapter has explained that a combination of domestic political dynamics that compel the government to take low-key approaches to counterterrorism and institutionalized practices that normalize the use of *preman* organizations for the provision of security influence the continued participation of *preman* organizations in port security in Indonesia. In the wake of the 9/11 attacks there was growing international concern over the security of Indonesia's waterways, coastlines and maritime facilities. In 2008, the United States issued PSAs to a majority of Indonesia's ports, exempting only sixteen port facilities from them. The issuance of PSAs by the United States meant that all vessels stopping at these facilities were required to go through additional security measures when calling at US ports. Responding to international pressure, Indonesia has sought to improve the security of its ports by allocating more financial resources to the country's key maritime agencies, conducting patrols and exercises, establishing a risk-profiling system and installing more scanners. These policy responses have enabled Indonesia to ensure the country's continued participation in international maritime trade. But despite rigorous efforts to improve port and maritime security in general, the Indonesian government faces challenges in enhancing security across thousands of small ports, ferry docks and coastal areas throughout the archipelago. The Indonesian government has only been able to focus its resources on the key ports responsible for handling the country's export and import activities. Faced with increasing international concern over maritime terrorism and a lack of resources, the government has used or encouraged the participation of *preman* organizations, which are present in most areas in Indonesia, including the capital city, border regions and the main tourist destinations. The war against terrorism has provided some justification for *preman* organizations to expand their activities in various small ports and coastal areas.

It is worthwhile to examine the dynamics of Indonesia's domestic politics. The involvement of non-state security providers in Indonesia can be traced to the early years of the republic. Civilian organizations and militias formed the basis of the Indonesian armed forces and they actively fought the Dutch forces for independence from 1945 to 1949. From the war of independence until the present day, the Total People's Defence and Security System continues to be the crux of Indonesia's defence and security doctrine. It lays the foundation and renders legitimacy for the participation of civilian organizations in Indonesia's security. The end of Suharto's authoritarian regime in 1998 provided opportunities for the development of various civilian organizations, including those that display militaristic traits. Some of these organizations form themselves along religious, ethnic or nationalistic lines.

After the events of 9/11, societal participation in improving port security and in patrolling and defending border areas and outlying islands has been encouraged by various parts of the Indonesian government and parliamentarians. The endorsement of *preman* organizations in port security by Indonesian bureaucracies and functionaries should not be seen as an exceptional measure adopted to deal with global terrorism. This is because the use of *preman* organizations in security is part of institutionalized practice in Indonesia. As part of everyday politics, Indonesian government agencies, local governments and businesses have engaged *preman* organizations to "fill the security gap" caused by shortages of government resources and manpower. Government officials and parliamentarians display a positive attitude towards *preman* organizations and their role in port security. This positive attitude towards *preman* organizations is also partly shaped by political support rendered by these organizations at the local and national levels to officials or parliamentarians. After 1998, *preman* organizations have provided support to national and local politicians who are affiliated with their organizations.

Notes

1. This part of the chapter draws heavily from the following publications: Febrica 2010, pp. 569–90; 2014, pp. 64–83; 2015, pp. 105–30; 2017a, pp. 27–28; pp. 36–40; 2017b; 2020; 2021.
2. Interview with Indonesian senior government official, 20 June 2008, Jakarta.
3. Interview with a senior government official at the Indonesian National Development Planning Agency, 28 September 2011, Jakarta.
4. Interview with a senior government official at the Indonesian Customs and Excise, Ministry of Finance, 4 November 2011, Jakarta.
5. Ibid.
6. Interview with senior government officials at the Indonesian Customs and Excise, Ministry of Finance, 3 November 2011, Jakarta.
7. Interview with a senior government official at the Indonesian Ministry of Transportation, 3 September 2010, Jakarta.
8. Interview with a senior official of the Agency for National Unity and Politics, Jakarta provincial government, 30 September 2016, Jakarta.
9. Interview with the chairman of Forum Betawi Rempug, 31 March 2016, Jakarta.
10. Interview with an Indonesian foreign policy expert at Universitas Indonesia, 15 April 2022.
11. Interviews with a senator from the Riau Island, Jakarta, 18 August 2015; senator from Jakarta, 18 August 2015, Jakarta.
12. Ibid.
13. Article 1(2) of Law No. 3/2002 on State Defence (UU No. 3/2002 *tentang Pertahanan Negara*).
14. Article 7(2) of Law No. 3/2002 on State Defence (UU No. 3/2002 *tentang Pertahanan Negara*).

15. Article 8(1) of Law No. 3/2002 on State Defence (UU No. 3/2002 *tentang Pertahanan Negara*).
16. Article 8(2) of Law No. 3/2002 on State Defence (UU No. 3/2002 *tentang Pertahanan Negara*).
17. Interview with an official from the Indonesian National Defence Council, 7 August 2015.
18. Interview with an official from the Indonesian Coordinating Ministry for Political, Legal and Security Affairs, 21 August 2015.
19. Ibid.
20. Interview with a senator from the Riau Islands, 18 August 2015, Jakarta.
21. Interview with a senator from Jakarta, 18 August 2015, Jakarta.

Chapter 2

Jakarta: *Preman* Organizations and Port Security in the Capital City

Jakarta is the capital city of Indonesia. The 7,659.02 square kilometres territory of Jakarta consists of 661.52 square kilometres of land, including 110 islands in Kepulauan Seribu, and 6,997.50 square kilometres of sea (Dinas Komunikasi, Informatika dan Statistik Pemprov DKI Jakarta 2017). Ports in Jakarta have played a crucial role as key gateways for both Indonesia's inter-island and international trade as well as the fishing industry. The busiest container port in Indonesia, Tanjung Priok, is located in Jakarta. Tanjung Priok Port alone is responsible for managing over 27 per cent of Indonesia's exports and more than 39 per cent of its import activities (Badan Pusat Statistik 2020a; 2020b, pp. 36–39). Jakarta is also home to six fishing ports. These include Cilincing, Samudera Nizam Zachman–Muara Baru, Pulau Pramuka, Muara Angke, Kamal Muara and Kali Adem (Kementerian Kelautan dan Perikanan 2013).

Security management across all ports in Jakarta, however, is not trouble free. The involvement of *preman* organizations in port security on the one hand has aided the security apparatus. On the other hand, it has brought various challenges, including violent conflicts among *preman* organizations and with the government security apparatus. Jakarta is home to many *preman* organizations that are competing for resources and influence in the country's capital city. As of 2016, there were 470 civil societies and 50 youth organizations formally registered with the Agency for National Unity and Politics (Badan Kesatuan Bangsa dan Politik) of the Jakarta provincial government.

These include those that adopt hyper-nationalist ideology such as Pemuda Panca Marga and Pemuda Pancasila (PP); ethnic-based organizations such as Forum Komunikasi Anak Betawi and Forum Betawi Rempug (FBR); and groups that exhibit Islamic ideology such as Forum Pembela Islam and Gerakan Pemuda Ka'aba. Among the many *preman* organizations operating in Jakarta, two are deemed the largest and have been involved in port security; these are PP and FBR. The involvement of these two CSOs in port security took place at different periods. PP played an important role in port security during the early decades of Suharto's regime up till the 1980s. FBR's involvement in port security only began in the years after Suharto stood down.

This chapter will provide a comprehensive explanation of the involvement of *preman* organizations in port security in Jakarta and the challenges this practice has brought. Analysis of interviews with government officials and representatives of *preman* organizations, government documents and media reports show that *preman* organizations have taken part in port security by working with licensed private security companies and providing information on the security situation and illicit activities in ports and surrounding areas to government authorities.

The participation of *preman* organizations in port security in Jakarta is very costly. This is because, first of all, violent clashes frequently occur between different *preman* organizations in various parts of Jakarta, and between these organizations and the government security authorities and the private security company in Tanjung Priok Port. Second, the involvement of *preman* organizations in local politics and their instrumental role in informing the course of the democratic process in Jakarta should be seen as a high price to pay for using *preman* organizations for security purposes. Third, the ambiguous role played by *preman* organizations in sustaining illicit activities at ports in Jakarta is another reason the participation of these organizations in port security could be deemed problematic.

To demonstrate the above arguments, the second part of this chapter will explain the involvement of PP in port security in Jakarta prior to Indonesia's democratic reform. It will provide an explanation for the historical trajectories of PP's involvement in Tanjung Priok Port and the changes in global and national maritime transport policies that transformed its control over the port. The third part of this chapter will analyse FBR's participation in port security after Suharto stood down in 1998. It will explain the existing partnership and support the government has provided to FBR. The fourth part of this chapter will account for the underlying tensions in using *preman* organizations for securing ports and port-related facilities in Jakarta. This section will explain the conflicts that have taken place between the government and FBR and clashes between FBR and different *preman* organizations. It will also provide an assessment of illicit activities at ports in Jakarta and the involvement of *preman* organizations in sustaining such activities. The conclusion of this chapter will highlight the involvement of *preman* organizations in port security in Jakarta and the underlying tensions that accompany it.

The Rise of Ethnic Betawi *Preman* Organizations and Port Security in Jakarta

The key *preman* organizations involved in port security and their mode of engagement in Jakarta saw significant changes following the introduction of the containerization policy by the Indonesian government. Containerization and the automation of port facilities has increased the speed of and reduced the expenses in the transportation of goods. The launching of the first container ship in 1956 marked the beginning of the container era in the world (Rodrigue and Notteboom 2009, p. 2). From the mid-1960s, the standardization of container sizes and the lashing system further assisted its diffusion within the global maritime system (ibid., p. 4). Containerization, however, only spread to developing countries such as Indonesia in the 1980s because of the lack of capital and technological and institutional capacity there to support container transport (Airriess 1989, p. 453). Indonesia was the last country among the ASEAN founding members to adopt containerization (ibid., p. 454).

Indonesia's largest port, Tanjung Priok, was the pilot site for the introduction of containerization and the automation of port facilities in the archipelago. Container operations formally began in Tanjung Priok in 1981 following pressure applied by Western markets and shipping firms, along with the Indonesian government's efforts to boost the country's non-oil exports (Airriess 1989, p. 454). In the 1970s, Indonesia was dependent on oil-based exports. A drastic fall in worldwide petroleum prices in the early 1980s pushed the Indonesian government to encourage non-oil exports (ibid., p. 457). The adoption of container technology was further supported by the introduction of Presidential Instruction 4 on 4 April 1985. The presidential instruction enabled the opening up of Indonesian ports to foreign vessels, introduced changes in the country's port clearance system that significantly reduced freight charges between Indonesia and Singapore, and shifted the inspection responsibilities of the national customs to the Societe Generale de Surveilance (ibid.). The adoption of the container transport system in Tanjung Priok also dramatically changed the participation of *preman* organizations in port security.

Historically, the groups that had control over ports in North Jakarta included migrants coming from Makassar, Banten, Madura and the Moluccas, which formed their own gangs, and PP, a more formally organized organization.[1] All these groups compete for the economic benefits that Tanjung Priok Port can offer, including in accessing the many employment opportunities there. Prior to the spread of container technology, a large number of labourers was required to handle the movement of break-bulk cargo and smaller unitized cargo in Tanjung Priok.[2] By controlling port labour, the ethnic-based gangs and PP could exercise influence over security at the port. They could maintain peace or instigate disturbances in port areas.

The ethnic-based gangs in Jakarta did not establish formal organizations to advance their interests. They were deeply segregated and often involved in turf wars with each other. During the New Order era, a government-registered *preman* organization that had significant influence over the security dynamics of Tanjung Priok Port was PP.[3] PP was the most influential *preman* organization during Suharto's New Order regime. During the New Order, this organization was involved in purging alleged members of the communist party, monitoring political demonstrations and guarding vital sites, including ports. PP was formed on 28 October 1959 in Jakarta as the youth wing of the Association of the Indonesian Independence Supporters (Ikatan Pendukung Kemerdekaan Indonesia), a political party formed by the Indonesian military in the 1950s (Sciascia 2013, p. 176). The patrons of PP have included prominent Indonesian military leaders such as General Ahmad Yani, General Abdul Haris Nasution and General Gatot Subroto (Majelis Pimpinan Nasional Pemuda Pancasila 2017). It is a semi-military organization, and members wear camouflage and a military-style beret. Because of the close link with the Indonesian army, the paramilitary wing of this organization—namely, the Core Command (Komando Inti/Koti)—has continued to receive martial arts training from the Indonesian army.[4] PP is registered with the Indonesian Ministry of Home Affairs and the provincial government as a legitimate non-governmental organization. It has secretariats in most cities and towns across Indonesia.

The introduction of containerization in Tanjung Priok Port posed significant limitations on PP's involvement in port security. At the local level, containerization brought significant changes to labour relations (Rodrigue and Notteboom 2009, p. 6). Labour-intensive port activities became thoroughly mechanized, transforming the role and function of port labour, and therefore affecting the involvement of *preman* organizations at the ports (ibid.). A senior figure of PP pointed out, for instance, that prior to the introduction of containerization in Tanjung Priok in the 1980s a large number of port labourers were members of PP. He asserted that

> in the past, many of our North Jakarta administrators *(pengurus)* controlled [Tanjung Priok] port labourers. Nowadays, there are only freelance labourers outside of the port, because inside the port everything has been containerized. Containers are then moved straight to trucks.[5]

The adoption of containerization and the opening of Indonesian ports to foreign vessels as prescribed by Presidential Instruction 4/1985 greatly reduced the number of port labourers in Tanjung Priok Port. Presidential Instruction 4/1985 particularly favoured newly established private stevedoring companies to "determine labor needs on a demand basis" (Airriess 1989, p. 458). Less-productive labourers were not called back to work, "leaving stevedoring companies with core productive workers" (ibid.). This circumstance further reduced the role of *preman* organization such as PP at Tanjung Priok Port.

The diffusion of containerization in Jakarta meant fewer labourers were needed to support the activities at the port. But it also opened employment opportunities beyond the port boundaries. Containerization led to the development of distriparks, logistic centres, free trade zones and other facilities to improve competitiveness (Lee, Song and Ducruet 2008, p. 3). The adoption of container technology in Indonesia paved the way for the development of inland container depots in Jakarta and at other port cities across the country, such as Surabaya, Semarang and Belawan. Given that Tanjung Priok Port could no longer provide the amount of employment it could in the past, labour forces—and the *preman* organizations that coordinated them—shifted their attention to container depots and warehouses (*pergudangan*) where goods were loaded into containers or unloaded from containers and stored.[6]

At present, PP does not exercise much influence at Tanjung Priok Port, and no port labourers or security guards are being recruited from PP.[7] PP continues, however, to display an interest in securing Indonesia's maritime concerns. In 2002 and 2005, for instance, when diplomatic tensions between Indonesia and Malaysia escalated over the maritime dispute in Ambalat block, PP declared to the media their readiness to be deployed in border areas (*Kompas*, 16 May 2002; 8 March 2005; 16 March 2005). PP has also continued to participate in port security by providing security protection and exercising control over some port areas outside of Java. As a senior figure of PP put it,[8]

> Until now, PP still has control [over port labour].... It is impossible to do so in Tanjung Priok Port, because everything has been mechanized and converted to an electronic mode of operation.... However, in ports that have no [automatic and electronic] devices, there are people who do the work. There are plenty [of such ports] in the hinterland, in remote areas.

PP has influence over port security in areas where it has a strong support base, such as Belawan, North Sumatra and Samarinda, East Kalimantan. Sciascia highlighted that in Belawan port, members of PP are employed to control access to the port, carry out patrols and secure ships and their cargoes (Sciascia 2013, p. 177). A former public relations official of the PP regional headquarter in North Sulawesi noted that "PP [has] significant influence in East Kalimantan port. Even workers who lift goods and secure the port are members of PP."[9] Two Indonesian officials from the Indonesian Ministry of Transportation confirmed this. An official pointed out that, "if you see PP in Samarinda, it is as if they own the city; they have more security posts than the police."[10] Another government official, who is responsible for managing Indonesian ports, further explains that,

> In Belawan port, PP is influential because historically the mass base of PP is located in Medan. The mass supporters of PP are already in that area.... In Bitung Port, Surabaya, and Batu Ampar, the presence of civil society and youth organizations is not that explicit. You need to look in certain areas that CSOs exist within in that area. In Medan, the [militarized] CSOs are very strong. The base of PP is there.[11]

In present day Jakarta, the *preman* organization actively involved in port security is an ethnic-Betawi-based organization known as

Forum Betawi Rempug (FBR). Betawi is an ethnic group that has lived in Jakarta for centuries, and they are known as the indigenous people of Jakarta. Betawi culture represents a hybrid of Sunda, Arab, Indian and Chinese practices (Noor 2012, p. 3). The end of the New Order provided opportunities for the rise of new *preman* organizations in Jakarta, including those that organized themselves along ethnic lines. Since Suharto resigned as Indonesia's president in May 1998, ethnic Betawi organizations have proliferated, from twenty to over seventy, most of which are affiliated with the Betawi consultative body (Badan Musyawarah Betawi, or Bamus) (Brown and Wilson 2007, p. 9). The Betawi consultative body is the umbrella institution for Betawi organizations.

FBR was established on 29 July 2001 by Kyai Haji Fadloli El Muhir and Kyai Haji Lutfi Hakim at Pondok Pesantren Ziyadatul Mukhtadi'ien, East Jakarta. The Pesantren Ziyadatul Mukhtadi'ien continues to be the headquarters of FBR. Kyai Lutfi became the chairman of FBR after the death of Kyai Fadloli El Muhir in March 2009. FBR was formed in response to what its members perceived as the growing marginalization of Betawi culture and identity (Noor 2012, p. 5). The marginalization of the Betawi began in the Dutch colonial era. The colonial power carefully maintained exclusive control over "education, government office and military command" and shared economic power with ethnic Chinese (Cribb 1991, p. 13, cited in Leksana 2008, p. 14). This politics of exclusion was maintained throughout Suharto's regime. Suharto's administration did not treat the Betawi as an ethnically authentic community, because of their "mixed ancestry, migrant status and their origin as a product of colonial rule" (Brown and Wilson 2007, p. 16).

The migration of various communities from different parts of Indonesia to Jakarta and the outbreak of ethnic-based violence throughout the archipelago after the end of Suharto's authoritarian regime contributed to the growing anxiety of FBR's founding members (Noor 2012, p. 6). To quote the current chairman of FBR,

> FBR was established by the late Kyai Haji Fadloli Al-Muhir and I as well as several friends who were concerned with the fate of Betawi people who were structurally and culturally marginalized; just like the stereotypical view that the people of Betawi are lazy and uncultured. That is what we are trying to address. Moreover, there are plenty of lands belonging to Betawi people that have been taken by immigrants, without a clear indication of whether they are renting or buying them.[12]

A conflict in 2001 between the Madurese, an ethnic group from the Island of Madura in East Java, and the Betawi in the urban neighbourhood of Cakung Barat, East Jakarta, prompted the establishment of FBR (Leksana 2008, p. s14).

FBR claims to represent ethnic Betawi interests, and it recruited the majority of its members from this ethnic group. There are also members who come from other ethnic groups, such as Batak and Padang, who have become leaders of this organization's branches at the sub-district (*kelurahan*) and district (*kabupaten/kotamadya*) levels.[13] Betawi members of FBR seek to reclaim economic and political resources that they were previously marginalized from, not only by peaceful means but also by coercion, intimidation and violence (Permana 2016, p. 79). FBR reaches out to and recruits their members from the poorer sections of the Betawi community (Noor 2012, p. 8). The majority of their members are males between the ages of twenty and forty years old (Brown and Wilson 2007, p. 9). Fifty per cent of FBR members are unemployed, and the rest have low-paying jobs such as motorcycle taxi (*ojek*) drivers, food stall (*warung*) owners and parking attendants (Noor 2012, p. 8; Brown and Wilson 2007, p. 9; Leksana 2008, p. 14). For these members, FBR could serve as an "employer" in informal markets (Altmeyer 2014, p. 126). FBR tries to reclaim financial resources by securing a parking lot, collecting debts, participating in security businesses and providing protection for marketplaces (Brown and Wilson 2007; Wilson 2010, cited in Permana 2016, p. 79). FBR offers a range of benefits to its members, including providing loans through the organization's saving and loan cooperative, entrepreneurial training, and education funds for the children of deceased members.[14]

FBR's area of activity is limited to Jakarta and its satellite towns, including Bogor, Tangerang and Bekasi. According to its current chairman, Kyai Lutfi, this is because FBR focuses primarily on the urban centres where the majority of Betawi people live.[15] By the end of March 2016, FBR had over one million members, making it the largest Betawi organization in Indonesia.[16] Each month, around three hundred new members join FBR.[17]

FBR is formally registered with the Jakarta provincial government as a CSO. Despite its legitimate status, the reputation of this organization is not untarnished. On numerous occasions, FBR has aligned itself with radical Islamic organizations and carried out attacks against minority groups and human rights organizations (*Jakarta Post*, 24 June 2008; 26 June 2008).

In 2002, FBR carried out attacks against the Urban Poor Community (Kelompok Miskin Kota, or KMK), an NGO representing the poorer members of Jakarta's urban society, at the courtyard of the National Human Rights Commission of Indonesia, in the process damaging the commission's office (*Kompas*, 27 June 2002; 30 March 2002; 13 September 2002). Seven members of FBR were arrested over this incident. KMK leader Wardah Hafidz has brought legal action through the central Jakarta court (Pengadilan Negeri Jakarta Pusat) against President Megawati and the governor of Jakarta, Sutiyoso, because of failures by the two leaders to address flooding in Jakarta. Hafidz claimed that FBR had been paid by the provincial government or by Sutiyoso to carry out the attack against KMK (*Kompas*, 30 March 2002). Prior to attacking KMK, FBR also attacked members of Aliansi Masyarakat Jakarta (AMJ) when Sutiyoso was reading his report before the Jakarta parliament in March 2002. Leaders of FBR and AMJ later discovered they actually supported the same cause, since both were supporting the former governor, Sutiyoso (*Kompas*, 30 March 2002). In 2008, FBR, alongside radical Islamic organizations such as Front Pembela Islam (FPI), attacked the Ahmadiyah minority group, who were campaigning for their freedom of religion in Indonesia.

Acts of violence are justified by FBR's loyalty oath, which calls on its members to "be ready to raid dens of vice and people who are unjust" (Noor 2012, p. 11). Often, however, pragmatic considerations outweigh FBR's moral concerns. For instance, FBR did not support calls by conservative Islamic organizations such as FPI for the closure of facilities producing alcohol, in order to protect the jobs of Betawi workers at these establishments (Noor 2012, p. 11).

Despite FBR's controversial record of vigilantism and violent behaviour over the years, the growth of this organization has received considerable attention from government officials and established political parties in Indonesia seeking support for election or re-election to public office. This can be seen from the presence of influential figures on the list of prominent leaders of FBR. They include Major General (retd.) H. Nachrowi Ramli and a parliamentarian from Partai Amanah Rakyat, Andi Anzhar Cakrawijaya (Noor 2012, pp. 13–14). FBR's first chairman, Fadloli El Muhir, was also a member of the Jakarta Supreme Advisory Council in 1998 and was reported to have a close relationship with Suharto's son (Leksana 2008, p. 30). FBR has a close connection with former Jakarta governor Sutiyoso, and it contributed to the re-election of Sutiyoso as the governor of

Jakarta from 2002 to 2007 (Widyanto 2005, p. 54, cited in Leksana 2008, p. 15). It also has close ties with Jakarta's governor Fauzi Bowo (Foke). It supported the Foke–Nachrowi Ramli gubernatorial campaign against Joko Widodo and his running mate Basuki Tjahaja Purnama in 2012 (Altmeyer 2014, pp. 121, 126). FBR capitalizes on these political connections to improve its control over the informal security market.

FBR uses its large membership and the organization's hierarchical command system as selling points in providing security services to government or private stakeholders. The central command of FBR consists of the chairman, a co-chairman and a treasurer (Leksana 2008, p. 30). FBR has command centres to manage its operations. It has thirteen command centres overall, and six of these are located in Jakarta (Noor 2012, p. 10). These command centres manage 300 operational branches, including 50 in Central Jakarta, 60 in East Jakarta, 32 in North Jakarta, 25 in West Jakarta and 15 in South Jakarta (Noor 2012, p. 10). FBR also has a surveillance team (Tim Wara Wiri), an investigation team (Tim Idik-Idik), a rapid-reaction force, and a search and rescue team (Satuan Relawan Bencana Betawi; Sarbeni) (Leksana 2008, p. 30; Brown and Wilson 2007, p. 25).[18] The surveillance team works to maintain peaceful relations among members and between FBR and other organizations (Leksana 2008, p. 30). The investigation team operates to gather intelligence for the chairman (ibid.). The FBR rapid-reaction team comprises members who are highly trained in martial arts. They are equipped with minivans "complete with sirens and flashing lights" and claim to be able to respond to a call in thirty minutes (Brown and Wilson 2007, p. 25). This is despite the use of sirens and flashing lights by non-military, police or state emergency services being strictly regulated by law, and with violations being punishable by imprisonment (Article 287 of Law No. 22/2009 on Traffic and Road Transport; see CNN, 18 June 2019).

FBR offers security services to finance the operational costs of their organization and meet the needs of its members (Leksana 2008, p. 32). On the pretext of offering protection, FBR extracts regular payments from local businesses (Brown and Wilson 2007, p. 24). Large and mid-sized companies operating in FBR's areas are the key targets of the organization (Leksana 2008, p. 32). FBR has established monopolistic control over the informal economy in significant areas of Jakarta, such as Pulo Gadung, Cakung and Pasar Senen (Brown and Wilson 2007, p. 24).

FBR operates in a semi-military style. Members wear black-coloured shirts as a uniform. FBR has extensive networks of security posts (*gardu*), which mirrors the Indonesian army's territorial command structure, and "troops" that are given training in martial arts (Brown and Wilson 2007, p. 10). At the security-post level, these troops are referred to as *Pitung*, a nineteenth-century heroic figure of the Betawi people who steals from the wealthy and gives to the poor (ibid.). These troops work under the coordination of a *pendekar*, a title taken from the martial arts culture of *pencak silat*, and an advisory council (ibid.). A security post is established at the sub-district level (*kelurahan*) only when there are at least a hundred members in the area.[19] The central leadership of FBR gives a mandate to each security post to seek funds and carry out action against "drug traffickers, alcohol vendors and entertainment venues" deemed immoral (ibid.). Each *pendekar* follows the command of a *jawara*, the highest title given within FBR, at the district level (ibid.). At the district level, this position of *jawara*, or district coordinator (*koordinator wilayah/korwil*), would only be established if at least fifty-one security posts have been built in the area.[20]

At Tanjung Priok, members of FBR are employed as security guards. FBR has no link to port authorities, including the Directorate General of Sea Transportation, PT Pelabuhan Indonesia or the Jakarta International Container Terminal. FBR has, however, established relations with private security companies involved in providing port security services. A private security company that wins a contract to secure a port will recruit members of FBR as security guards. As the chairman of FBR explained,

> if they [private security companies] do not take their entire security personnel from FBR, they will take half or a percentage of their total employees from this organization. For instance, if they need 100 personnel, they will take 50 from us. We still follow [their recruitment procedures]. We ask to be prioritized, because we live in the area. I think this is reasonable.[21]

A senator from the Jakarta Regional Representative Council (Dewan Perwakilan Daerah) went further to argue that the use of local *preman* organizations for port security should be seen as a form of corporate social responsibility on the part of the port operator or private security company towards the local community.[22] This view is echoed by an expert (*staf ahli*) on the senator's team, who pointed out that

> FBR ... brings benefits to Jakarta because they could provide extra security services to their clients. One of their advantages is their loyalty to their leader and the Betawi ethnic group. They are local people who have local knowledge regarding their territory. For instance, if you ask someone from Depok to guard Tanjung Priok, they will not know the area well. If there are problems, they will not know who to talk to when they need to coordinate with local communities. I joined *Bamus* before the local elections (*Pilkada*). The recruitment of FBR members for port security has been going on for a long time, from year to year. The *Bamus* itself only began to flourish a year before Mr Fauzi Bowo became a governor [of Jakarta], if I am not mistaken in 2007.... However, the use of FBR elements for port security had begun years before that. It is necessary for a port or company to recruit members of FBR as their form of corporate social responsibility.[23]

According to a senior official who has been with the Jakarta provincial government since 2014, under the leadership of Basuki Tjahja Purnama, also known as Ahok, the provincial government of Jakarta has implemented measures to improve law and order in ports in Jakarta and limit the involvement of *preman* organizations in port security.[24] The Purnama administration removed the guard posts of various organizations from port areas or locations adjacent to ports. To cite a senior official at the Jakarta provincial government,

> Prior to Jokowi's [term as the governor of Jakarta, a] mass organization could serve as the executor of security not only in ports but also in every aspect of life. The government official who [dealt with this issue] also did not fully understand societal concerns over *preman* organizations' participation in security. Civilian groups and mass organizations controlled the security of Tanjung Priok. Now, their control is lessened.... In the past, the system was more open. It was possible to ask a certain organization to guard a certain piece of land [at the port]. There were also posts and shelters of [*preman* organizations] in ports. In 2014, a new policy was implemented to remove these guard posts and shelters. It began in 2014 because of the incredible leadership and commitment of Ahok.... If we want to compromise with mass organizations that intimidate us, Mr Ahok would not let us. He found it unacceptable.[25]

Despite consistent government measures to limit the involvement of *preman* organizations in providing security in ports in Jakarta, these organizations continue to play their role in port security. A government official noted that although there have been changes as a result of the no-compromise policy on the part of the government to maintain law and order at ports and the areas surrounding them, these changes have not been drastic.[26] Stakeholders with interests in maintaining port security continue to "recruit members of ethnic-based organizations as security personnel. Security companies recruit their personnel from ethnic-based groups such as Betawi or Madura."[27]

As part of FBR involvement in port security in Jakarta, this organization has also established cooperation with the Indonesian police and armed forces. Members of FBR, especially those that are part of the organization's intelligence unit, provide information to state security authorities about the security situation of areas close to Tanjung Priok Port. As explained earlier, FBR includes a surveillance team (Tim Wara Wiri). According to FBR chairman Kyai Lutfi, his organization has developed partnerships with the police, armed forces and the national intelligence body (Badan Intelijen Nasional). To quote Kyai Lutfi:

> We are close with intelligence [agencies].... with the Indonesian Police's intelligence and security agency (Intelkam), the Indonesian armed forces' Intel Kramat Tujuh and with the national intelligence agency's regional community.[28]

An expert (*staf ahli*) member of staff of the senator from Jakarta corroborated the FBR chairman's statement as he pointed out that "in some instances FBR has been asked to carry out undercover tasks, for instance, to go undercover as street vendors to monitor conditions near Tanjung Priok Port and gather information".[29]

The continued involvement of FBR in port security in Jakarta is facilitated by the existence of various Indonesian government programmes that encourage the participation of *preman* organizations in social and security sectors. According to a senior member of staff at the Agency for National Unity and Politics of the Jakarta provincial government, some of these organizations have carried out positive actions in areas of law enforcement and social issues.[30] The provincial government of Jakarta has established several forums to encourage and monitor the participation of *preman* organizations supporting government programmes, including those within the security sector. These include the local intelligence committee (Komite Intelijen Daerah), the coordinating forum for the prevention of terrorism (Forum Kooordinasi Pencegahan Terorisme), the state defence programme (Bela Negara), and de-radicalization initiatives.[31] In 2008, the Agency for National Unity and Politics of the Jakarta provincial government established an early awareness forum (Forum

Kewaspadaan Dini).³² This forum includes members of *preman* organizations who are expected to provide information about potential social unrest or security problems in their area. These early awareness forums are established at the provincial, district and village levels. The chairman of FBR explained his organization's involvement in supporting government programmes to address radicalization and to counter terrorism as follow:

> FBR's principle is to guard our village (*jaga kampung*). Guarding the place where we live. For instance, during Idul Fitri, Christmas and Waisak celebrations we guard our areas.... No matter how good government intelligence officers are, sources of [their information] come from the community. We are part of the community. Information will flow to those who side with the community. FBR helps to counter terrorism. We identified whether a person is a resident or not. We have assisted the arrest of terrorists in the south of Tangerang twice, in 2008 and 2009. In dealing with terrorism, we share information [with government authorities].³³

The government provides support to registered CSOs in various ways, including by giving them permission to use gymnasiums, auditoriums or provincial government buildings, and to cover the cost of catering for certain events organized by these organizations. As shown in Table 1, the provincial government also provides financial support in the form of grants and social assistance. This practice is in line with Rule No. 14/2016 of the Indonesian Ministry of Home Affairs.

Rule No. 14/2016 allows the local government to provide grants in the form of money, goods or services to the central government or other local governments, state-owned enterprise, institutions or CSOs that are registered as a legal entity.³⁴ The same rule allows the local government to provide social assistance in the form of money or goods to an individual, family or organization.³⁵ Article 6 of the rule stipulates that only CSOs with the status of a legal entity, that have been verified by the Indonesian Ministry of Law and Human Rights and that have obtained a certificate of registration from the Ministry of Home Affairs, governor or mayor can apply for a government grant.³⁶ The leader of FBR explained in an interview that his organization has never asked for funding from the government, since they want to be independent in financing all their activities.³⁷ Table 1 shows that the Jakarta provincial government has provided funding for several *preman* organizations, including Forum Komunikasi Putra Putri Purnawirawan dan Putra Putri TNI Polri (FKPPI) and

Pemuda Panca Marga (PPM). It also shows that from 2014 to 2016 FBR had not received funding from the provincial government of Jakarta.

Table 1, however, shows allocations of provincial government funding in 2014 and 2015 to Badan Musyawarah Masyarakat Betawi (Bamus Betawi). This institution is the parent organization of FBR. A senior official from the Jakarta provincial government claimed there is a possibility that FBR gained access to the grant, but there is no precise data about the percentage FBR might have received. In 2016, the Jakarta provincial government stopped allocating grants or social assistance to Bamus Betawi because of the organization's involvement in the 2017 gubernatorial election. To quote a senior member of staff in the provincial government,

> We stopped grant and social assistance for Bamus Betawi because of their involvement in politics. Based on the law, they are not allowed to be affiliated with any political party. They supported a certain candidate for governor in the local election, *Pilkada*. They use their organization's name [for this purpose].[38]

Underlying Tensions in the Use of *Preman* Organizations

The use of *preman* organizations such as FBR in port security has created significant tensions between these organizations and the Indonesian government. A senior official from the Indonesian Directorate General of Sea Transportation expressed her disapproval of the involvement of *preman* organizations in port security as follow: "It is a lie [that] *preman* organizations help to secure port areas.... PP and FBR, they are thugs. Their purpose is to seek money."[39] Sources of tensions between *preman* organizations and the government entail, first, the frequent violent conflicts between the two parties; second, the involvement of *preman* organizations in politics; and third, their participation in illegal activities.

In terms of conflict in Jakarta, clashes between *preman* organizations and government agencies, including the police and the local government, are frequent. The term *bentrok*, or "clash", was featured twenty-two times in *Kompas* articles published from 2008 to October 2016. The word *bentrok* was mentioned in articles reporting clashes between government authorities and *preman* organizations, conflicts between different CSOs, and attacks launched by *preman* organizations against human rights organization such as KMK.

TABLE 1
Provincial Government Grants and Social Assistance to Civil Society Organizations

Name of Organization	Allocated Budget (IDR)
2014 Grants	
1 Badan Musyawarah Masyarakat Betawi (BAMUS Betawi)	5,000,000,000
2 Forum Komunikasi Umat Beragama Provinsi dan 6 wilayah Kota/Kabupaten	2,000,000,000
3 Forum Koordinasi Pencegahan Terorisme (FKPT) Provinsi	2,000,000,000
4 Dewan Perwakilan Daerah (DPD) Prov. DKI Jakarta	1,500,000,000
5 Persatuan Purnawirawan dan Warakawuri TNI dan Polri (DPD PEPABRI)	750,000,000
6 Persatuan Purnawirawan TNI-Angkatan Darat Provinsi DKI Jakarta dan sekitarnya	300,000,000
7 Legiun Veteran Republik Indonesia DKI Jakarta	200,000,000
8 Kerukunan Keluarga Indonesia Gorontalo Jakarta	200,000,000
9 Komisi Pemilihan Umum Daerah Provinsi DKI Jakarta	16,500,000,000
10 DHD 45 Provinsi DKI Jakarta	300,000,000
11 Forum Komunikasi Putra Putri Purnawirawan dan Putra Putri TNI Polri	200,000,000
12 Pemuda Panca Marga	200,000,000
13 Perkumpulan Masyarakat Indonesia Peduli Pendidikan dan Kesehatan	300,000,000
2014 Social Assistance	
1 Kel. Besar Wirawati Catur Panca PD. DKI Jakarta (Wanita pejuang 45)	150,000,000
2 Ikatan Keluarga Pahlawan Nasional Indonesia (IKPNI)	150,000,000
3 Wanita Veteran RI DKI Jakarta	100,000,000
4 Persatuan istri veteran Republik Indonesia (PIVERI) DKI Jakarta	100,000,000
5 Korps Cacad Veteran DKI Jaya	95,000,000
6 Lembaga Indonesia Membangun	50,000,000
7 Forum Komunikasi Mahasiswa Betawi	50,000,000
8 Forum Betawi Bersatu Sejabodetabek	50,000,000
9 Lingkar Studi Mahasiswa	100,000,000
10 Lembaga Pendidikan Penerapan Hukum Indonesia	30,000,000
11 Institusi Proklamasi	30,000,000
12 LSM Gerakan Pemuda Nusantara Indonesia	30,000,000
13 Lembaga Anak Bangsa Centre	100,000,000
14 Yayasan Pengembangan Intelektual Bangsa Jakarta	50,000,000
15 Yayasan Lembaga Bantuan Hukum dan Kemanusiaan Duta Keadilan Indonesia	30,000,000

TABLE 1 (cont.)
Provincial Government Grants and Social Assistance to Civil Society Organizations

	Name of Organization	Allocated Budget (IDR)
16	Paguyuban Purwo Widodo Makmur	30,000,000
17	Keluarga Mahasiswa Minangkabau Jaya	100,000,000
18	Lembaga Partisipasi Pemuda Indonesia	30,000,000
2015 Grants		
1	Badan Musyawarah Betawi	2,500,000,000
2	Forum Kerukunan Umat Beragama Provinsi dan 6 wilayah Kota/Kabupaten	2,000,000,000
3	Forum Koordinasi Pencegahan Terorisme Provinsi DKI	1,500,000,000
4	Dewan Perwakilan Daerah Republik Indonesia Provinsi DKI Jakarta	1,500,000,000
5	Legiun Veteran Republik Indonesia	250,000,000
6	Persatuan Purnawirawan Warakawuri TNI dan Polri	200,000,000
7	Komite Intelijen Daerah DKI Jakarta	1,300,000,000
2015 Social Assistance		
1	Ikatan Keluarga Pahlawan Nasional Indonesia	150,000,000
2	Keluarga Besar Wirawati Catur Panca PD DKI Jakarta (Wanita Pejuang 45)	150,000,000
3	Muyawarah Kekeluargaan Gotong Royong	150,000,000
4	Gerakan Ekonomi dan Budaya Minang	100,000,000
5	Komunitas Jakarta Baru	50,000,000
6	Korps Cacad Veteran	150,000,000
7	Persatuan Istri Veteran Republik Indonesia DKI Jakarta	100,000,000
8	Wanita Veteran RI DKI Jakarta	100,000,000
2016 Grants		
1	Forum Komunikasi Umat Beragama Provinsi DKI Jakarta dan 6 wilayah Kota/Kabupaten Administrasi Kep. Seribu	2,000,000,000
2	Forum Komunikasi Pencegahan Terorisme Provinsi DKI Jakarta	1,500,000,000
3	Legiun Veteran Republik Indonesia	250,000,000
4	DPD RI Provinsi DKI Jakarta	1,500,000,000
2016 Social Assistance		
1	Korps Cacat Veteran DKI Jaya	150,000,000

Source: Kesbangpol DKI Jakarta, 2016. Grants provided to Bamus Betawi, PPM and FKPPI are highlighted.

The most common cause of clashes between the government authorities and *preman* organizations are land disputes. In 2003, for instance, FBR was involved in a conflict with Jakarta's provincial government following the issuance of a government decision to dismantle fourteen huts and thirty-two semi-permanent buildings in Billy Moon complex in East Jakarta (*Kompas*, 2 October 2003). Two government security officers (Ketentraman, Ketertiban dan Perlindungan Masyarakat) were injured. The police arrested twelve members of FBR and another Betawi-based *preman* organization called Forum Komunikasi Anak Betawi (Forkabi) in this incident. Another major dispute between FBR and the government took place in 2008 when hundreds of FBR members rallied in front of Senayan City, a shopping mall located in Jakarta's business district. FBR demanded the restoration of rights of ownership of the land of Senayan City to the Marzuki family, a Betawi family (*Jakarta Post*, 6 August 2008).

The two largest *preman* organizations in Jakarta, FBR and PP, are also often in conflict with each other. In August 2014, FBR reportedly attacked the PP secretariat and guard posts in the south of Jakarta (Liputan6, 10 August 2014). A year later, in August 2015,

FIGURE 5
Locations of FBR Posts and the Secretariat Office around Tanjung Priok Port, Marunda Port and Surrounding Areas

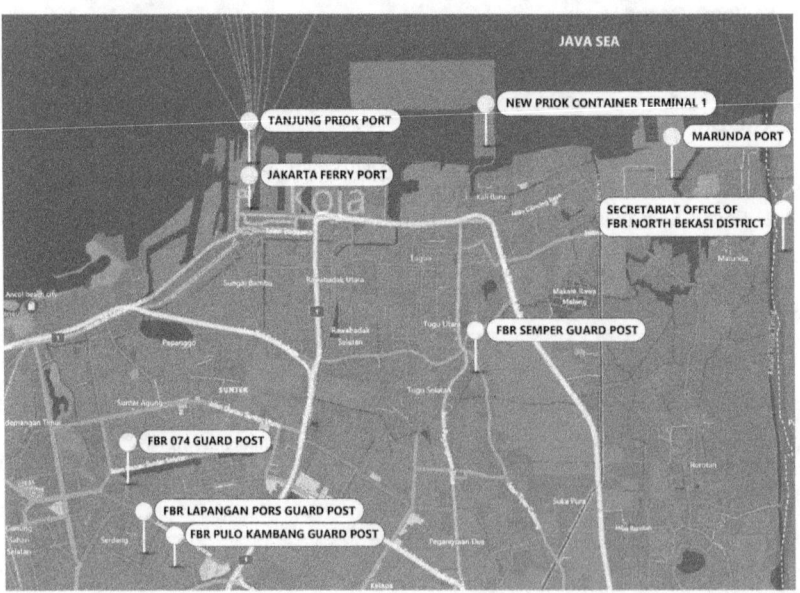

members of FBR attacked a resident of Gembrong Market, East Jakarta, who wore a PP shirt (*Tempo*, 11 August 2015). This incident instigated a fight between local residents and FBR. Fights between FBR and PP largely take place in the south or east of Jakarta and rarely in the north of Jakarta. The chairman of FBR deemed that FBR and its rival organization "understand that the north of Jakarta is an important area given that vital government installations such as Tanjung Priok Port and the PT Pertamina Plant, a state-owned oil and gas operator, are located in this area. Therefore, it is crucial to avoid conflict between organizations in the area."[40] This could be seen as consensus among the *preman* organizations to avoid provoking a strong government reaction.

In Tanjung Priok Port and areas adjacent to the port, small and large-scale conflicts involving FBR and government security authorities have taken place. A large-scale conflict involving FBR, the police and the Jakarta provincial government security guards took place in 2010. In that year, port authority PT Pelindo II and the provincial government of Jakarta sought to remove the tomb of Mbah Priok—which is deemed sacred by the local community—from Koja, an important port facility in Tanjung Priok.

The presence of a tomb complex inside Koja had implications for the security of the port facility. In 2008, the US Coast Guard issued a port security advisory (PSA) to this facility. The presence of the tomb complex made it difficult for security guards to limit public access to the facility. As a consequence of the issuance of the PSA, any vessels calling at Koja were obliged to go through extensive security procedures before being granted permission to enter US ports. Koja lost millions of dollars after the PSA was issued because most of its major clients withdrew their contracts from the port facility.[41]

The decision by the government to relocate the tomb to outside the port facility was met with fierce opposition from the local community, and the volatile situation was exacerbated by FBR involvement in the public protests. Claiming that several FBR members were victims of attacks carried out by the police and the provincial government security unit—Satpol Pamong Praja—FBR sent more members to guard the tomb (*Oke Zone*, 15 April 2010). Reports of the numbers of deaths as a result of this clash varied from 3 to 25 members of Satpol Pamong Praja (*Detik*, 21 August 2013).[42] The chairman of FBR highlighted that the clash caused significant destruction, as 32 police cars, 16 Satpol Pamong Praja cars, 2 shipping containers and a water canon were destroyed.[43] The involvement of *preman* organizations in this clash is confirmed by a statement made by a member of Satpol Pamong Praja. He explained that "2,000 members of the police force and the Satpol Pamong Praja were facing a mob three times more than their number. Many of them were members of mass organizations in Jakarta who opposed the eviction" (Detik, 21 August 2013). The chairman of FBR recalled this incident as follow:

> The attempt to remove Mbah Priok tomb was rowdy. Their [port authority] concept was to turn the place into a garden. They would only leave a small area for pilgrimage around the garden, perhaps around 100–200 metres. I refused it. I would not help if that is the case. For me, the government … is too naïve…. The government should have allocated one hectare of land to build a heritage place, [and] equip the tomb area with a parking lot. Give one hectare, allocate a budget to build fences, [and] infrastructures. Tidy the place and provide a parking lot and washing ritual (*wudhu*) space. However, they did not want to do this and preferred to build a garden. Yeah, it could not [happen]. What would happen to pilgrims as they are reciting their prayers and closing their eyes? They could suddenly be hit by a container on the head and die. Demonstration, clashes,… the clashes were severe. Sixteen Satpol PP cars were destroyed. Many people who died were from Satpol PP…. I was then asked to stop it [the clashes]…. There were many businessmen who phoned [me]. I said it was enough for today. Tomorrow I would carry out peaceful demonstration, and after that there would be no more movement because the situation was very chaotic…. The clashes were ended. Until today nothing could be done regarding the tomb.[44]

Six years later, FBR was involved in a clash with a legitimate private security company at Tanjung Priok Port. In 2014, FBR closed the access road to Tanjung Priok Port following a fight at the port between members of FBR and security guards working for PT Philia Citra Sejahtera, a security company that provides port security services. The incident led to the death of a member of FBR. This issue was resolved only after PT Philia Citra Sejahtera agreed to provide compensation to FBR (Polda Metro Jaya, 21 January 2015).[45] The commandant of North Jakarta military district, Lieutenant Colonel Stefy Yance Mamuya, and the head of North Jakarta police headquarters, Mohammad Iqbal, were involved to broker a peaceful arrangement between the parties to the conflict (Polda Metro Jaya, 21 January 2015).

The second source of tension between *preman* organizations and government authorities is derived from the involvement of these organizations in politics. That Basuki Tjahaja Purnama lost in his bid for re-election to Anies Baswedan in April 2017 illustrated this particularly well. Despite *preman* organizations only playing a fringe role in coordinating activities, such as spreading a doctored version of Purnama's speech and manipulating the issue that led to Purnama's electoral loss and his two-year prison sentence for blasphemy, they were actively involved in staging large-scale protests and pressing the government authorities to arrest and try him (see Parameswaran, 18 February 2017).

Preman organizations such as FBR and Forkabi had openly opposed Basuki Tjahaja Purnama, Jakarta's former governor. Since the early years of his gubernatorial stint, Purnama had opposed the presence and activities of *preman* organizations in Jakarta. Purnama pointed out that members of these organizations "act as gangsters (*preman*)" (CNN Indonesia, 11 April 2016). In a public demonstration held in July 2013, hundreds of members of *preman* organizations demanded that Purnama resign as the vice-governor of Jakarta (Merdeka, 29 July 2013). FBR and the Joint Betawi Forum (Forum Betawi Bersatu) conducted another public rally to push for Purnama's resignation in February 2015 (*Tempo*, 26 February 2015). Action like this was not uncommon. Since Purnama's inauguration as the governor of Jakarta in 2014 until his resignation in 2017, a group of *preman* organizations—including FBR and FPI—had constantly made public demands for him to step down (Oke Zone, 4 April 2016; Detik, 12 February 2014).

In the 2017 gubernatorial election, Basuki Tjahja Purnama, an ethnic Chinese and non-Muslim, was competing for the public office along with two other candidates. They were Anies Baswedan, who was supported by Prabowo Subianto, President Joko Widodo's main political rival in the 2014 and 2019 presidential elections, and Agus Harimurti Yudhoyono, the son of former president Susilo Bambang Yudhoyono (Parameswaran, 18 February 2017). Indonesia has a history of appointing leaders from minority groups to public office. For instance, the governor of Jakarta from 1964 to 1965, Hendrik Hermanus Joel Ngantung, and the mayor of Solo from 2012 to 2021, Fransiskus Xaverius Hadi Rudyatmo, are both Catholic (see CNN, 19 November 2014; Merdeka, 30 July 2022; Prameswaran, 18 February 2017). In the case of the 2017 Jakarta gubernatorial election, however, religion served as a catalyst in mobilizing support

FIGURE 6
Convoy of Front Pembela Islam Members Heading to Central Jakarta to Take Part in Protests against Basuki Tjahja Purnama on 14 October 2016

Photos: Senia Febrica.

against Purnama. In the run up to the election, during his campaign in Kepulauan Seribu, Purnama stated that his Islamist opponents who used the Koranic verse Al Maidah 51 to dissuade people from supporting him were deceiving voters (BBC, 16 November 2016; Parameswaran, 18 February 2017). Some clerics interpret the verse as prohibiting Muslims from electing a non-Muslim leader (*Jakarta Post*, 9 May 2017). Purnama's political opponents quickly seized on the opportunity to help them win the election. In the run up to the election, there were allegations that the Yudhoyono camp requested the head of the Indonesian Ulema Council, Ma'ruf Amin, to issue a blasphemy fatwa against Purnama and funded the large "411" protest movement against him on 4 November 2016 (*Kompas*, 2 February 2017).

Most surprisingly, Anis Baswedan, previously known as a progressive and pluralist candidate, sought to garner more conservative votes by visiting Habib Rizieq Shihab, leader of FPI, a radical Islamic organization, in January 2017 (Parameswaran, 18 February 2017). Despite a government ban on FPI from carrying out its activities being in place since 2014, the organization continued its operations. In 2020, the Indonesian Coordinating Ministry for Political, Legal and Security Affairs issued a statement banning FPI from carrying out its activities. The government further warned people from taking part in FPI activities and using attributes or symbols of this organization (Detik, 30 December 2020). This decision was made because of FPI support for the Islamic State of Iraq and Syria, the participation of 35 of its members in terrorist acts and 209 of its members in various crimes, and acts of vigilantism carried out by the organization (ibid.).

Under the banner, "Action to Defend Islam (*Aksi Bela Islam*)", ethnic Betawi *preman* organizations, such as FBR and Forkabi, joined hard-line Islamic organizations, including FPI, Persaudaraan Muslimin Indonesia and Forum Umat Islam, to stage a series of large-scale protests, some of which were accompanied by acts of violence against government authorities, on 14 October 2016, 4 November 2016, 2 December 2016, 11 February 2017, 21 February 2017, 31 March 2017 and 5 May 2017 (Antara, 14 October 2016; CNN, 22 January 2019). These organizations called for the arrest of and the death penalty to be awarded to Purnama (Antara, 14 October 2016). In the end, the blasphemy allegation against Purnama contributed to his defeat to Anies Baswedan in the April 2017 gubernatorial election. In May 2017, the North Jakarta district court found Purnama guilty of blasphemy and sentenced him to two years in prison (*Jakarta Post*, 9 May 2017).

The third source of tension between the government and *preman* organizations is the participation of such organizations in illicit activities. In Jakarta, the port of Tanjung Priok has complied with the International Ship and Port Facility Security Code. Smaller ports in Jakarta, however, do not have the same security system in

FIGURE 7
Locations of FBR Guard Posts around Muara Baru Port, Samudera Fishing Port

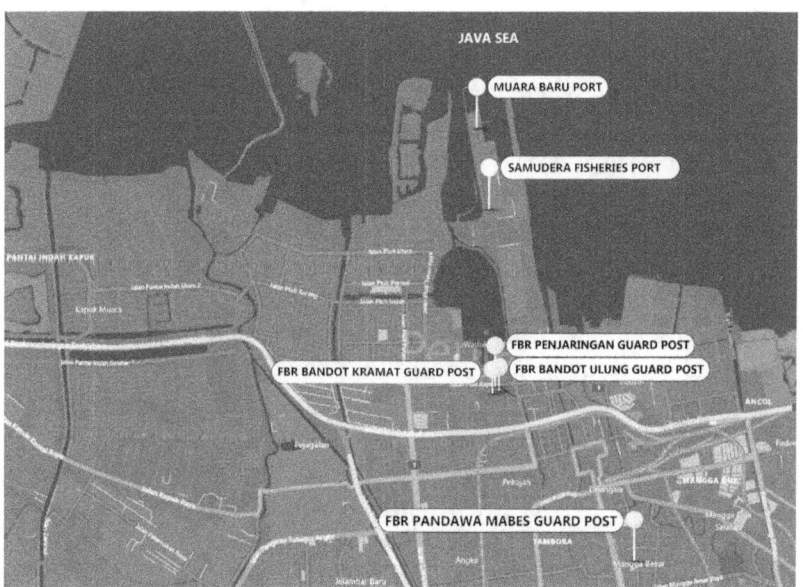

place, and illicit activities such as drug smuggling are rampant. In February 2017, the Indonesian government unravelled the smuggling of drugs from Malaysia to Jakarta through Muara Angke fishing port in North Jakarta (*Kompas*, 4 February 2017). Of twenty-one tonnes of drugs smuggled into Indonesia, over fifty-four per cent came from Malaysia (*Kompas*, 4 February 2017). The Indonesian National Narcotics Bureau announced in February 2017 that international drugs syndicates have changed their mode of smuggling from using aeroplanes and container ships to using the wooden vessels of fishermen. Smugglers navigate from Malaysia to Jakarta via Tembilahan, the east coast of Sumatra and the Gulf of Jakarta. The Indonesian Directorate General of Customs is enhancing its monitoring capacity in the Gulf of Jakarta and deploying patrol vessels from the eastern coast of Sumatra to Kepulauan Seribu, Jakarta (*Kompas*, 4 February 2017).

Despite the illicit activities in ports in Jakarta, not many references have been made by national newspapers to link the *preman* organizations with efforts to combat or support illicit economic activities at ports in Jakarta. The chairman of FBR claimed his organization has assisted Indonesian customs by providing information about the smuggling of small amounts of alcohol through Marunda Port. Liquor smuggled from Kalimantan or Borneo is normally shipped to Jakarta through Marunda Port.[46]

The lack of media coverage of efforts by *preman* organizations to curb or support illicit activities is interesting given that they have control over small ports in Jakarta. The *Jakarta Post* reported that in North Jakarta, where container and fishing ports are based, five gangs rule the area. Three of them control Samudera port, Muara Baru fish market and several nearby traditional markets; one controls warehouses in the area; and a leader of FBR is in charge of the small kiosks near Samudera port (*Jakarta Post*, 3 July 2008). These gangs provide jobs and cash to local residents during the Idul Fitri holiday or when they face economic difficulties as a result increasing oil prices (*Jakarta Post*, 3 July 2008). Local residents of North Jakarta explained that the gangs controlling the ports and fish market worked alongside local businessmen who seek protection from them (*Jakarta Post*, 3 July 2008).

Despite the involvement of FBR in port security in Jakarta, interviews with government officials and members of *preman* organizations in Jakarta, as well as an analysis of media reports, did not reveal the involvement of FBR in illicit activities in ports in Jakarta. Media reports do, however, point to the involvement of *preman* organizations—namely, Laskar Merah Putih, in providing protection for illicit activities in a container depot area. In October 2015, members of Laskar Merah Putih—a hyper-nationalist *preman* organization—stopped, intimidated and attacked twenty customs officials who were going to check twenty containers of zinciferous sand in Kawasan Berikat, North Jakarta (Detik, 8 October 2015; Sindo, 8 October 2015). The police deemed that the containers of sand would be exported illegally from the country (Detik, 8 October 2015; Sindo, 8 October 2015). Despite this incident, Laskar Merah Putih continues to operate as a registered organization in Jakarta.

According to Article 60 of Law No. 17/2013 on CSOs, the central and local governments have the authority to implement administrative sanctions against an organization that carries out violent action, disturbs the peace or public order, or destroys public facilities. These sanctions range from issuing a written warning, stopping grants or assistance, temporary bans on the activities of an organization, to revoking the organization's certificate of registration or legal status.[47] However, as a government official explained in an interview, the implementation of such sanctions is not an easy task. Article 62 of Law No. 17/2013 regulates that prior to implementing sanctions the government must provide up to three written warnings. The written warnings must be delivered in stages, and each stage could last up to thirty days.[48] If an organization that has violated the law abides by the government's warning before the end of the thirty-days' window, the central or local government could revoke their warning.[49] As a consequence, this circumstance can be manipulated by *preman* organizations to avoid government punishment. In most cases entailing acts of violence or violations of the law, government authorities tend to punish individual members of the organizations involved and issue criminal charges against them rather than against the organization as a whole.

Conclusion

This chapter has discussed the participation of *preman* organizations as security providers in ports in Jakarta. Although in the past PP exercised control over Tanjung Priok Port, at present, ethnic-based organization such as FBR play a more active role in port security in Jakarta. FBR provides information to government authorities about security conditions and illicit activities in port areas. Security companies operating at Tanjung Priok Port also recruit their port security staff from FBR. FBR maintains its position of importance in ports through its ability to provide jobs and cash to local residents (as shown in the case of Samudra Port), settle or prolong disputes (as seen in the case of Mbah Priok), and connect with government or private companies that seek their services.

The involvement of *preman* organizations in port security is not always trouble free. Members of *preman* organization Laskar Merah Putih had provided protection for smuggling activities in Kawasan Berikat, North Jakarta. And violent clashes occurred in Tanjung Priok Port between the provincial government and *preman* organizations, and between these organizations and a private security company. Clashes also took place in various parts of the city between rival organizations.

Despite the continual involvement of *preman* organizations in providing security for ports in Jakarta, it is interesting to note that during the Basuki Tjahja Purnama administration there was a consistent effort to limit the control of these organizations over vital infrastructure such as ports. Purnama issued warnings to *preman* organizations that carried out attacks and intimidation, stopped providing grants to those who broke the law, removed their posts and shelters from areas in and around ports, and denied them access to land adjacent to ports. During the 2017 gubernatorial election, the accusation by Islamic *preman* organizations of blasphemy against Purnama was instrumental in his defeat. It shows the influence of uncivil elements within Indonesian society in informing the course of the democratic process. This raised another question. Do the provincial governments in other parts of Indonesia also seek to limit the engagement of *preman* organizations in security, particularly port security? And do *preman* organizations continue to participate in port security in different parts of Indonesia? In order to address these questions, Chapter 3 will examine port security in North Sulawesi.

Notes

1. Interview with the head of the National Leadership Assembly of Pemuda Pancasila, 19 September 2016, Jakarta.
2. Interview with staff of the Port Directorate, Indonesian Ministry of Transportation, 6 August 2015, Jakarta.
3. Interview with the head of the National Leadership Assembly of Pemuda Pancasila, 19 September 2016, Jakarta.

4. Interview with the chairman, vice chairman and secretary of Pemuda Pancasila Batam, 17 February 2016, Batam.
5. Interview with the head of the National Leadership Assembly of Pemuda Pancasila, 19 September 2016, Jakarta.
6. Ibid.
7. Ibid.
8. Ibid.
9. Interview with the public relations official of Milisi Waraney, North Sulawesi, and the former public relations official of Pemuda Pancasila, North Sulawesi, 5 August 2016, Manado.
10. Interview with staff of the Port Directorate, Indonesian Ministry of Transportation, 6 August 2015, Jakarta.
11. Ibid.
12. Interview with the chairman of Forum Betawi Rempug, 31 March 2016, Jakarta.
13. Ibid.
14. Ibid.
15. Ibid.
16. Ibid.
17. Ibid.
18. Ibid.
19. Ibid.
20. Ibid.
21. Ibid.
22. Interview with a senator from DKI Jakarta, 18 August 2015, Jakarta.
23. Interview with an expert staff member of a senator from Jakarta, 18 August 2015, Jakarta.
24. Interview with a senior official of the Agency for National Unity and Politics, Jakarta provincial government, 30 September 2016, Jakarta.
25. Ibid.
26. Ibid.
27. Ibid.
28. Interview with the chairman of Forum Betawi Rempug, 31 March 2016, Jakarta.
29. Interview with an expert staff member of a senator from Jakarta, 18 August 2015, Jakarta.
30. Email correspondence with a senior staff member of the Agency for National Unity and Politics, Jakarta provincial government, 21 November 2016.
31. Interview with a senior official of the Agency for National Unity and Politics, Jakarta provincial government, 30 September 2016, Jakarta.

32. Interview with a senior official of the Agency for National Unity and Politics, Jakarta provincial government, 30 September 2016, Jakarta.
33. Interview with the chairman of Forum Betawi Rempug, 31 March 2016, Jakarta.
34. Indonesian Ministry of Home Affairs Rule No.14/2016, p. 6.
35. Ibid.
36. Ibid., p. 9.
37. Interview with the chairman of Forum Betawi Rempug, 31 March 2016, Jakarta.
38. Interview with a senior official of the Agency for National Unity and Politics, Jakarta provincial government, 30 September 2016, Jakarta.
39. Interview with a senior government official at the Indonesian Ministry of Transportation, 7 August 2015, Jakarta.
40. Interview with the chairman of Forum Betawi Rempug, 31 March 2016, Jakarta.
41. Interview with a senior government official at the Indonesian Ministry of Transportation, 3 September 2010, Jakarta.
42. Interview with the chairman of Forum Betawi Rempug, 31 March 2016, Jakarta.
43. Ibid.
44. Ibid.
45. Ibid.
46. Ibid.
47. Article 60 of Law No. 17/2013 on civil society organizations.
48. Article 61 of Law No. 17/2013 on civil society organizations
49. Article 62(3) of Law No. 17/2013 on civil society organizations.

Chapter 3

Preman Organizations in North Sulawesi: To Guard *Tanah Toar Lumimuut*

North Sulawesi is situated in the most northern part of Indonesia. This border province encompasses 15,472,98 square kilometres, and the length of its coastline is 1,837 kilometres (Dewan Maritim Indonesia 2007a, p. 31). North Sulawesi consists of a large number of islands, including Manado Tua, Bangka, Lembeh, Siau, Tagulandang, Karakelang, Karabuan, Salibabu, and 124 smaller islands (ibid.). These smaller outlying islands are grouped into the following three categories: the Talaud Islands, the Sangir Besar Islands, and Siau Tagulandang and Biaro (ibid.).

North Sulawesi shares a maritime border with the Philippines to the north and a land border with the Indonesian Gorontolo province to the west. It faces the Tomini Gulf to the south and the Moluccas Sea to the east (Dewan Maritim Indonesia 2007a, p. 32). Located strategically between the Sulawesi Sea and the Pacific Ocean, North Sulawesi has grown to be the economic centre for the eastern part of Indonesia. The port sector presents commercial opportunities that contribute significantly to the North Sulawesi economy (ibid., p. 62). Thus, the security of ports in North Sulawesi is crucial to developing the economic potential of this border province and to maintaining the safety of maritime gateways that connect the east and west parts of Indonesia.

The transport of goods and people to and from North Sulawesi ports face various challenges from trans-border criminal and terrorist activities. In order to secure ports and the many outlying islands in

North Sulawesi, government authorities have formed close partnerships with *preman* organizations. This chapter will explain the participation of *preman* organizations in port security in North Sulawesi. The next part of this chapter will map the existing *preman* organizations in North Sulawesi that take part in securing ports and outlying islands in the province. It will explain their cooperation with state authorities and identify government agencies that collaborate with *preman* organizations. The third part will elaborate on the relatively low degree of tensions within North Sulawesi society that occur as a result of the involvement of *preman* organizations in the security sector. The fourth part of the chapter will outline the illicit trans-border activities that are rampant at North Sulawesi's maritime borders. It will provide details of the involvement of *preman* organizations in seeking to deter these illicit activities. The key findings in the chapter reveal that the participation of ethnic *preman* organizations in securing ports and coastal areas in North Sulawesi has received unusually welcoming support from the local government, the government security apparatus and the media. This is something that did not occur in the other port-cities studied—Jakarta and Batam—where the government authorities and media exhibited negative or mixed perceptions of *preman* organizations. But despite the lack of a negative portrayal of *preman* organizations, the involvement of these organizations in providing protection to businesses that act unlawfully poses a challenge to government authorities seeking to maintain order in North Sulawesi and other provinces in the archipelago.

The Rise of Ethnic *Preman* Organizations in North Sulawesi

The participation of *preman* organizations in assisting government law enforcement agencies to secure ports and coastal areas is not a new practice in North Sulawesi. During Suharto's New Order regime, Pemuda Pancasila (PP) was the key *preman* organization involved in securing ports in this province. To quote a former member of the North Sulawesi parliament,

> During the New Order government, PP was strong.... they acted like the one who owns the kingdom, because they had the armed forces behind them. Therefore, they had no fear. In the New Order era, PP was the one who held [control] over port security. Just bring PP in and everything could be taken care of. However, now this is no longer the case.[1]

This view was also shared by a retired police officer in Manado. He claimed that,

> in the Golkar period or the New Order era, PP had an incredible role. They controlled lots of development projects, like a contractor. Now you do not hear much about them.... They controlled everything at that time, including ports, although it was not visible and you could not see it physically, but they had access to everything. They had influence. They had control over port labour associations and port security units.

PP lost their influence in North Sulawesi as the result of a combination of factors, including a leadership vacuum within the organization, the end of the New Order era and the rise of new ethnic *preman* organizations in the province. PP still exists in North Sulawesi, but it is not as influential as it was in the past.

As the current head of the North Sulawesi PP branch explained,

> Since I joined PP, this organization has been inactive. Even the management of the North Sulawesi PP has not been inaugurated. As a consequence, the contributions of this organization in various fields could not be materialized. The former chairman ... did not show his existence in leading this organization. The PP in East Kalimantan and Medan are fantastic in all aspects. The best one is the [PP] in East Kalimantan. The PP in North Sulawesi was most progressive during the era of Mr Edy Waleleng. This is why Mr Yapto is concerned about the PP in North Sulawesi, because in the past the performance of the PP in North Sulawesi was just like [the PP] in East Kalimantan. We had many members. When we went for a parade [our] cars were lining from the airport to the city centre of Manado.... According to our elders, the PP in North Sulawesi is not dead, it is just sleeping.[2]

A senior figure of PP in Jakarta confirmed that the PP branch in North Sulawesi has been in a vacuum for a long time. To quote him,

> In North Sulawesi, PP is a little in a vacuum, a bit in a vacuum. If you go there perhaps [PP] is in a vacuum. They are present in small towns and on a small-scale. This is despite in the past PP in North Sulawesi being in competition with [PP] in North Sumatra. [The PP branch in] North Sulawesi used to be militant. This was because the first chairman of PP came from North Sulawesi.[3]

Analysis of interviews and local news articles has pointed to the existence of a few large *preman* organizations currently active in

North Sulawesi. These include Brigade Manguni Indonesia, Milisi Waraney and Ansor. The development and dynamics of large *preman* organizations such as Brigade Manguni and Milisi Waraney have been overlooked in scholarly works and also the media. These organizations are not discussed much in the Indonesian national media. Articles published by *Kompas* from 2008 to 2022 did not mention Brigade Manguni or Milisi Waraney. From 2008 to 2022, there was only one article published in the *Jakarta Post* that mentioned Brigade Manguni, despite the prominence of this *preman* organization in North Sulawesi.

Brigade Manguni Indonesia is the largest *preman* organization in North Sulawesi.[4] In North Sulawesi alone, this organization has around ten thousand members (*Harian Jaya Pos*, 7 February 2016). The second-largest ethnic-based *preman* organization in North Sulawesi is Milisi Waraney, with five thousand members.[5] These organizations claim to represent the Minahasan ethnic group. In total there are thirty ethnic-affiliated *preman* organizations in North Sulawesi,[6] although some of them are no longer active. These ethnic-based *preman* organizations share the aim of safeguarding North Sulawesi as the land of their ancestors, or *tanah toar lumimuut* in the Minahasan language.

The establishment of ethnic based *preman* organizations in North Sulawesi began in the late 1990s when sectarian violence flared in the central and eastern parts of Indonesia, including in Ambon, the North Moluccas and Central Sulawesi. Many internally displaced Christians and Muslims who fled the conflict sought refuge in North Sulawesi. Against this backdrop, fighting between villages began to occur in North Sulawesi. Brigade Manguni and Milisi Waraney were established to maintain peace and prevent sectarian violence in the province.[7] Manguni and Waraney have worked together with the police and Ansor.[8] Ansor and its paramilitary wing, called Banser, is also an influential group in North Sulawesi. Ansor is part of Nahdlatul Ulama, the largest Islamic organizations in Indonesia, which has a membership of ninety million (Sebastian 2003, p. 432; *Kompas*, 7 April 2016; NU Online, 19 December 2021). Brigade Manguni, Milisi Waraney and Ansor are officially registered as CSOs at the city, provincial and national levels.[9] They are involved in maintaining security in North Sulawesi, along with government law enforcement agencies, especially during Eid, Christmas and New Year.[10] As a senior official from the Manado city administration put it, "They safeguard us. During religious festivals, a day before and after [Hari

Raya] they will help to monitor the security situation."[11] Of the three organizations, it is Milisi Waraney and Brigade Manguni that have been involved in securing ports and coastal areas across the province.

The funding for *preman* organizations comes from various sources, such as government grants, payments from providing protection

FIGURE 8
Brigade Manguni

A. Banner for inauguration ceremony of Brigade Manguni's leaders in 2016 in Manado; B. Car adorned with Brigade Manguni's symbols; C. Headquarters and ambulance of Komando Bela Negara, Brigade Manguni's paramilitary wing; D. Headquarter of Brigade Manguni in Manado; E. Brigade Manguni's anniversary in Tondano, 2015.

Image credits: Photos A to D by Senia Febrica; photo E by a member of Brigade Manguni. For ethical reasons, his name will not be revealed in this book.

services and donations from members (*Jakarta Post*, 16 November 2013; Indonesian National Human Rights Commission, 17 February 2014).[12] An editor of a local newspaper in North Sulawesi explained that,

> in the past, prior to Pastor Hanny Pantouw's chairmanship, Brigade Manguni had provided protection services. As the organization also supports the implementation of some government programmes, a government grant became [one of the sources] of their funding. Brigade Manguni's leaders are also successful people. For instance, the current head of Brigade Manguni is Nicholas Undap, a wealthy mining businessman.[13]

This editor of a local North Sulawesi newspaper implied that generous donations to the organization are often made by the leader.

As Brigade Manguni and Milisi Waraney are formally registered as legitimate CSOs, they have access to government grants (*hibah*) at the provincial and city levels. Evidence shows, however, that these two organizations rarely apply for government funding. Both an official from the Regional Financial and Property Management Agency, Bitung city government (Badan Pengelolaan Keuangan dan Barang Milik Daerah), and the head of the Agency for National Unity and Politics (Badan Kesatuan Bangsa dan Politik) of Bitung stated that the local government has never allocated funds to Milisi Waraney or Brigade Manguni Indonesia.[14] This is despite the strong presence of Milisi Waraney and Brigade Manguni in Bitung, the main port city of North Sulawesi.[15] Data on recipients of government grants and social assistance in Bitung for 2012–15 confirmed that neither Milisi Waraney nor Brigade Manguni received funding from the Bitung city government (Pemerintah Kota).[16]

Brigade Manguni and Milisi Waraney also have a strong presence in Manado, the capital city of North Sulawesi. An official responsible for the allocation of grants and social assistance by the Manado city government (Pemerintah Kota Manado) claimed that in recent years neither Brigade Manguni nor Milisi Waraney have received funding from her office.[17] She further explained that between 2011 and 2012 the city government only provided Brigade Manguni a small grant worth Rp10 million (US$684) for a meeting and less than Rp10 million (US$684) to Milisi Waraney just after 2012.[18]

At the provincial level, the head of the North Sulawesi Regional Financial and Property Management Agency claimed that Brigade Manguni and Milisi Waraney have not asked for grants or social assistance from the provincial government. She explained that her office has only received requests for funding from farmers' associations, orphanages and some foundations (*yayasan*).[19] A senior official at the North Sulawesi provincial government responsible for verifying CSO grant applications noted, however, that both Brigade Manguni Indonesia and the Milisi Waraney have applied for provincial government funding in the past. To quote him,

> The office of the Agency for National Unity and Politics verifies grant and social assistance applications. Milisi Waraney and Brigade Manguni have applied for grants. We verified whether or not they are registered and have a clear [secretariat] address. The data is available at the provincial finance office. We are the ones to do the monitoring and evaluation. Brigade Manguni Indonesia applied for grants several times. It is now is my third year working here dealing with government grants.[20]

Data from the provincial government detailing the allocation of grants and social assistance to CSOs was not made available to the author. It is therefore difficult to verify the conflicting statements made by the provincial government officials. Having reviewed news articles and interview results, however, it could be concluded that large *preman* organizations such as Brigade Manguni and Milisi Waraney do not depend on government funding as their main source of funding. The majority of their funding comes from members of the organizations, especially wealthy and influential members. Pride and prestige, protection of businesses, and political support could be among the factors encouraging financial contributions to *preman* organizations.[21] Despite the claim of neutrality in politics, in the 2014 presidential election, for instance, Brigade Manguni lent their support to presidential candidate Prabowo Subianto, who is also one of the founders (*Pembina*) of the organization (*Berita Manado*, 10 March 2013; 12 June 2014).

In North Sulawesi, *preman* organizations such as Brigade Manguni and Milisi Waraney could be categorized as high-profile organizations. The involvement of the two organizations in security is widely discussed in local newspapers in North Sulawesi. Brigade Manguni was mentioned 12 times in *Manado Post* articles published from 1 January 2014 to 14 August 2016 and 196 times in articles published by *Tribun Manado* from 1 January 2012 to 14 August 2016.

An analysis of *Manado Post* articles shows that the word "secure" (*aman*) appeared three times and the word "security" (*keamanan*) was used three times in news discussing Brigade Manguni. The word "secure" (*aman*) was mentioned twice to refer to Brigade Manguni's vision to establish a secure and peaceful environment for all residents of North Sulawesi and once to explain the invitation by Police Brigadier General Wilmar Marpaung, the head of the North Sulawesi police force, to organizations such as Brigade Manguni and Ansor to assist the government in efforts to combat terrorism and with problems related to alcohol abuse in the province. Brigadier General Marpaung's statement was made at a meeting between the Indonesian law enforcement agencies and various *preman* organizations in North Sulawesi (*Manado Post*, 11 April 2015). The word "security" (*keamanan*) was used twice in *Manado Post* to refer to the commitment by the North Sulawesi community to maintain security in their province and once to explain the pledge by the leader of Brigade Manguni to help police in improving security in border areas and ports throughout the province (*Manado Post*, 11 April 2015; 28 March 2015).

Analysis of *Tribun Manado* articles that discuss Brigade Manguni reveals that the word "security" (*keamanan*) appeared 26 times to explain Brigade Manguni's participation in maintaining stability and security in North Sulawesi and coordination between this organization and government authorities. *Tribun Manado* used the phrase "guarding security" (*jaga keamanan* or *menjaga keamananan*) 11 times when referring to Brigade Manguni Indonesia. The word "secure" (*aman*) was mentioned 12 times. In *Tribun Manado* articles that discussed Brigade Manguni, the following terms appeared once each: "involvement in maintaining the region's security" (*terlibat dalam keamanan*), "the guardian of peace and security" (*penjaga perdamaian dan keamanan*) and "assisting security authorities" (*membantu aparat keamanan*).

Tribun Manado reported that the support Brigade Manguni provided to the government authorities ranged from efforts to prevent fighting between inebriated youth groups to counterterrorism (*Tribun Manado*, 5 May 2015; 7 November 2012). On the matter of counterterrorism, *Tribun Manado* reported various coordination meetings between Brigade Manguni Indonesia and high-profile provincial government officials, the police and the military (*Tribun Manado*, 7 November 2012; 5 February 2015). The word "terrorism" was mentioned four times among all the *Tribun Manado* articles that discussed Brigade Manguni. It was used three times to refer to the coordination meeting between the government authorities and Brigade Manguni to deter terrorism. The word "terrorism" also appeared once in an article in September 2011 telling how Brigade Manguni condemned a suicide bomb attack on a church in Solo (*Tribun Manado*, 25 September 2011).

Articles published by *Tribun Manado* from 1 January 2012 to 14 August 2016 mentioned Milisi Waraney 22 times. *Tribun Manado* has reported the engagement by Milisi Waraney in various activities, including organizing a sports tournament at the provincial level, cleaning the environment, providing social assistance to street sweepers in Bitung, monitoring the use of a government fund to build a public facility, and participating in anti-radicalization efforts (*Tribun Manado*, 5 September 2015; 11 August 2012; 21 December 2011; 15 August 2014; 8 August 2014).

The word "radical" (*radikal*) was used five times in articles that discussed Milisi Waraney (*Tribun Manado*, 15 August 2014; 8 August 2014). The term "radical" was used three times when referring to the readiness of Milisi Waraney to guard South Minahasa (Minahasa Selatan), an administrative region in North Sulawesi, from militant and radical groups (*Tribun Manado*, 8 August 2014). The trans-Sulawesi highway that connects North Sulawesi with Poso, an area that has been destabilized by Islamic terrorism, passes through South Minahasa. One of the leaders of Milisi Waraney, Sonny Sariowan, has called on the local government at the village level to register its residents (*Tribun Manado*, 8 August 2014). The aim of this registration is to anticipate the entry of outsiders that have the potential to introduce radical views and disturb the harmony of the region. The term "radical" was used once to point out Waraney's peaceful demonstration before the Bitung Mayor's office to refuse the Islamic State of Iraq and Syria (ISIS) and their radical views (*Tribun Manado*, 15 August 2014). It was also used once to explain Milisi Waraney's rejection of radical CSOs being established in North Sulawesi and its call to the government to shut down such organizations (*Tribun Manado*, 7 June 2013). *Tribun Manado* did not mention the name of the radical CSO. But from interviews with officials and members of Milisi Waraney in North Sulawesi it could be concluded that the radical organization opposed by Milisi Waraney was Front Pembela Islam (FPI). FPI is a radical Islamic-based *preman* organization that has a long record of vigilantism and violent behaviour. The provincial government of North Sulawesi and the Manado city administration have rejected the establishment of this organization in their jurisdiction.[22]

FIGURE 9
Location of Brigade Manguni Secretariat Office near
Bitung Container Port and Bitung Passenger Port

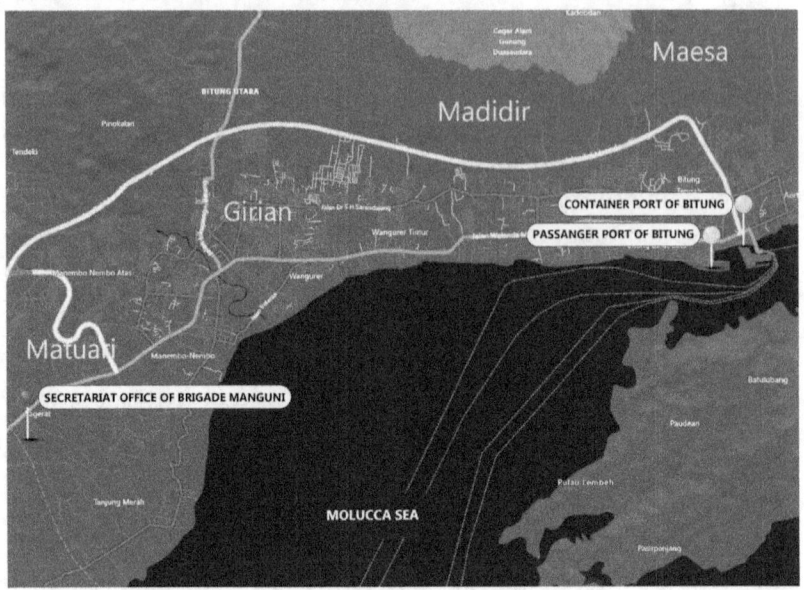

The above analysis of coverage by the *Manado Post* and *Tribun Manado* shows the significant role played by Brigade Manguni and Milisi Waraney in the security of North Sulawesi and the positive portrayal of the two organizations by the local media and government.

Brigade Manguni Indonesia and Milisi Waraney enjoy harmonious relations with government authorities. High-profile government officials attend special events organized by these organizations (*Berita Manado*, 9 March 2015; 10 November 2013; 25 February 2013; 28 May 2011; 25 June 2013; *Berita Manguni*, 9 March 2013). The inauguration of Nicholas Undap as leader of Brigade Manguni Indonesia in February 2016, for instance, was attended by North Sulawesi governor Sony Sumarsono, the deputy chief of the regional police (Wakapolda), the commander of the military headquarters (Danrem) and the commander of the Indonesian eastern fleet naval base (*Harian Jaya Pos*, 7 February 2016). A senior government official also explained that many government officials have joined Brigade Manguni.[23] Periodically, government authorities also meet with Brigade Manguni and Milisi Waraney to discuss security concerns and coordinate ways to address them with these organizations (*Berita Manado*, 25 June 2013; 4 February 2015; 8 March 2013).

Brigade Manguni and Milisi Waraney have built partnerships with the Indonesian authorities to secure ports in North Sulawesi. Members of these organizations are recruited to be security guards in ports. Members of Komando Bela Negara, the paramilitary wing of Brigade Manguni, are given priority to work as security guards in ports in Bitung and Manado.[24] According to a local leader of Komando Bela Negara, the Indonesian port authority, Pelindo, in Bitung has recruited members of the Manguni paramilitary wing as port security guards.[25] This recruitment was made possible because various port authority officials are also members of Brigade Manguni.[26]

Occasionally, certain members of Manguni and Waraney are also involved in monitoring port security and carrying out joint operations at ferry or passenger ports when there are special events that require the presence of more security guards.[27] During joint operations, members of these groups work alongside the police, the armed forces and Satpol Pamong Praja—the local government security unit.[28] Members of Brigade Manguni and Milisi Waraney assist government security personnel in checking passengers' identities and belongings. They are not assigned as permanent guards in the passenger or ferry ports where the joint operations are held. Rather, Brigade Manguni and Milisi Waraney only take part if the state intelligence agency (Badan Intelijen Negara, or BIN) or the police request their assistance.[29] As a member of Milisi Waraney suggested, "we are not involved on a regular basis"; for instance, during the Marine Day festival (Festival Hari Bahari), Milisi Waraney assisted the police and armed forces in guarding a passenger port in Bitung.[30] A member of Milisi Waraney who had taken part in securing a port in the past stated that if the port authorities asked for say, 25, 50 or 100 personnel, their leaders would provide that exact number.[31] He further explained that,

> In Bitung we have our commander. We can monitor the situation in the port if there are suspicious people.... We intervene in port security in order to reduce peoples' fear when a big event is held. Passengers at the port can observe "tight security measures" being delivered by the armed forces, the police and Milisi Waraney. They will witness how good the security is.[32]

The head of the Bitung Agency for National Unity and Politics claimed that CSOs such as Milisi Waraney and Brigade Manguni assisted the government in monitoring port security at Bitung passenger port. To quote him,

> Yes, they [Milisi Waraney and Brigade Manguni] help in monitoring ports. We have a regional intelligence community (Komunitas Intelijen Daerah, or Kominda). From Kominda we established the community early awareness forum (Forum Kewaspadaan Dini Masyarakat, or FKDM). At FKMD there are intelligence [agents] that are ready to help the government. We get plenty of information from CSOs. The armed forces and police often carry out sweeping if they receive information that actors who threaten security are traveling to Bitung via sea, land or air routes. CSOs carry out monitoring, not sweeping, unless they are asked to by the police or armed forces. There were times when CSOs and youth organizations were invited by the police to help sweeping vehicles.[33]

A senior official at the North Sulawesi Agency for National Unity and Politics viewed the coastal population, CSOs and youth organizations as "the guards, the reserve component of Indonesian law enforcement agencies".[34]

The role of *preman* organizations in port security in North Sulawesi is also confirmed in media reports. It was reported that on 31 December 2012, Brigade Manguni assisted the Indonesian police and armed forces in guarding Bitung Port on New Year's Eve (Viva, 31 December 2012). The main purpose of their involvement in the joint operation was to assist the authorities in preventing a terrorist attack. In the run up to the 2013 New Year's celebration, the North Sulawesi police deployed over three thousand armed personnel and speedboats to secure the coastal areas from Bitung to North Minahasa from potential terrorist attacks (ibid.).

A secretariat staff of Milisi Waraney confirmed that there is coordination between her organization and government authorities at Bitung Port.[35] Milisi Waraney has assisted in monitoring security at the Bitung passenger port, Amura port in South Minahasa and ports in the outer islands of North Sulawesi, including Siau and Sanger.[36] At Bitung passenger port, the civilian groups have assigned thirty people to monitor security.[37] According to the vice-chairman of Milisi Waraney, around ten per cent of his members (roughly five hundred people) have provided assistance for port security in the province, including in the outer islands.[38] Not all such members were specifically assigned by the organization to work there;[39] many of them were already working at the ports as ship crew, porters, fishermen, ships captains, drivers, and businessmen in the fishing sector.[40]

Neither Milisi Waraney nor Brigade Manguni have been involved, however, in joint operations with the government security authorities at Bitung international container port. Former president Megawati Soekarno Putri inaugurated Bitung container port on 12 October 2004 (Pelindo IV Cabang Bitung, 18 November 2018). It is one of Indonesia's main export-import ports in the eastern part of the country that has met the International Ship and Port Facility Security (ISPS) Code requirements.[41] For this reason, the port administrator (Administrator Pelabuhan), coastguard (Kesatuan Penjaga Laut dan Pantai) from the Directorate General of Transportation, the navy, and the port security guards are the ones strictly responsible for security in this area.

Brigade Manguni and Milisi Waraney have coordinated closely with the police.[42] As part of Brigade Manguni's cooperation with the police, a team of volunteers from Brigade Manguni provides information on various matters—from vehicle thefts to radicalization—through social media such as Facebook to the police team called Tim Manguni Polda Resort.[43] At ports, Milisi Waraney is working under the coordination of the local police.[44]

In contrast to *preman* organizations operating in Batam and Tanjung Pinang that regularly receive basic military training from the government security authorities, members of Brigade Manguni and Milisi Waraney do not receive such training. The vice-chairman of Milisi Waraney, a leader of the organization's youth wing and a member of this organization pointed out that the majority of Waraney members work as miners and other professions that are deemed as rough. Thus, they know how to fight and defend themselves.[45] The police, however, have provided select members of Brigade Manguni and Milisi Waraney with intelligence training. A retired senior police officer confirmed that,

> for counter terrorism, Brigade Manguni and Milisi Waraney are trained for early detection. They become the ears of the security apparatus and are trained for that purpose. North Sulawesi is the gateway for terrorists travelling from the Philippines. They [members of Brigade Manguni and Milisi Waraney] are everywhere. Therefore, if there are problems they can gather really quickly.[46]

The role of Brigade Manguni and Milisi Waraney has been acknowledged by politicians and officials. Overall, they found that these CSOs are not aggressive and are able to neutralize conflicts or disturbances.[47] A senior government official from Bitung argued that personnel of Brigade Manguni and Milisi Waraney could respond to trouble quickly and can help to secure places of worship during special celebrations such as Idul Fitri, Christmas and New Year.[48] These *preman* organizations are also deemed useful as they have their own search and rescue team and an ambulance team that could assist the community when natural disasters strike—such as when flooding occurred in Manado in 2014—and help with burials.[49] As a former member of the North Sulawesi parliament and a senior politician from the Golkar Party put it, "I do not know precisely the arrangement on port security.... Nevertheless, if there are problems, Brigade Manguni will catch the perpetrators and hand them to the police. If you see in the newspapers, it is widely reported how Manguni has been helping the police."[50] He further stated that the role of *preman* organizations in North Sulawesi is very positive, "unlike in Java, where the CSOs conduct demonstrations on a daily basis".[51] Taken as a whole, these statements illustrate the positive portrayal of *preman* organizations by active and retired officials and politicians.

A North Minahasa (Minahasa Utara) parliamentarian explained that in North Sulawesi the mode of operation of *preman* organizations in securing ports is not fixed because it depends on the specific request made by the local office of the Ministry of Transportation. If a group has connections with the Ministry of Transportation, then that group will be the one that participates in port security. "So, it is not certain whether it will be Brigade Manguni or Milisi Waraney or perhaps other groups such as Pemuda Pancasila or Ansor [who will help to secure the port] because it depends on ... their relations with the relevant authorities."[52] He further suggested that "in North Minahasa there is a ferry/passenger port.... Here, Brigade Manguni and Milisi Waraney have been most helpful in guarding this port."[53] Members of the two organizations do not wear uniforms, and they "mingle with the rest of the people in the port. Therefore, their involvement in securing the port is not apparent to the public."[54]

The Lack of Conflict?

In contrast to the situation in Jakarta, at present there has been no large-scale open confrontation between *preman* organizations in North Sulawesi or between these organizations and the police or armed forces.[55] A retired senior police official claimed that there was a conflict between the police and members of Brigade Manguni in the year after the group was established, between 1999 and 2000.[56] According to him, this clash between the police and Brigade Manguni took place when Brigade Manguni ran convoys across town. He recalled that,

> during a convoy in Kairagi district, some members of Brigade Manguni stopped the traffic and began to hit cars that would not give way to their convoy with bamboo sticks. Since this incident, relations between the police and Brigade Manguni Indonesia have improved significantly.[57]

At present, it is rare for a conflict to occur between the police and members of *preman* organizations. A parliamentarian suggested that "sometimes members of CSOs oppose government evictions that involve their relatives or family members. This could lead to a confrontation in the field between the police and CSOs."[58] But such incidents are rare.[59] Analysis of local media reports confirms this. Local newspapers, including *Tribun Manado* and *Manado Post*, did not feature any reports on conflicts between Brigade Manguni or Milisi Waraney with the government authorities or local communities, or any participation of these organizations in illicit activities at the ports. Overall, the local media provides a positive portrayal of the roles of Brigade Manguni and Milisi Waraney in North Sulawesi.

In North Sulawesi, *preman* organizations have relatively peaceful relations with the port authorities. The *preman* organizations had staged a demonstration at Manado Port following the decision by the port administration in June 2013 to ban street vendors from entering the port. According to a senior government official at the Manado Port administration, one of the *preman* organizations involved in the demonstration only wrote a letter of complaint to his superior at the Ministry of Transportation in Jakarta.[60]

Preman organizations have also protested and written letters of complaint to the Directorate General of Sea Transportation because the Manado Port administration has often allowed large ships to stop and stay in areas outside the port or the special terminal. They found that such a situation created a nuisance for local communities and fishers. An official with the Manado Port administration suggested this was a decision that had to be made on a regular basis because in Manado there is only one special terminal, which is located in Malalayang.[61] If, therefore, there were many large vessels arriving at Manado on the same day, he would ask some of the vessels that could not find a berthing space to stop outside the port or the terminal location.[62] Protests and complaints aimed at the port authorities, however, have never escalated to violent conflict between *preman* organizations and government authorities.

The absence of any significant conflict between *preman* organizations and the government authorities in North Sulawesi is partly the result of acknowledgment by government officials of the usefulness of these *preman* organizations in securing the "border province". Various remarks have been made to the media by government officials about Brigade Manguni's role as a partner of the police force in North Sulawesi. Charles Ngili, the vice head of the police (Wakil Kepala Kepolisian Daerah, or Wakapolda) of North Sulawesi, expressed in a statement to *Tribun Manado* that,

> Brigade Manguni can be the pioneer [to maintain] security and order in society and avoid violating the law. We want Brigade Manguni to be a partner and not a troublemaker. To be [an instrument] for social control for the government, including the police (*Tribun Manado*, 5 February 2015a).

Ngili compared the role of Brigade Manguni with the *Pecalang*, traditional security officers in villages in Bali. As he put it,

> In Bali, if there are events, the one to secure [these events] is the *Pecalang*. All the police need to do is to coordinate. In Bali, one police, many [members of] the *Pecalang*. In Bali, the *Pecalang* is deeply trusted by society because they can maintain their credibility to create an orderly society. [They] have never backed illicit activities that deviate from the law. (*Tribun Manado*, 5 February 2015a)

Acknowledgement of Brigade Manguni as a partner of the police was also made by Krisno Siregar, the police commissioner of North Sulawesi. In a meeting with Brigade Manguni in February 2015, Siregar stated his expectation that "a large CSO such as Brigade Manguni" can serve as a partner to the police. He warned Brigade Manguni not to let members of society fear their organization. In Tangerang, Banten [the city where he worked previously], CSOs have turned into something frightening, often viewing law enforcement agencies not as a partner but as an enemy (*Tribun Manado*, 5 February 2015b).

A local newspaper, *Berita Manado*, reported a claim made by the former chairman of Brigade Manguni that several generals from the Indonesian armed forces had encouraged the establishment of Brigade

Manguni's intelligence division because of the close proximity of North Sulawesi to the southern Philippines (*Berita Manado*, 8 March 2013). This suggests the presence of security functions that can be filled by *preman* organizations such as Brigade Manguni. To quote the newspaper article,

> The largest ethnic organization in North Sulawesi, Brigade Manguni Indonesia (BMI), has a central role in defending the country. Related to this, Tonnas Wangko of the BMI, Decky Maengkom, claimed that he has received guidance from several Indonesian armed forces generals to strengthen [his organization]. One [way to do this is] by forming the intelligence division, because North Sulawesi is directly adjacent to the Philippines. (*Berita Manado*, 8 March 2013).

Despite the absence of violent conflict with government authorities, *preman* organizations such as Brigade Manguni have on several occasions provided security support to private companies that have broken the law. This practice presents challenges for government authorities seeking to maintain order in North Sulawesi and other parts of Indonesia. It is worth noting that the more critical views on the use of *preman* organizations in North Sulawesi are from non-local sources. This contrasts with the more positive coverage in local sources, such as *Manado Post* and *Tribun Manado*. The *Jakarta Post* reported that Brigade Manguni provided protection services for land reclamation projects carried out by PT Gerbang Nusa Perkasa and PT Kembang Utara (*Jakarta Post*, 16 November 2013). The developers had illegally closed the open space that fishers needed to gain access to the sea (ibid.). A clash then broke out between the fishers and security guards for the reclamation site on 19 October 2013. Less than a year later, on 17 February 2014, the Indonesian National Human Rights Commission sent a letter to the head of the North Sulawesi police force reporting that Brigade Manguni, together with members of the North Sulawesi police force, had escorted a shipment of heavy machinery equipment from Bitung Port to Bangka Island (Indonesian National Human Rights Commission, 17 February 2014). The equipment belonged to a mining company called PT Mikgro Metal Perdana. The company's mining licence had been revoked by the Indonesian Supreme Court on 24 September 2013 in decision number 291K/TUN/2013 (ibid.). The shipment and placement of heavy machinery equipment by PT Mikgro Metal Perdana was therefore deemed provocative and illegal (ibid.). The

Indonesian Human Rights Commission requested the head of the North Sulawesi police to ban members of Brigade Manguni from entering Bangka Island and to remove members of his force that had taken part in escorting the shipment. The commission expressed concern over potential conflict between the local communities of Bangka Island with the members of Brigade Manguni and the police used by the mining company (ibid.).

Combating Illegal Activities

A range of illicit activities—including the smuggling of weapons, drugs and fake dollar bills; human trafficking and armed robbery against ships—take place in the waters and outlying islands of North Sulawesi (Dewan Maritim Indonesia 2007a, p. 33). The partnership between the Indonesian authorities and the two *preman* organizations—Brigade Manguni and Milisi Waraney—touches on efforts to address illegal activities in the North Sulawesi maritime domain. These include activities to deal with terrorism, human trafficking and illegal fishing.

In terms of terrorism, the province of North Sulawesi is located close to Mindanao, the southern part of the Philippines. The Indonesian minister of home affairs, Tjahjo Kumolo, stated that North Sulawesi is not a recruitment target area for ISIS, but it serves as a gateway for radical views (or people bringing radical views) to enter Indonesia (*Manado Post*, 11 April 2015). Members of Jamaah Islamiyah, a terrorist organization based in Southeast Asia, and other Islamic militant organizations have travelled from Indonesia to terrorist training camps in the Philippines through ports in North Sulawesi and from the Philippines to central Sulawesi, small islands in North Sulawesi such as Miangas, Sanger or Siau, and other parts of Indonesia. The government authorities regularly hold meetings with *preman* organizations to coordinate action and to ask for their cooperation in reporting suspicious activities to the police (*Manado Post*, 11 April 2015). According to a senior official of the Manado city government, Milisi Waraney and Brigade Manguni participate in the local government early awareness forum (Forum Kewaspadaan Dini), which seeks to address human trafficking, social disturbances and radicalization.[63] He explained that,

> We use CSOs and youth organizations as sources of information.... from this forum, the government seeks information from CSOs.

CSOs are expected to play a crucial role in raising early awareness by dealing with security problems through monitoring and providing information.[64]

In a meeting with *preman* organizations, including Brigade Manguni, Pemuda Pancasila and Ansor, the head of the North Sulawesi police, Brigadier General Wilmar Marpaung SH, stated that,

> supporters of Philippines' radical groups are likely to enter North Sulawesi through traditional ports.... members of radical groups in Poso who are targeted by the police and military can [also] escape to North Sulawesi. Thus, to anticipate these activities, CSOs need ... to provide information if they see anything suspicious. (*Manado Post*, 11 April 2015)

Joint security operations between government authorities and *preman* organizations to prevent smuggling of weapons and halt militants travelling from Mindanao to Sulawesi and vice versa are common. A senior official at the North Sulawesi provincial government verified that many smuggling attempts had failed because the *preman* organizations reported such activity to the police. According to him,

> members of the CSOs reported smuggling activities to their organizations. These organizations reported them to us, to the armed forces and the police.... The CSOs and youth organizations, they are like intelligence ... they report to us. It will be more difficult for officials [to find information].[65]

The senior official further explained that the recent discovery by the government of a new smuggling route utilized by terrorists and criminal organizations was thanks to reports made by a *preman* organization (which he refused to name).[66] Given the close proximity of North Sulawesi to the Philippines, and the great distance between the capital and the many outlying islands in the northern regencies (Talaud, Sangihe and Sitaro), assistance from *preman* organizations and youth organizations in combating illicit activities is highly valued by the Indonesian government. To further quote the official,

> If we are travelling from the centre of Manado to Talaud, we will arrive in Talaud the next day. From Miangas to Davao [the Philippines] it will only take three hours at the longest. From the capital town of Talaud to Miangas, it will take six hours. Smuggling activities are carried out from the Philippines [to Indonesia]. Smugglers would not go through Miangas, because of the tight security now that there is a naval base there. They

navigate a little further to the west, to Gorontalo. From Gorontalo they travel to Toli-Toli in Central Sulawesi, which is located close to East Kalimantan.... There is a ferry route from Toli-Toli to East Kalimantan, so the route is Gorontalo–Toli-Toli–East Kalimantan.[67]

The senior provincial official implied that the military presence at Miangas caused the smuggling route to change, so the role of *preman* organizations in helping to monitor and provide information is therefore deemed important.

The Indonesian national anti-terrorism board and the police have established connections with *preman* organizations for their assistance in counterterrorism intelligence and anti-radicalization. A member of Brigade Manguni explained that the organization assisted the police in 2015 to unravel the smuggling of weapons by terrorists from the Philippines.[68] As he described it,

> There had been cases where efforts to halt trafficking had been carried out by Brigade Manguni. This happened more or less two years ago. Brigade Manguni had also dismantled terrorist networks.... the terrorist group came from the Philippines. Brigade Manguni assisted to stop the smuggling of weapons from the Philippines. The last incident took place a year ago, where the weapons were quickly confiscated and the perpetrators were handed over to the police.... We have to find evidence and ambush them. During the ambush, we only provide support [to the police]. The police were on the front line because if the terrorists were armed that would be dangerous.[69]

The presence of close coordination between the government and *preman* organizations is confirmed in various articles published by local newspapers, which cited both the leaders of the *preman* organizations and government officials. On 7 November 2012, *Tribun Manado* reported, for example, that a meeting aimed at preventing terrorism took place between representatives of the provincial government, the leaders of Brigade Manguni, two senior government officials from the Indonesian armed forces (Markas Besar Tentara Nasional Indonesia, or Mabes TNI) and a senior government official from the Indonesian police (Markas Besar Kepolisian Republik Indonesia, or Mabes Polri) at the North Sulawesi Agency for National Unity and Politics (Kesatuan Bangsa dan Politik Sulawesi Utara). Cited by *Tribun Manado*, Pastor Hanny Pantouw, the former leader of Brigade Manguni's representative board for North Sulawesi, explained how

> there has been indication that these people [the terrorists] had entered [North Sulawesi] as they are looking for the opportunity

to make their move.... North Sulawesi is a target. These two major generals and one brigadier general have come to North Sulawesi because North Sulawesi is important, and to remind [us], so that the situation in Poso will not take place here (*Tribun Manado*, 7 November 2012).

In February 2015, during a meeting with the police commissioner of North Sulawesi, Pastor Hanny Pantouw pointed out the need for his organization to coordinate with the police on various issues, specifically "to prevent the occurrence of terrorism in North Sulawesi" (*Tribun Manado*, 5 February 2015). On 28 March 2015, following a meeting with the head of the North Sulawesi police force and his team, the leader of Brigade Manguni, Daecky Maengkom, in his statement to *Manado Post*, claimed that his organization would help the police to strengthen security in "the border areas and ports across the province to halt the smuggling of weapons and deter terrorists from travelling from the southern Philippines to North Sulawesi and vice-versa" (*Manado Post*, 28 March 2015). The statements made by Brigade Manguni's leaders were confirmed by Brigadier General Wilmar Marpaung, the head of North Sulawesi's police force, who expressed his expectation that Brigade Manguni could help the police in addressing security problems in this province (*Manado Post*, 28 March 2015).

In North Sulawesi, Brigade Manguni and Milisi Waraney have also assisted the police in halting the trafficking of girls, mainly teenagers, from Manado and Bitung seaports to other parts of Indonesia—in particular, Sorong, Papua, and Jakarta—and abroad.[70] These organizations are often informed by the victims' families, and they are sometimes tipped off by the police.[71] In some incidents, the organizations have intervened and stopped the perpetrators before the police arrived.[72] A leader of Brigade Manguni's paramilitary wing in Bitung claimed the organization would stop an average of eight trafficking attempts a year.[73] According to him, in 2014 Milisi Waraney halted the trafficking of twelve North Sulawesi women at Bitung passenger port following information received from the victims' families.[74]

These statements by Brigade Manguni and Milisi Waraney were confirmed by a parliamentarian, retired and active police officers, and senior local government officials at the township and provincial levels. A parliamentarian from Minahasa Utara noted that Brigade Manguni and Milisi Waraney "have contributed to halting human trafficking". He pointed out that, in January 2016, Brigade Manguni stopped a case of trafficking where women were going to be trafficked to Sorong, Papua, from Bitung.[75] A retired senior police official confirmed that "it is true that Brigade Manguni and Milisi Waraney have helped the police to stop the trafficking of people via seaports and airports in North Sulawesi".[76] An active police official in Manado also corroborated this statement, pointing out that

> Groups such as Brigade Manguni and Milisi Waraney are very helpful to the police. There were cases of women trafficking through ports that were stopped because of information given by these CSOs. In 2016 there were five women who were lured by a trafficker with the promise of good jobs in Jakarta with a monthly salary of ten million rupiah [less than US$1,000].[77]

The head of Bitung Township's Agency for National Unity and Politics acknowledged the crucial role of CSOs in providing information to halt trafficking. As he put it,

> In terms of trafficking, mass organizations such as Milisi Waraney and Brigade Manguni and NGOs provide lots of information.... In Bitung, some of them were discovered when they were already onboard ships in the harbour or along the coast. Law enforcement officials have received information from members of society, including from mass organizations and NGOs. Some victims of trafficking reached their destination, but the Bitung local government and police returned them to Bitung.... Mass organizations supply plenty of information. This is because each individual organization has their own intelligence division.[78]

A senior official from the provincial government of North Sulawesi further highlighted the role of *preman* organizations in assisting the government in addressing human trafficking. To quote him,

> They help in dealing with trafficking.... Not only Brigade Manguni Indonesia; there are also other organizations. In port areas at Bitung Port and Manado Port they halt trafficking. They help the work of government. Their work has also been acknowledged by the police. However, they do not carry out action [against the traffickers]. Just regular intelligence [role].... They provide information. They can secure [the victims and perpetrators] to be handed over to the police.[79]

The role of these *preman* organizations in maritime security has seemingly extended beyond port areas. On their own initiative, Generasi Muda (Garda) Milisi Waraney, the youth wing of

Waraney, has actively carried out undercover activities to capture boats conducting illegal fishing in the waters of North Sulawesi. According to one leader of Garda Milisi Waraney, each of their operations to tackle illegal fishing involves fifteen to twenty people. The participants wear fishers' outfits and use two fishing boats to surround the illegal fishers. He claimed that in 2016 they managed to capture a fishing vessel from the Philippines. The captured boat was then handed over to the marine police.[80] *Preman* organizations involved in campaigns to tackle illegal fishing perceive that they need to act to help local fishers and safeguard the land of their ancestors (*"tanah toar lumimuut"* in the Minahasan language). There is rampant illegal, unreported and unregulated (IUU) fishing in North Sulawesi. Vessels coming from the Philippines, Taiwan and Thailand often conduct IUU fishing in the waters of North Sulawesi. The abundance of tuna in the Sulawesi Sea has drawn perpetrators of IUU fishing to these waters. Local fishers from Bitung, North Minahasa, and the outer islands, including Siau, claim that illegal fishers do not hesitate to kill, kidnap or use violence against any local fishers they encounter at sea to prevent the reporting of the IUU fishing to the Indonesian authorities.[81] One fisher from the North Sulawesi town of Minahasa Utara stated that at least twenty of his fellow fishers had been killed by perpetrators of IUU fishing.[82]

Conclusion

The analysis of *preman* organizations in North Sulawesi shows that the participation of these organizations in port security is largely welcomed by the local government authorities and the media. Large *preman* organizations such as Brigade Manguni and Milisi Waraney were established in the late 1990s by local communities to prevent the spread of sectarian violence from the neighbouring conflict zones of the Moluccas, North Moluccas and Central Sulawesi to North Sulawesi. Since their establishment, these organizations have formed close relations with the local government and security authorities.

The presence of *preman* organizations is deemed useful by the government authorities for maintaining order and security. This positive attitude towards them is shaped by a combination of North Sulawesi's geographical location and the existing security gap. North Sulawesi is located close to the Southern Philippines and consists of hundreds of outlying islands. Given its location, ports in North Sulawesi face challenges of cross-border illicit activities by criminal and terrorist groups. Against this background, the leaders and members of *preman* organizations, local parliaments, provincial and town government authorities, and police forces view the partnership between the government and *preman* organizations as essential to maintaining port, border and coastal security. The government authorities would not be able to manage this task alone.

Local media, parliamentarians and officers from the local government and state security apparatus hold a positive view of the role of *preman* organizations in dealing with trans-border illicit activities, including terrorism and human trafficking. This perspective is partly informed by the lack of clashes between *preman* organizations and the government. Whilst there have been several reported conflicts between members of society and CSOs, large violent clashes between different *preman* organizations or between these organizations and the government have not taken place.

This is not to suggest, however, that the involvement of *preman* organizations in security in North Sulawesi has been trouble free. Protection services provided by *preman* organizations to businesses that act unlawfully pose a challenge for government authorities seeking to maintain order in North Sulawesi and other parts of Indonesia. Such practices have also led to conflict between members of *preman* organizations and the local community whom they claim to protect. More critical views regarding the use of *preman* organizations in North Sulawesi tend to come from external rather than local sources. This has raised the question of how *preman* organizations affect democratization, given the significance of a free media in democracy.

This chapter has examined the involvement of *preman* organizations in port security in North Sulawesi. The chapter has shown that these organizations form an integral part in monitoring and maintaining security not only at ports but also at border and coastal areas of the province. The next chapter will explore whether the centrality of *preman* organizations in security also applies to ports in the Riau Islands, an Indonesian border province located close to the Straits of Malacca and Singapore.

Notes
1. Interview with the head of Komando Bela Negara Maesa District Brigade Manguni Indonesia, 6 February 2016, Bitung.
2. Interview with the head of Pemuda Pancasila in North Sulawesi, 11 February 2016, Manado.

3. Interview with the head of the national leadership assembly of Pemuda Pancasila, 19 September 2016, Jakarta.
4. Discussion with a government official living in Bitung, 6 August 2016. Interviews with a retired police official, 12 February 2016, Manado; the public relations official of Milisi Waraney and a former public relations official of Pemuda Pancasila Manado, 12 February 2016, Manado; a former member of the North Sulawesi parliament and former head of Pemuda Pancasila in Nusa Utara, 13 February 2016, Manado; one of the leaders of the Milisi Waraney youth organization, 5 February 2015; and the head of the Agency for National Unity and Politics, Manado city government, 10 November 2016, Manado.
5. Interview with one of the leaders of the Milisi Waraney youth organization, 5 February 2015, Manado.
6. Interviews with the public relations official of Milisi Waraney and a former public relations official of Pemuda Pancasila Manado, 12 February 2016, Manado; a former member of the North Sulawesi parliament and the former head of Pemuda Pancasila in Nusa Utara, 13 February 2016, Manado; and a member of the Minahasa Utara parliament, 13 February 2016, Manado.
7. Interviews with the vice-chairman of Milisi Waraney, 5 February 2016, Manado; the public relations official of Milisi Waraney and a former public relations official of Pemuda Pancasila Manado, 12 February 2016, Manado; and a former police official, 12 February 2016, Manado.
8. Interviews with the vice-chairman of Milisi Waraney, 5 February 2016, Manado; a former police official, 12 February 2016, Manado; and the public relations official of Milisi Waraney and a former public relations official of Pemuda Pancasila Manado, 12 February 2016, Manado.
9. Interview with the head of the Agency for National Unity and Politics, Manado city government, 10 November 2016, Manado.
10. Ibid.
11. Ibid.
12. Interviews with an official from the Regional Financial and Property Management Agency (Badan Pengelolaan Keuangan dan Barang Milik Daerah), Manado city government, November 2016, Manado; an official from the Regional Financial and Property Management Agency, Bitung town government, 14 November 2016, Bitung; the head of Security Facilitation, Arts, Culture, Economics, Religion and Society Section, North Sulawesi provincial government Agency for National Unity and Politics, 17 November 2016, Manado; and two editors of *Tribun Manado*, 10 November 2016.
13. Interview with an editor of *Tribun Manado*, 10 November 2016.
14. Interviews with an official from the Regional Financial and Property Management Agency, Bitung town government, 14 November 2016, Bitung; and the head of the Agency for National Unity and Politics, Bitung government, 14 November 2016, Bitung.

15. Interview with an official from the Regional Financial and Property Management Agency, Bitung town government, 14 November 2016, Bitung.
16. Data of Bitung city government's allocation of grants and social assistance was provided to the author in Bitung by an official from the Regional Financial and Property Management Agency, Manado city government, 16 November 2016, Manado.
17. Interview with an official from the Regional Financial and Property Management Agency, Manado city government, November 2016, Manado.
18. Ibid.
19. Interview with the head of the Regional Financial and Property Management Agency, November 2016, Manado.
20. Interview with the head of Security Facilitation, Arts, Culture, Economics, Religion and Society Section, North Sulawesi Agency for National Unity and Politics, 17 November 2016, Manado.
21. Interviews with an editor of *Tribun Manado*, 10 November 2016; and a retired police official, 12 February 2016, Manado.
22. Interview with the head of the Agency for National Unity and Politics, Manado city government, 10 November 2016, Manado.
23. Ibid.
24. Interviews with the head of the Komando Bela Negara Maesa District Brigade Manguni Indonesia, 6 February 2016, Bitung; and a member of Milisi Waraney, 5 February 2016, Manado.
25. Interview with the head of the Komando Bela Negara Maesa District Brigade Manguni Indonesia, 6 February 2016, Bitung.
26. Ibid.
27. Interviews with a staff member of Milisi Waraney headquarters, 5 February 2016, Manado; and the head of the Komando Bela Negara Maesa District Brigade Manguni Indonesia, 6 February 2016, Bitung.
28. Interview with the head of the Komando Bela Negara Maesa District Brigade Manguni Indonesia, 6 February 2016, Bitung.
29. Ibid.
30. Interview with a member of Milisi Waraney, 5 February 2016, Manado.
31. Ibid.
32. Ibid.
33. Interview with the head of the Agency for National Unity and Politics, Bitung government, 14 November 2016, Bitung.
34. Interview with the head of Security Facilitation, Arts, Culture, Economics, Religion and Society Section, North Sulawesi Agency for National Unity and Politics, 17 November 2016, Manado.
35. Interview with a staff member of Milisi Waraney headquarters, 5 February 2016, Manado.

36. Interviews with one of the leaders of the Milisi Waraney youth organization, 5 February 2015; the vice-chairman of Milisi Waraney, 5 February 2016, Manado; and a staff member of Milisi Waraney headquarters, 5 February 2016, Manado.
37. Interview with one of the leaders of the Milisi Waraney youth organization, 5 February 2015.
38. Interview with the vice-chairman of Milisi Waraney, 5 February 2016, Manado.
39. Interview with one of the leaders of the Milisi Waraney youth organization, 5 February 2015, Manado.
40. Interviews with one of the leaders of the Milisi Waraney youth organization, 5 February 2015; and the vice-chairman of Milisi Waraney, 5 February 2016, Manado.
41. Interview with a senior government official at the Indonesian Ministry of Transportation, 7 August 2015, Jakarta.
42. Interviews with the head of Komando Bela Negara Maesa District Brigade Manguni Indonesia, 6 February 2016, Bitung; the vice-chairman of Milisi Waraney, 5 February 2016, Manado; one of the leaders of the Milisi Waraney youth organization, 5 February 2015; and a member of Milisi Waraney, 5 February 2016.
43. Interview with the head of Komando Bela Negara Maesa District Brigade Manguni Indonesia, 6 February 2016, Bitung.
44. Interviews with the vice-chairman of Milisi Waraney, 5 February 2016, Manado; one of the leaders of the Milisi Waraney youth organization, 5 February 2015, Manado; and a member of Milisi Waraney, 5 February 2016, Manado.
45. Interviews with the vice-chairman of Milisi Waraney, 5 February 2016, Manado; one of the leaders of the Milisi Waraney youth organization, 5 February 2015, Manado; and a member of Milisi Waraney, 5 February 2016, Manado.
46. Interview with a retired senior police official, 12 February 2016, Manado.
47. Ibid.
48. Interview with a senior government official from Bitung, 9 February 2016.
49. Interviews with a member of the Minahasa Utara parliament, 13 February 2016, Manado; a police officer, 8 February 2015, Manado; and a retired senior police officer, 12 February 2016. Author's personal observation while in Manado, February 2015.
50. Interview with a former member of the North Sulawesi parliament and the former head of Pemuda Pancasila in Nusa Utara, 13 February 2016, Manado.
51. Ibid.
52. Interview with a member of the Minahasa Utara parliament, 13 February 2016, Manado.
53. Ibid.

54. Ibid.
55. Interviews with a retired senior police official, 12 February 2016, Manado; two editors of *Tribun Manado*, 10 November 2016; the head of the Agency for National Unity and Politics, Bitung government, 14 November 2016, Bitung; and the head of Security Facilitation, Arts, Culture, Economics, Religion and Society Section, North Sulawesi Agency for National Unity and Politics, 17 November 2016, Manado.
56. Interview with a retired senior police official, 12 February 2016, Manado.
57. Ibid.
58. Interview with a member of the Minahasa Utara parliament, 13 February 2016, Manado.
59. Ibid.; interview with a senior government official in Bitung, 9 February 2016.
60. Interview with the head of the Manado Port Administration, 5 February 2016, Manado.
61. Ibid.
62. Ibid.
63. Interview with the head of the Agency for National Unity and Politics, Manado city government, 10 November 2016, Manado.
64. Ibid.
65. Interview with the head of Security Facilitation, Arts, Culture, Economics, Religion and Society Section, North Sulawesi Agency for National Unity and Politics, 17 November 2016, Manado.
66. Ibid.
67. Ibid.
68. Interview with the head of Komando Bela Negara Maesa District Brigade Manguni Indonesia, 6 February 2016, Bitung.
69. Ibid.
70. Interviews with a member of the Minahasa Utara parliament, 13 February 2016, Manado; and the head of Komando Bela Negara Maesa District Brigade Manguni Indonesia, 6 February 2016, Bitung.
71. Ibid.
72. Ibid.
73. Ibid.
74. Interview with the vice-chairman of Milisi Waraney, 5 February 2016, Manado.
75. Interview with a member of the Minahasa Utara parliament, 13 February 2016, Manado.
76. Interview with a retired senior police officer 12 February 2016, Manado.
77. Interview with a police officer, 8 February 2015, Manado.
78. Interview with the head of the Agency for National Unity and Politics, Bitung government, 14 November 2016, Bitung.

79. Interview with the head of the Agency for National Unity and Politics, North Sulawesi Provincial government, 17 November 2016, Manado.
80. Interview with the leader of the Milisi Waraney youth organization, 5 February 2016, Manado.
81. Interview with three retired local fishermen from North Sulawesi, Bitung, Manado and Minahasa Utara, 8 February 2016.
82. Interview with a retired local fisherman from Minahasa Utara, 8 February 2016.

Chapter 4

Riau Islands: *Preman* Organizations in the Cross-Border Region

The Riau Islands were part of Riau Province from 1957, but on 1 July 2004 they officially became a distinct province of Indonesia. The Riau Islands consist of 1,350 islands, which are divided into four regencies (Kepulauan Riau, Natuna, Karimun and Lingga) and two cities (Batam and Tanjung Pinang). They are strategically located close to the Straits of Malacca and Singapore (Dewan Maritim Indonesia 2007a, p. 26). The Riau Islands are located at the border between Indonesia and Singapore, Vietnam and Malaysia. Around ninety-six per cent of the territory of the province consists of waterways (ibid., p. 26). Thus, ports play a crucial role in the economic development of the Riau Islands. Ports are the gateways for inter-island trade within the Riau Islands and a point of interaction that links this province and other parts of Indonesia. The ports of the Riau Islands also serve as trading hubs that connect Indonesia with Malaysia and Singapore. Export and import activities take place at nearly every port in this province (ibid., p. 56).

The large number of ports and outlying islands in the Riau Islands has posed enormous challenges for the Indonesian government to monitor and secure the transport of goods and people coming in and out of the province. Areas within and around the ports are rampant with criminal activities. These include smuggling, human trafficking, illegal logging, illegal fishing, and armed robbery against ships. The government authorities have involved *preman* organization to secure the ports and outlying islands in this province.

FIGURE 10
Small Ports in Batam and Tanjung Pinang

The first two pictures at the top are examples of small ports in Batam and the last two pictures are examples of small ports in Tanjung Pinang. (Photos: Senia Febrica.)

This chapter will explain the role of *preman* organizations in the Riau Islands, focusing primarily on Batam, the largest port city in this province, and Tanjung Pinang, the capital city of this province. The chapter comprises four parts. The first part will outline the competing *preman* organizations in the Riau Islands and explain their cooperation with government authorities to guard ports and outlying islands. The second part will examine conflicts between *preman* organizations and government authorities. This section will also analyse the reasons underpinning the tensions between *preman* organizations, the government and society. The third part of this chapter will account for the participation of *preman* organizations both in support of illicit activities and in efforts to address them. Finally, the conclusion of the chapter points to the ambiguous role of *preman* organizations in port security. It argues that *preman* organizations have played a role in securing ports and outlying islands. However, the involvements of *preman* organizations in illicit activities and tensions between them, government authorities and members of society have generated insecurity in port areas and other parts of the port cities of the Riau Islands.

Port Security in the Riau Islands and Competing *Preman* Organizations

In the Riau Islands, *preman* organizations are competing in an informal market of security. Most *preman* organizations involved in port security in Batam are registered officially. There are 377 organizations registered as CSOs at both the local and national levels in Batam alone.[1] These include Pemuda Pancasila (PP), Pemuda Panca Marga (PPM), Gerakan Pemuda Ansor and Ikatan Pemuda Karya (IPK) (see Figure 11).

These organizations have formal structures and each has a secretariat. Among these groups, PP is the largest and is the most established organization in Batam.[2] It has between 15,000 and 17,000 members in Batam alone.[3] Ansor Batam has 5,000 members.[4] IPK has a total of 50,000 members across the Riau Islands, and PPM has around 3,000 members in various parts of the province.[5]

In Tanjung Pinang, the groups that have control over ports are varied. As shown in Figures 13 and 14, these groups include several *preman* organizations—such as the Tanjung Pinang branches of PP,

FIGURE 11
Locations of Pemuda Pancasila and Ikatan Pemuda Karya Posts and Headquarters near Batu Ampar Port, Batam

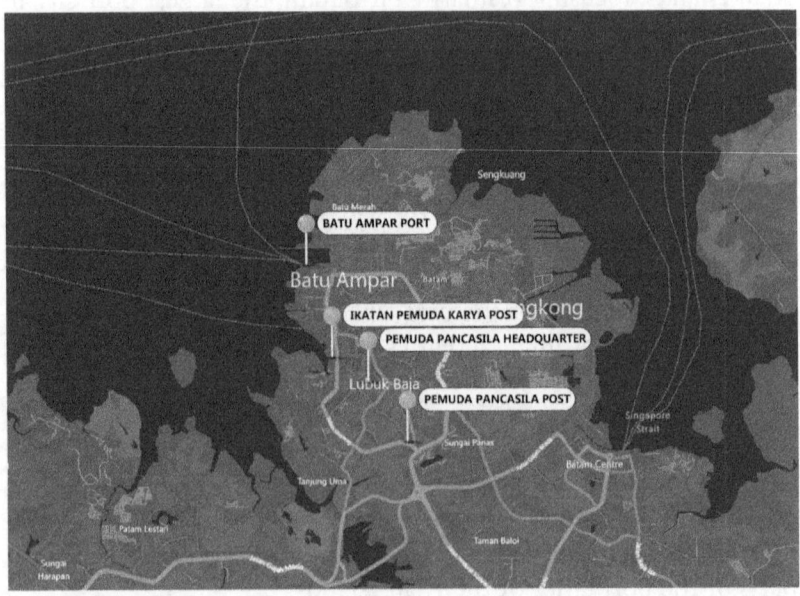

FIGURE 12
Preman and Youth Organizations in Batam

(A) Pemuda Pancasila's headquarters in Batam; (B) banner of Forum Komunikasi Putra–Putri TNI/Polri showing their leaders dressed in military-style outfits placed alongside the main road in Batam; (C) Garda Nusantara's headquarters in Batam; (D) car adorned with Garda Nusantara's symbol, one of the hyper-nationalist *preman* organizations in Batam; (E) Pemuda Pancasila's post in Batu Ampar, Batam; (F) gathering of Persatuan Pemuda Tempatan, an ethnic-based youth organization in Batam; (G) headquarters of Ikatan Pemuda Karya in Batam; (H) banner of Ansor in Batam. (Photos: Senia Febrica.)

PPM and IPK—and local youth gangs. The local youth gangs are comprised primarily of male residents of nearby villages. These gangs are in charge of coordinating and supplying security personnel and porters that work at the ports. The relations between local gang, with each other and with other villages are deeply segregated. As a former member of a local gang explained,

> Pelantar Dua Port is ... located just across from the Kampung Bugis [Bugis village].... In this port, youth organizations such as Perpat [Persatuan Pemuda Tempatan] or other mass organizations are not involved in providing port security or porter services. The village youth coordinates and controls [the security and porter services]. Similarly, in Tanjung Unggat Port, the one that coordinates port security and porter services is the Tanjung Unggat youth.

Despite the prominent role of local gangs at ports, the vice-chairman of the Tanjung Pinang parliament and a maritime security expert at Universitas Maritim Raja Ali Haji noted that in certain ports in Tanjung Pinang hyper-nationalist *preman* organizations such as PP exercise control over all activities in that port. In others,

FIGURE 13
Locations of Preman and Youth Organization Posts around Tanjung Pinang Port and Tanjung Unggat Port

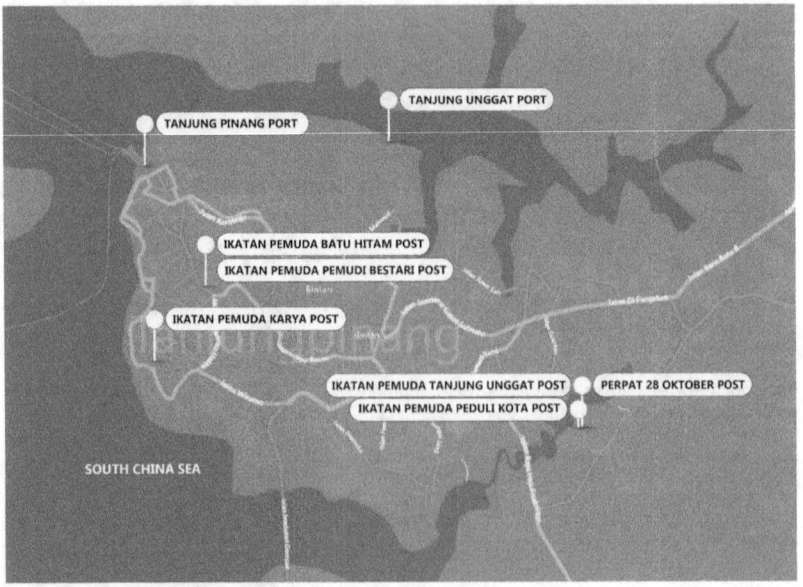

FIGURE 14
Location of Pemuda Pancasila Office near Bulang Linggi Speed
Boat Port and Roro Tanjung Uban Port, Tanjung Pinang

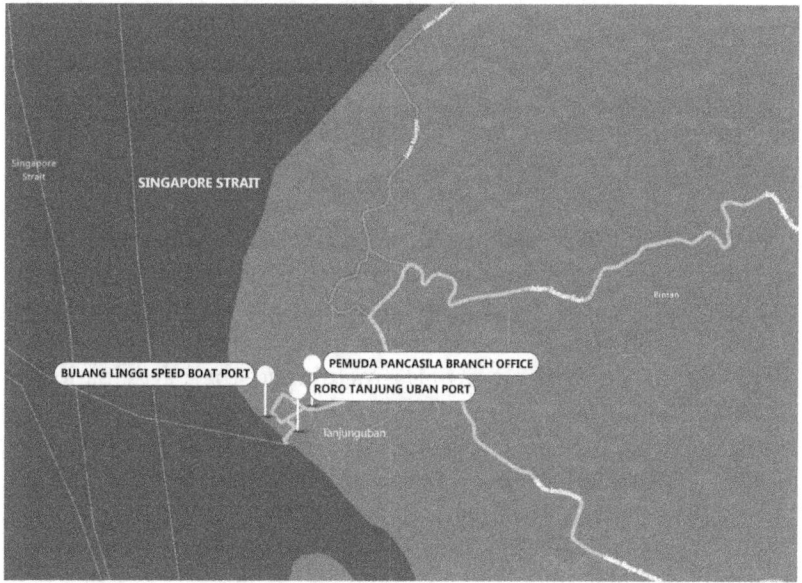

however, the local gangs are the influential ones.⁶ The local gangs are notorious for their involvement in illicit activities at ports in Tanjung Pinang. PP, according to the Tanjung Pinang parliamentarian, is in charge of a small port near the Batu 8 Bridge.⁷ The presence of PP in this port is noticeable. The organization has established the headquarters for their paramilitary wing, Komando Inti, opposite the port.

Of all the *preman* organizations that operate in the Riau Islands, PP is deemed the most prominent not only in terms of the number of its members but also in regard to the media attention it receives. The prominence of PP in the Riau Islands is reflected in the reports of the local newspaper *Tribun Batam*. The words "Pemuda Pancasila" appeared 108 times in articles published by this paper from 1 January 2012 to 31 August 2016. PP's involvement in providing protection during special occasions such as labour demonstrations and local government elections in the Riau Islands was widely reported. In 2013, *Tribun Batam* reported that members of PP were employed alongside the police and armed forces to guard Batam's industrial complexes, including the Executive, Lytech, Citra Buana, Sarana

Industrial Point and Tunas Industri during a labour rally in the city (*Tribun Batam*, 31 October 2013a; 31 October 2013b). In the run up to the 2015 gubernatorial elections, the secretary of Tanjung Pinang city government (Sekretaris Daerah Kota Tanjung Pinang), Riono, highlighted that "cooperation between the city government and PP has been good" (*Tribun Batam*, 23 December 2014). He further asked for "PP participation to keep Tanjung Pinang conducive … for the 2015 gubernatorial elections" (*Tribun Batam*, 23 December 2014).

Although local media in the Riau Islands have widely reported the engagement of *preman* organizations in security, the participation of these organizations in port security has not received adequate media coverage. The word "port", for example, appeared 905 times in articles published by *Tribun Batam* from 1 May 2015 to 1 March 2017. But none of these articles mentioned the participation of *preman* organizations in securing ports in Batam, Tanjung Pinang or other parts of the Riau Islands. An article published by *Kompas*, Indonesia's largest national newspaper, sheds some light on the role of *preman* organizations in port security of the Riau Islands. *Kompas* reported that in May 2002 one hundred members of PP from the province participated in guarding Tanjung Pinang Port together with police officers from Polres Kepri Timur, the navy and the provincial government security force (Satuan Polisi Pamong Praja, or Satpol PP) (*Kompas*, 16 May 2002). PP and government security officers were engaged in securing the port from student demonstrators. From noon to three in the afternoon, two hundred university students blocked an international seaport that served the Tanjung Pinang–Malaysia–Singapore routes (*Kompas*, 16 May 2002). These students demanded the Indonesian central government to ratify the draft legislation for the establishment of the Riau Islands Province (RUU Provinsi Kepri) within seventy-two hours (*Kompas*, 16 May 2002). This incident serves as an example of the use of *preman* organizations in securing ports in the Riau Islands.

In Batam and Tanjung Pinang, security measures at domestic and international ports are implemented strictly by the Indonesian port authorities, the sea and coastguard unit of the Directorate General of Sea Transportation, the police, the navy and the port security guards. International ports in these cities have complied with the International Ship and Port Facility Security (ISPS) Code requirements of the International Maritime Organization. *Preman* organizations have only limited roles in these restricted areas. The involvement of *preman* organizations at the ports managed by government authorities or state-owned enterprises is confined to three forms of participation. First, members of *preman* organizations participate in port security by establishing or joining private security companies who win the bid to secure certain ports. One of the leaders of PPM in Batam, for instance, has set up a legitimate private security business and recruited members of his organization and rival organizations to work for him. In the past, his company has won contracts to secure nearly all the seaports in Batam. He claimed that,

> I am responsible for port security in Batam Centre Port.... so security guards are provided with training on the ISPS Code in Batam Center Port. In the past I was responsible for security in almost all sites, including Hang Nadim Airport. This is my business. I also recruit my security personnel from various organizations that want to entrust their members to me. It is a mix—some come from PP, PPM; there are also [members] of other organizations. I will also recruit the underlings of those people who are categorized as a big man (*pentolan*) in the field to be my security personnel. When they start to work, there are no more disputes. We train those who are members of mass organizations and those who are not members of any organization—free men. My company is in charge of providing security in Sekupang and Batam Centre Seaports and Hang Nadim Airport.[8]

A senior police officer confirmed that some *preman* organizations have established security companies specializing in port areas, or some of their members become port security guards.[9] These *preman* organizations are largely registered with the government as youth organizations (*organisasi kepemudaan*) or CSOs (*organisasi kemasyarakatan*). As one senior police officer stated,

> This type of arrangement is made between them [*preman* organizations] and parties who need the security services. It is related to Pasukan Pengamanan Masyarakat [PAM] Swakarsa, which is assisted by the police.[10] We only provide training on services that [they] must provide to the public.... In order to provide security services, [an individual or organization] must set up a specific business entity called Badan Usaha Jasa Pengamanan. The police will then provide training and allocate limited police tasks to the entity.[11]

A senior government official at the Batam Naval Base pointed out how members of *preman* organizations could be used for security purpose. As he put it,

There are negative and positive consequences in involving [*preman* organizations]. If we do not involve them, there will be positive and negative consequences as well. They can be formed as security associations. So they can be trained as internal security [personnel]. Youth organizations (Organisasi Kepemudaan/OKP) are also part of society and are registered. OKPs are registered with the district military command (Komando Distrik Militer/Kodim) and the local government (Pemerintah Daerah/Pemda).[12]

Second, *preman* organizations are involved in securing ports and other vital locations in the run up to Eid, Christmas and the New Year holiday or other special events such as local elections or public rallies on the basis of requests made by the police or the local government. For this type of engagement, the *preman* organizations would carry out their tasks alongside the police and armed forces. As pointed out by a local government official, "On a day-to-day basis, there is no direct involvement of CSOs or youth organizations [in port security]. [These organizations] only take part in securing the ports when asked."[13] A senior police officer in Batam confirmed this. To quote him,

> For security purposes, they [*preman* organizations] help by joining us [police]. This depends on our needs. They help to guard police sub-stations during special events. For instance, the *Ketupat* Operation that is held in the run-up to and after the Idul Fitri celebration and the *Lilin* Operation that is conducted during Christmas and New Year. They [*preman* organizations] work in service sub-stations in seaports and airports alongside the police. During those operations, they are given the same tasks as policemen. They are assigned to help the members of society.... their task is to guard them. During these operations, we involved all governmental agencies, including the police and the armed forces, as well as the youth organizations.... the *Ketupat* Operation is carried out once a year, and the *Lilin* Operation is conducted once a year.... We do not have a formal MoU with the OKP. We have a mutual agreement with OKP to work together to maintain a conducive atmosphere in Batam.[14]

Third, *preman* organizations are involved indirectly in port security through their control over labour associations in ports. These labour organizations maintain order by providing jobs as porters to unemployed youth and those who are considered potential troublemakers. The *preman* organizations also facilitate negotiations between the labour and port authorities when disputes occur. The vice-head of IPK, a lawyer and also the vice-chairman of the Riau Islands Chamber of Commerce, confirmed this point in an interview. He asserted that,

> IPK is active in ports across the Riau Islands. In Sekupang, one of the largest domestic ports in Batam, IPK gathered all the porters to form a cooperative mechanism.... The chairman of the cooperative mechanism in Sekupang has been part of the IPK working committee for ten years. The cooperative mechanism offers services for saving and borrowing money to its members and serves as an umbrella organization to establish the expedition/transportation business.[15]

IPK has carried out similar functions in most ports of the Riau Islands, including in Makobar Port, Batu Ampar.[16] According to the vice-head of IPK, the presence of his organization helps to resolve conflict. As he argued,

> When a conflict took place, the head [IPK] would intervene. Thus, conflict will be resolved. In Batu Ampar, we set up a special branch in Makobar Port.... Our friends seek refuge there. They form a porter organization. Therefore, those who are often involved in fights stop fighting. We asked troublemakers to join us. What can you do? You can work as porters.[17]

This practice carried out by IPK at Sekupang and other ports in Batam is not unique. The secretary of PP Batam explained that the labour association of PP has resolved labour disputes on many occasions.[18] The head of the organization also added that "for a long time the majority of porters in Sekupang Port have been members of PP. Therefore, if a conflict arises the organization can resolve it through consensus-making."[19] According to the vice-head of PP Batam, their trade union covers various industries, including heavy industries such as shipyards and steel, light industries such as electronic devices, and tourism, including hotels and restaurants.[20]

In Batam and Tanjung Pinang, *preman* organizations provide information to the government authorities about the security of many small ports that are not managed by government agencies. The Indonesian government does not have enough resources to monitor and secure all ports, including small and unofficial ports, which are often referred to as "rat ports" (*pelabuhan tikus*). The Batam customs office, for example, has only thirty-five prosecution officials and three patrol boats (*Batam Pos*, 16 September 2016). *Preman* organizations, therefore, provide additional resources to the local government. Most rat ports are located near shipyards or fishing villages (*Batam Pos*, 26 September 2016). These ports can be found spread throughout the area, from Batuaji, Sagulung, through to Galang. In Sagulung, rat ports are scattered from Dapur 12, Tanjung Undap, all the way through to Jembatan I, Barelang (*Batam Pos*, 26 September 2016). These areas are rampant with the smuggling of sugar, wood and diesel (ibid.). Small and unofficial ports dotted around Galang are known as smuggling points for electronic devices and second-hand goods from Singapore, staple foods and people (ibid.).

Given the proximity of the outer parts of the Riau Islands with Batam and Tanjung Pinang, the government also recruited members of *preman* organizations to secure border areas and to serve as a reserve component for the armed forces. A senior official from the Batam local government made the following remark to highlight the relations of *preman* organizations with the Indonesian military:

> PP has an affiliation with the military and the armed forces. When we held the state defence training [*diklat bela negara*], we recruit members of IPK, PP and PPM. I often recruit members of these groups to join events organized by the National Defence Council (Dewan Ketahanan Nasional) … we bring [participants] from IPK, PP and PPM.[21]

His statement is corroborated by an official responsible for recruiting members of CSOs for various government programmes. As she put it,

> the Ministry of Defence has established "the state-defence" [*bela negara*] programme…. The district military command (*Kodim*) enlisted members of PP and PPM to join the programme…. PP and PPM sent their members.[22]

A senior representative of PPM in Batam pointed out that his organization has assisted the armed forces (Tentara Nasional Indonesia) in guarding the outlying Natuna Regency and the border between West Kalimantan and Sarawak.[23] To quote him,

> When the armed forces asked [for our members to be dispatched], we will send [them]. We were once asked to help guard Natuna. We were provided with training on how to guard the border. We were also requested to help guard the border between West Kalimantan and Sarawak. At the border between West Kalimantan and Sarawak, the mud was knee-deep.[24]

A senior figure of PP in Jakarta made a similar point:

> ... so, I met these government officials. Not recently; this was twenty years ago. From the government minister, governor, head of village (*lurah*), [they] always said to me ... thank you for PP. I asked, "Why, Sir?" According to a village head, [members of] PP are everywhere, even in places his administration had never reached before. Therefore, if you ask about the outlying islands, I can guarantee I have more members there than any other organization. I can even guarantee that to the government security apparatus (*aparat*). PP is not in cooperation [with the government security apparatus]. [Rather], PP is used by the government security apparatus. If [we talk about] cooperation, there will be a contractual bond. They [PP] are not [like that]. If needed, they are called to come. They are asked; they help.[25]

The involvement of *preman* organizations in border security is corroborated by an article published by *Batam Pos* on the inauguration ceremony of the head of PPM, Haji Lulung, which was attended by the chief of the Indonesian armed forces, Admiral TNI Suhartono, in March 2012 in Nipah, an outlying island adjacent to Malaysia and Singapore (*Batam Pos*, 3 March 2012). Lulung—who has recruited two thousand members of PPM to work in the several companies he owns—in his statement to the press, indicated the participation of PPM in border security. He explained that,

> Nipah is an outer island of Indonesia that directly shares a border with Singapore and Malaysia. Nipah must be introduced, guarded, and transformed into a tourism and economic zone.... This inauguration helps to introduce Nipah at the national and international levels. (*Batam Pos*, 3 March 2012)

Batam Pos reported that the key theme highlighted at the inauguration ceremony was the role of PPM in Indonesia's security (*Batam Pos*, 3 March 2012).

In the Riau Islands, *preman* organizations were also used to display force at Indonesia's outlying islands when there are disputes or political tensions between Indonesia and neighbouring countries such as Malaysia and Singapore. Under the banner of "Alert Meeting" (*Apel Siaga*), the local government and the navy have coordinated several large-scale ceremonial meetings attended by different *preman* organizations in Natuna Regency and on Nipah Island. The head of the IPK maintained that his organization took part in the "Alert Meeting" held at Nipah Island.[26] The leader of another *preman* organization, Forum Komunikasi Putra Putri Purnawirawan dan TNI Polri (FKKPI), emphasized a similar point. He claimed that members of FKPPI had also visited Nipah Island to raise the Indonesian flag.[27] He went further to state that FKPPI is very proactive when it comes to border security. In his view, the Riau Islands are located close to what he defined as a "war zone" because of their close proximity to Malaysia, Singapore and the disputed maritime areas of the South China Sea.[28] Therefore, "civilians should become the spearhead of the state defence, and if it is necessary, they should be positioned in those [outlying] islands to guard the country".[29]

The partnership between the Indonesian government and *preman* organizations is maintained through institutionalized training for these organizations. The Indonesian army has provided training to select organizations such as PP and PPM. A senior leader of PP Batam, for instance, recalled that the Indonesian special forces (Komando Pasukan Khusus, or Kopassus) had always provided military training to Komando Inti (Koti), the paramilitary unit of PP.[30] According to him, PP's Koti continues to receive military training from the Indonesian armed forces at the district military command (Kodim).[31]

Military training provided by government authorities to *preman* organizations is not an uncommon practice. The Indonesian national media has recently provided wide reporting on the training provided by the Indonesian military regional command (Kodam) III/Siliwangi in Lebak, Banten, on 5–6 January 2017 to 120 members of Front Pembela Islam (FPI) (*Tempo*, 7 January 2017; 8 January 2017; Media Indonesia, 8 January 2017; *Tempo*, 8 January 2017). The army received fierce criticism from the public for this as the FPI is notorious for perpetrating violence and vigilante acts in Indonesia. The commander of Lebak military district command was removed from his post for failing to report the training to his superiors: Danrem and Pangdam III/Siliwangi (Media Indonesia, 8 January 2017).

Representatives of PP, IPK, Garda Nusantara and Ansor also mentioned that members of their organizations have participated in search and rescue training workshops organized by the National Search and Rescue Agency (*Badan SAR Nasional, or Basarnas*) in the Riau Islands.[32] *Preman* organizations in Batam and Tanjung Pinang have established their own search and rescue teams, which could fill a gap in public emergency services and serve as the first responder when natural disasters strike.[33]

Media reports have corroborated interview results that show the existence of collaboration between the government and CSOs. *Tribun Batam*, for instance, reported that *preman* organizations have carried out several activities in cooperation with local governments in Batam and Tanjung Pinang, such as dealing with flooding, cleaning the environment (*gotong royong*)—including coastal and marine areas (*bersih laut*)—providing social assistance to orphans, conducting AIDS awareness campaigns, sponsoring sports tournaments and donating blood to the Indonesian Red Cross (Palang Merah Indonesia) (*Tribun Batam*, 23 December 2014; 10 February 2016; 18 April 2016; 30 October 2011; 7 August 2016; 21 July 2014; *Batam Pos*, 18 May 2005).

Extensive Tensions

There are no large-scale conflicts between different *preman* organizations or between *preman* organizations and the government authorities in the port areas of Batam and Tanjung Pinang. But small-scale conflicts between CSOs and members of local communities often take place. Small-scale conflicts that are reported in the local media include acts of violence by members of *preman* organizations during evictions, including shootings and stabbings (*Tribun Batam*, 6 March 2016; 1 May 2011; 1 April 2011a; 1 April 2011b). Local media tend to disassociate violent incidents from the names of certain *preman* organizations by referring to those involved as merely "*oknum*", which can be translated in English as a person with an unsavoury character, or the "bad apples" from these organizations. As a deputy chief editor of a Batam media organization pointed out,

> In Batam, lots of [*preman* organizations] are fighting over territories. I do not report these—these conflicts that involved members of CSOs and youth organization.... PP has lots of members. So, there are lots of *oknum*. I phoned its chairman, Mr Ucok Cantik. He said he does not know [about the conflicts]. "Yes, but brother (*abang*), your subordinates are *preman*."[34]

The absence of large conflicts around Batam and Tanjung Pinang is interesting, because in major port cities such as Jakarta and Medan, large-scale conflicts between different *preman* organizations and between these organizations and government security authorities are not unusual. As explained in Chapter 2, a conflict in Jakarta between FBR and government security authorities over the removal of a tomb complex from a port facility in Tanjung Priok Port led to the deaths of several members of Satpol Pamong Praja. In Medan, a clash between police and Islamic *preman* organizations—including Front Pembela Islam, Majelis Mujahidin Indonesia and Jaringan Penyelamat Umat Islam—in April 2013 had a knock-on effect on port activities in Belawan (*Sumut Pos*, 13 April 2013). In protesting the arrest of eighteen Rohingya refugees accused of murder, these Islamic *preman* organizations blocked the road to Belawan International Container Port. As a consequence, no containers could enter or leave the port for two hours, and this incident created vehicle queues of three kilometres (ibid.).

According to a government official with the Batam city government, each organization in Batam and Tanjung Pinang confines their activities to areas deemed their own territory.[35] To quote this official,

> In Medan, conflict between youth and mass organizations have taken place.... If they divide the existing territory, there would be no conflict. In Batam, there is no clash between organizations.... Since their leaders are smart, they do not fight over territory. If A comes to an area, the others will not go there.[36]

Despite the absence of large-scale conflicts, there are frictions between the government authorities and *preman* organizations in Batam and Tanjung Pinang. The underpinning reasons for these frictions can be grouped into three categories. First, some members of the *preman* organizations are involved in illicit activities at the ports, including smuggling, human trafficking and illegal logging. A senior representative of Ansor explained that "we must be careful when we talk about human trafficking in Batam.... some youth and mass organizations are involved in backing this activity."[37] The director of security of the Batam Concession Agency (Badan Pengusahaan Batam, or BP Batam) pointed out that in several criminal cases he investigated, he discovered that *preman* organizations had provided security services to businessmen carrying out illegal logging activities in the Riau Islands.[38]

Second, members of *preman* organizations have been involved in instigating disturbances or extorting money from the public. One incident in particular is worth noting as it happened in a port facility. *Tribun Batam* reported a disturbance caused by members of PP at a port facility owned by PT Dua Karya Abadi, a mining company, in December 2010 (*Tribun Batam*, 13 December 2010). The paper reported that members of PP prevented PT Dua Karya

Abadi from loading bauxite onto a ship located at the company's mining facility (ibid.). A representative of PT Dua Karya Abadi claimed the company lost thousands of dollars as a result (ibid.). The police arrested thirteen members of PP for entering the mining area without permission and preventing the operations of PT Dua Karya (ibid.).

It has also been reported that members of *preman* organizations have on several occasions extorted money from the public. Instances of the extortion of money range from asking for money from passers-by to blackmailing businessmen. A local government official claimed that *preman* organizations "like to build huts on the roadside and ask for money from passers-by".[39] A senior police officer contended that *preman* organizations in Batam sometimes used information they have on certain companies—for example, on a company's violation of environmental regulations—to blackmail business owners.[40] He has received many reports of such conduct. This policeman recalled that in one case the police managed to arrest members of a *preman* organization (which he refused to specify) just before a large sum of money was handed over from a victim of blackmail to the organization.[41] This is hardly surprising. From my fieldwork in Batam, I discovered that some members—or even the district leaders—of *preman* organizations have day jobs as journalists or environmental activists, which enabled them to transfer the information they learned from their formal profession to the *preman* organization they are affiliated with.

The third activity that has become a sticking point between the local government, the security authorities and *preman* organizations in Batam and Tanjung Pinang is the involvement of these organizations in misusing and/or selling land owned by the state, or providing security support to those who carry out these acts. Government officials from the police, the Directorate of Security of BP Batam and the Batam local government mentioned that the participation of *preman* organizations in this type of activity has led to clashes between these organizations and the security authorities.[42]

On Illicit Activities: Ambiguous Role of *Preman* Organizations

Batam and other port towns in the Riau Islands such as Tanjung Pinang and Tanjung Balai Karimun are well-known transit points for trafficking of Indonesian workers seeking to enter Singapore or

Malaysia illegally and the smuggling of illicit goods (*Tribun Batam*, 19 July 2016; 16 December 2016; 24 January 2017; 29 July 2016; 28 April 2016). That there are many outlying islands throughout the Riau Islands and the fact that the law enforcement agencies are underequipped combine to limit the capacity of the government to control various private networks that operate across the country's borders. This has led government authorities to use *preman* organizations to fill this security gap.

According to one anti–human trafficking activist, every week through rat ports in just Batam alone, at least two to three organized sea voyages embark to take Indonesian workers seeking to enter Malaysia illegally.[43] Each boat normally takes around a hundred people.[44] The main points in Batam and Tanjung Pinang used as transit locations for undocumented Indonesian workers to travel to Malaysia include Nongsa Pantai, Teluk Mata Ikan and Tanjung Bemban.[45] Traffickers will use rafts to move people from Teluk Punggur, Batam, to Tanjung Pinang before continuing to Malaysia if they find that the security conditions are not conducive.[46] Malaysia is one of the main destination countries for Indonesian migrant workers. This is because Malaysia is near to Indonesia and there is a perceived cultural closeness between the two in terms of language and traditions. The cost of travel from Indonesia to Malaysia is also cheaper compared to other destinations as the country can be reached by boat. Migrant workers travel from Surabaya to Pare-Pare, Nunukan, East Kalimantan, and Tawao before navigating to Malaysia (Badan Koordinasi Keamanan Laut 2010, p. 65). They also use other alternative sea routes via Medan, Tanjung Balai Karimun and Batam to reach Malaysia. Indonesian workers travelling illegally to Malaysia face a high risk of accident as the boats taking them are often not seaworthy. This danger was illustrated by a boat accident that took place on 2 November 2016 in Tanjung Bemban, Batam, where eighteen migrant workers were killed and forty-four went missing, presumed dead (CNN Indonesia, 2 November 2016).

In term of smuggling, most goods are smuggled across the Strait of Malacca to the Riau Islands to avoid prohibitions or taxes (Valencia 2006, p. 92). Smuggled goods include second-hand clothing, steel, liquor, cigarettes, subsidized fuel, rice and endangered species (Cribb and Ford 2009, p. 15; Nik and Permal 2008, pp. 193–94). Consumer goods such as cigarettes are smuggled from Indonesia to Malaysia, but items of concern including small arms and light weapons flow in the opposite direction (Valencia 2006, p. 92).

Several small rat ports in Batam are owned by individuals (*Batam Pos*, 25 June 2012; 30 April 2012). Such ports are used mainly for importing second-hand goods from neighbouring countries such as Malaysia and Singapore. Illicit activities, including smuggling of goods and people, often take place in these small ports, and these are not easily detected.

The significance of the problem of smuggling of goods in Batam is clearly reflected by local media attention on this issue. *Tribun Batam* noted that ports in Batam—such as Beton Sekupang Port, Batam Centre International Port and most rat ports—are the areas most prone to the smuggling of drugs to Indonesia (*Tribun Batam*, 14 February 2017). The majority of smuggled goods, particularly drugs, enter Batam through rat ports (*Tribun Batam*, 17 February 2017). The head of the Riau Islands National Narcotics Agency, Ajun Komisaris Besar Polisi Bumbung Pramiadi, claimed that 95 per cent of the drugs entering the province came from Malaysia (*Tribun Batam*, 14 February 2017). Drugs smuggled from Stulang in Johor, Malaysia, and cannabis from Aceh first enter ports in Batam or Karimun before being channelled to the Port of Tanjung Priok, Jakarta, and other areas in Indonesia (*Tribun Batam*, 11 January 2016; 11 March 2016; 24 December 2015). By mid-September 2016, the Batam customs office had prevented 241 smuggling activities (*Batam Pos*, 16 September 2016). A fifth of those entailed the smuggling of drugs. This was an increase from 182 smuggling activities in 2015 (ibid.). In 2021, the number of smuggling activities stopped by the Batam customs office that year reached 496 activities (Bea Cukai, 10 January 2022).

In Tanjung Pinang, local gangs have control of the rat ports and are involved in smuggling networks. Local gangs that have influence in small ports in Tanjung Pinang are mobilized around traditional village networks or family ties where the ports are located.[47] Leadership is often passed down from one generation to the next within the same family. Members who are part of this informal network work for the organization as porters or security guards. As porters they would take part in loading and unloading smuggled goods coming to ports or waterways close to their village. According to a former member of a local gang involved in smuggling, each person is paid Rp300,000 (US$20.7) for an operation. In one week, it is estimated that members of the local gangs will carry out between three and five operations, depending on the arrival of vessels carrying smuggled goods to the ports or waterways adjacent to their villages.[48]

According to a member of a local parliament in Tanjung Pinang, there are four small ports where smuggling activities are controlled by local gangs.[49] These are Koperasi Unit Desa (KUD), Gudang Minyak, Tanjung Unggat and Dompak Lama ports.[50] Goods smuggled to these ports are mainly staple foods such as rice, mobile phones and construction materials (*Batam Pos*, 5 August 2005).[51] Both a parliamentarian and a maritime expert based in Tanjung Pinang believe that closing these small rat ports would not resolve the problem. Rather, they deemed that legalizing these small, unofficial ports would offer a solution.[52] By legalizing them, the government would then be able to impose taxes on goods coming from abroad to these ports.

As a measure to deal with the smuggling of consumer goods through rat ports, leaders of large *preman* organizations in Batam and Tanjung Pinang have hinted that they have signed MoUs with relevant government agencies. Key leaders of PP in Batam claimed that the PP National Leadership Council (Majelis Pimpinan Nasional) in Jakarta has signed an arrangement with the national logistics agency (Badan Urusan Logistik, or Bulog) to develop a cooperative mechanism with PP for rice distribution across the archipelago. The vice-head of PP Batam explained that, as part of the agreement, the PP National Leadership Council has instructed their secretariat in Batam to deal with the problem posed by the smuggling of rice from other countries in Southeast Asia. To quote the vice-head of PP Batam,

> The National Leadership Council (Majelis Pimpinan Nasional) has signed an MoU with the Indonesian national logistics agency (Bulog) to reactivate their cooperative mechanism. The head of the economics section and vice-head II [of PP Batam] had attended training workshops with Bulog. The cooperative will manage "the house of food". The name of the cooperative is Koperasi Abadi.... all over Indonesia it will be called Koperasi Abadi. It will handle the distribution of nine staple foods.[53]

Further, the secretary of PP Batam made the following claim:

> Batam is located at the border. Thus, there are lots of perpetrators of economic crime. [The smuggling activities] are beneficial for society but costly for the state. Staple foods coming from Jakarta are more expensive than imported foods from foreign countries. For instance, imported rice from Thailand and Vietnam is cheaper than those transported from Jakarta. Here, there are many active

rat ports [*pelabuhan tikus*].... There is an instruction from the PP's National Leadership Council that when the cooperation with Bulog is implemented it will be our task to deal with smuggling activities in the Riau Islands Province. So, we help to address smuggling. In terms of cooperation with Bulog, at this stage we have received training. We are in the process of applying for our licence and preparing our IT system.

Leaders of IPK in Batam and Tanjung Pinang claimed that similar deals had been reached between their organizations and the Riau Islands Chamber of Commerce. The head of IPK Batam implied that his organization had established a partnership with the chamber of commerce and the police, but he did provide any specifics. The leaders of IPK in Tanjung Pinang were willing to provide a more detailed account of the MoU between their organization and the Riau Islands Chamber of Commerce. The head of IPK Tanjung Pinang highlighted that, "with regard to port security", at the provincial level IPK is "going to sign an MoU with the chamber of commerce" after the inauguration of IPK officials in March 2016.[54] The vice-head of IPK Tanjung Pinang indicated that "under the chamber of commerce there are various companies. Thus, as part of the MoU, IPK can assign its members to work as security guards for these companies", including those operating in ports.[55]

On the matter of countering human trafficking activities, according to the head of IPK Batam, members of IPK have been involved in thwarting several human trafficking attempts via the sea in their city. He mentioned the following:

> Our involvement in stopping seaborne human trafficking took place in 2011 and 2012. These [incidents] happened in the city of Batam. Our members provided information to the police.... In Batam there are a lot of human trafficking cases. We received reports from members of the public.[56]

The involvement of IPK in assisting the police in curtailing human trafficking is not unique. A senior representative of Ansor Batam pointed out the active engagement of Ansor in dealing with human trafficking carried out through rat ports, not only on Batam but also at other islands throughout the Riau archipelago.[57] As he explained,

> We always assign Ansor troops for surveillance purposes in rat ports or areas where ships can be anchored. The assignment of our members to small ports throughout the Riau Islands will continue. I am one of the founders of the anti-trafficking movement. We

[Ansor] once raided a building that was used to hold Indonesian workers that were going to be trafficked abroad. This was in the early 2000s.... Before the local government decided to send them to their place of origins, we provided food and shelter for nearly two hundred of them. They come from almost all parts of Java: West Java, East Java and Central Java.... My members ... I give them the task of guarding rat ports. Sometimes some of them caught dengue fever or malaria when guarding those areas.[58]

Some of the leaders of *preman* organizations claimed that the involvement of members of the government security apparatus and officials in human trafficking activities often put off local communities from reporting trafficking activities to the police as they fear for their safety.[59] The head of PP Batam implicitly stated that

... sometimes in trafficking there are "the watchmen". Those who know [about the trafficking activities] report them to PP because they feel safe to do so. We emphasize this point during our visits to the Rukun Tetangga and Rukun Warga (local neighbourhoods). The local neighbourhoods are pleased with the PP presence in their areas.[60]

Echoing the above statement, a senior representative of Ansor Batam pointed out the following:

Why do members of the public report human trafficking to youth or mass organizations and not the police? Sometimes members of the security authorities or government officials are involved...[61]

Senior policemen have corroborated the claim regarding the usefulness of *preman* organizations in assisting the Indonesian government in dealing with trafficking and smuggling. A senior police officer from Batam suggested that "in the area of countering human trafficking, there are *preman* organizations that provide information. These include some ethnic, national and religious-oriented organizations."[62] Another senior policeman verified that "it is true that" the police use members of *preman* organizations "(*ormas* and OKP) for their information networks".[63] He explained, however, that for such services the police do not pay the organizations that their informants are affiliated with.[64] Rather, they pay the informants directly.[65] A senior official working for the Batam local government maintained that *preman* organizations have participated in a partnership forum with the police called the Police Partners' Communication Centre (Sentra Komunikasi Mitra Polisi).[66] According to him, *preman* organizations join this forum and provide information to the police intelligence service.⁶⁷

However, in the Riau Islands the presence of *preman* organizations is not always part of the solution to address illicit activities. Interviews with government officials, journalists and religious figures point to the involvement of members of *preman* organizations in illicit activities in this border province. A senior representative of Ansor Batam pointed out that,

> When we talk about human trafficking, we must be careful, because there are many interests at stake there. There are government officials, members of the armed forces and CSOs who take part..... We must be careful.⁶⁸

A Catholic priest who became a key anti-trafficking figure in Batam claimed that

> Friends that are working in the anti-trafficking movement are NGOs such as Gerakan Anti-Trafficking, Embun Pelangi and Rumah Faye. These NGOs are our partners. We carry out discussions and cooperation with them. I have never heard about the [*preman* organizations] and youth organizations working in anti–human trafficking.⁶⁹

Labelling some members of *preman* organizations as "freemen", this priest further noted that

> These freemen, lots of them are working with mafias. Those who provide information [related to human trafficking] are those who already got promising jobs.⁷⁰

The involvement of *preman* organizations in illicit activities in the Riau Islands was also corroborated in a statement made by the director of security of Badan Pengusahaan (BP) Batam (Batam Free Zone Authority) and the deputy chief editor of a local newspaper in Batam. As the BP Batam director of security put it,

> We do not have partnerships with mass and youth organizations. We only have partnerships with relevant government institutions. Here [Batam], mass and youth organizations tend to be negative.... The growth of these organizations tends to put a burden on development, security.... I carry out operations against illegal logging. Sometimes, they [*preman* organizations and youth organizations] respond to it in a negative way. They protect and even become the bodyguards of businessmen who conduct illegal logging.

To quote a deputy chief editor of a local newspaper in Batam,

> [We] hear a lot about [the involvement of *preman* organizations in illicit activities]. However, if we report it, we will be in trouble.... There are many illicit activities, such as controlling land, using organizations to advance private interests, participating in smuggling—plenty of cases.... Here, social organizations have a profit motive. This is a story behind a story. If we reveal all, we will be dead.... People said that Batam is the city of mafia, smuggling, drugs.... Story behind a story is scary. The Riau Islands is among five provinces with the best freedom of press in Indonesia. This is awarded by the Press Board (Dewan Pers). In my heart I question how come it is one of the best. The press in the Riau Islands is seemingly polite, growing, but if we look inside, it is under pressure, cannot be open-honest. We could be found in Jembatan Empat, dumped. I am often being terrorized.[71]

The deputy chief editor of a local newspaper in Batam further explained that *preman* organizations are often used as a vehicle by smugglers. According to him, "if the chairman of a *preman* organization is a smuggler, his peers are part of his gang. Those who play [in the smuggling business] are only the leaders. Some of them are land brokers (*calo lahan*) [some others are] smugglers of staple food."[72]

Conclusion

To summarize, in Batam and Tanjung Pinang, *preman* organizations have taken part in maintaining port security, both through direct and indirect participation. Direct participation involves the establishment of security firms and the recruitment of informants by government security authorities. Some members of *preman* organizations have established security firms and recruited personnel from their own organizations as well as rival groups as port security guards. The Indonesian security authorities have also recruited their informants from *preman* organizations and formally engaged these organizations in police and local government forums to improve information sharing, prevent security disturbances and deal with trans-border crimes, especially smuggling of people and goods.

Indirect involvement takes the form of cooperation between government authorities and *preman* organizations to enable these organizations to set up their cooperative mechanisms for the distribution of staple foods. Although the cooperation mechanism is not directly related to port security, it entices *preman* organizations to collaborate in curbing the smuggling of staple foods, especially rice, which is rampant in the Riau Islands.

Another form of indirect engagement by *preman* organizations in maintaining port security was found in the control of port labour associations by these organizations. Organizations such as PP and IKP, for instance, maintain control over labour associations in port areas such as Sekupang. This endows them with the ability to settle disputes between the port authorities and labour.

Local media reports and interviews with local government officials, representatives of the police, activists and journalists highlight the ambiguous role *preman* organizations play in securing ports in Batam and Tanjung Pinang. On the one hand, *preman* organizations are seen as offering useful assistance when extra security personnel are required, such as during festivals like Eid, Christmas and New Year, or when student or labour demonstrations are taking place. Because of the location of the Riau Islands bordering Singapore, Malaysia and Vietnam, *preman* organizations in Batam and Tanjung Pinang are also deemed useful in monitoring and maintaining the security of border areas. On the other hand, *preman* organizations are also seen as a source of insecurity. There are widespread perceptions that *preman* organizations provide protection for illegal businesses and perpetrate criminal activities such as smuggling and illegal logging. This ambiguous perception results in tensions between the government and *preman* organizations. As a consequence, despite the absence of any large-scale clashes between the government and *preman* organizations, tensions between the two parties continue to exist.

Taken as a whole, this chapter has examined the role and perception of the participation of *preman* organizations in port security in Batam and Tanjung Pinang. The findings echo the arguments presented in Chapters 2 and 3 about the continued involvement of *preman* organizations in port security in Indonesia. The next chapter will provide a conclusion to this research. It will provide a systematic comparison of the role of *preman* organizations in port security across the three provinces of Jakarta, North Sulawesi and the Riau Islands.

Notes

1. Interview with a government official, 26 February 2016, Batam.
2. Interviews with the head of the local branch of Pemuda Pancasila Batu Ampar, 17 February 2016, Batu Ampar, Batam; a staff member of the Batam Agency for National Unity and Politics (Kesatuan Bangsa dan

Politik/Kesbangpol), Batam local government, 26 February 2016; two staff members of the Pemuda Pancasila Batam secretariat, 16 February 2016; and a local resident of Batam, 18 February 2016.
3. Interviews with the head, vice-head and secretary of Pemuda Pancasila Batam, 17 February 2016, Batam.
4. Interview with a senior representative of Gerakan Pemuda Ansor/secretary of Komite Nasional Pemuda Indonesia Batam, 15 February 2016, Batam.
5. Interviews with a senior representative of Pemuda Panca Marga Batam/the head of Komite Nasional Pemuda Indonesia Batam, 15 February 2016, Batam; and the head of Ikatan Pemuda Karya Batam, 16 February 2016, Batam.
6. Interview with the vice-head of the Tanjung Pinang parliament, February 2016, Tanjung Pinang.
7. Ibid.
8. Interview with a senior representative of Pemuda Panca Marga Batam/the head of Komite Nasional Pemuda Indonesia Batam, 15 February 2016, Batam.
9. Interview with a senior official from the Batam Police, 18 February 2016, Batam.
10. Pasukan Pengamanan Masyarakat translates as "public security forces". Members of PAM Swakarsa are drawn from the civilian population. PAM Swakarsa was widely used during the New Order regime to maintain order and security across the country.
11. Interview with a senior official from the Batam police, 18 February 2016, Batam.
12. Interview with the commander of Batam Naval Base, 19 February 2016, Batam.
13. Interview with two staff members of the Agency for National Unity and Politics, Batam local government, 18 February 2016, Batam.
14. Interview with a senior official from the Batam Police, 18 February 2016, Batam.
15. Interview with the vice-head of Ikatan Pemuda Karya Tanjung Pinang, February 2016, Tanjung Pinang.
16. Ibid.
17. Ibid.
18. Interview with the secretary of Pemuda Pancasila Batam, 17 February 2016, Batam.
19. Interview with the head of Pemuda Pancasila Batam, 17 February 2016, Batam.
20. Interview with the vice-head of Pemuda Pancasila Batam, 17 February 2016, Batam.
21. Interview with a senior official from the Society Guidance Division, Batam Police, 19 February 2016, Batam.

22. Interview with a staff member of the Agency for National Unity and Politics, Batam local government, 26 February 2016, Batam.
23. Interview with a senior representative of Pemuda Panca Marga Batam/ the head of Komite Nasional Pemuda Indonesia Batam, 15 February 2016, Batam.
24. Ibid.
25. Interview with the head of the National Leadership Assembly of Pemuda Pancasila, 19 September 2016, Jakarta.
26. Interview with the head of Ikatan Pemuda Karya Batam, 16 February 2016, Batam.
27. Interview with the head of Forum Komunikasi Putra Putri Purnawirawan dan Putra Putri TNI Polri, 3 February 2016, Jakarta.
28. Ibid.
29. Ibid.
30. Interview with the secretary of Pemuda Pancasila Batam, 17 February 2016, Batam.
31. Ibid.
32. Interviews with a senior representative of Gerakan Pemuda Ansor/ secretary of Komite Nasional Pemuda Indonesia Batam, 15 February 2016, Batam; a staff member of the Garda Nusantara secretariat, 17 February 2016, Batam; the head and secretary of Ikatan Pemuda Karya Batam, 16 February 2016, Batam.
33. Interviews with a senior representative of Gerakan Pemuda Ansor/ secretary of Komite Nasional Pemuda Indonesia Batam, 15 February 2016, Batam; a staff member of the Garda Nusantara secretariat, 17 February 2016, Batam; the head and secretary of Ikatan Pemuda Karya Batam, 16 February 2016, Batam.
34. Interview with a deputy chief editor of a local newspaper in Batam, 5 November 2016, Batam.
35. Interview with a staff member of the Agency for National Unity and Politics, Batam local government, 26 February 2016, Batam.
36. Ibid.
37. Interview with a senior representative of Gerakan Pemuda Ansor/ secretary of Komite Nasional Pemuda Indonesia Batam, 15 February 2016, Batam.
38. Interview with the director of BP Batam and two of his staff, 16 February 2016, Batam.
39. Interview with a senior official from the Batam Police, 18 February 2016, Batam.
40. Ibid.
41. Ibid.
42. Interviews with the director of BP Batam and two of his staff, 16 February 2016, Batam; a senior official from the Batam Police, 18 February 2016,

Batam; a staff member of the Agency for National Unity and Politics, Batam local government, 26 February 2016, Batam.
43. Interview with a Catholic priest who become a leading figure in anti-trafficking in Batam, 8 November 2016, Batam.
44. Ibid.
45. Ibid.
46. Interviews with a Catholic priest who has become a leading figure in anti-trafficking in Batam, 8 November 2016, Batam; and the deputy chief editor of a local newspaper in Batam, 5 November 2016, Batam.
47. Interviews with an academic from Universitas Maritim Raja Ali Haji, February 2016, Tanjung Pinang; the vice-head of the Tanjung Pinang parliament, February 2016, Tanjung Pinang; a former member of a local militarized CSO, February 2016, Tanjung Pinang.
48. Interview with a former member of a local militarized CSO, February 2016, Tanjung Pinang.
49. Interview with the vice-head of the Tanjung Pinang parliament, February 2016, Tanjung Pinang.
50. Ibid.
51. Ibid.
52. Interviews with an academic from Universitas Maritim Raja Ali Haji, February 2016, Batam; and the vice-head of the Tanjung Pinang parliament, February 2016, Tanjung Pinang.
53. Interview with the vice-head of Pemuda Pancasila Batam, 17 February 2016, Batam.
54. Interview with the head of Ikatan Pemuda Karya Tanjung Pinang, February 2016, Tanjung Pinang.
55. Ibid.
56. Interview with the head of Ikatan Pemuda Karya Batam, 16 February 2016, Batam.
57. Interview with a senior representative of Gerakan Pemuda Ansor/ secretary of Komite Nasional Pemuda Indonesia Batam, 15 February 2016, Batam.
58. Ibid.
59. Interviews with a senior representative of Gerakan Pemuda Ansor/ secretary of Komite Nasional Pemuda Indonesia Batam, 15 February 2016, Batam; and the head, vice-head and secretary of Pemuda Pancasila Batam, 17 February 2016, Batam.
60. Interview with the head, vice-head and secretary of Pemuda Pancasila Batam, 17 February 2016, Batam.
61. Interview with a senior representative of Gerakan Pemuda Ansor/ secretary of Komite Nasional Pemuda Indonesia Batam, 15 February 2016, Batam.
62. Interview with a senior official from the Society Guidance Division, Batam Police, 18 February 2016, Batam.

63. Interview with a senior official from the Batam Police, 18 February 2016, Batam.
64. Ibid.
65. Ibid.
66. Interview with a senior official from the Agency for National Unity and Politics, Batam local government, 26 February 2016, Batam.
67. Ibid.
68. Interview with a senior representative of Gerakan Pemuda Ansor/ secretary of Komite Nasional Pemuda Indonesia Batam, 15 February 2016, Batam.
69. Interview with a Catholic priest who has become a leading figure in anti-trafficking in Batam, 8 November 2016, Batam.
70. Ibid.
71. Interview with a deputy chief editor of a local newspaper in Batam, 5 November 2016, Batam.
72. Ibid.

Conclusion

This book has examined the involvement of *preman* organizations in securing ports and coastlines across three provinces in Indonesia, including Jakarta, North Sulawesi and the Riau Islands. The involvement of *preman* organizations in port security shows a continuation of Indonesia's old security practices from the times of Suharto's authoritarian regime. The main finding is that the involvement of *preman* organizations in port security is problematic and hinders Indonesia's transition to be a fully functioning democracy. The use of *preman* organizations for security by government authorities plays an instrumental role in strengthening the position of power these organizations have in society. An analysis of interviews, media reports and government documents shows that this position of power has not always been used by *preman* organizations for the betterment of society. This is the case even in areas where there is a great degree of acceptance by officials and societal actors of the role of *preman* organizations in security. The evidence in all empirical chapters in this book confirms that *preman* organizations have been involved in various unlawful activities, ranging from providing protection to businesses that violate laws to conducting violent attacks against the government security apparatus. These unlawful activities are the key source of tensions between *preman* organizations and the government.

Findings

There are six key findings of this book. First, the decision to use *preman* organizations for port security in Indonesia cannot be traced to a single decision made by the country's political leader or senior defence officials in response to terrorist threats in the aftermath of the 9/11 attacks and 2002 Bali bombings. The evidence shows that participation of *preman* organizations in monitoring and, on some occasions, physically guarding ports and coastal areas in the three case study regions—Jakarta, North Sulawesi and the Riau Islands—is a product of continued action by government bureaucracies at the national and local levels, and the history of these actions date back to Suharto's New Order era (Indonesian Ministry of Defense 2008, p. 86; *Jakarta Post*, 29 June 2006; Kemenkopolhukam 2006b, pp. 40, 57; Dewan Maritim Indonesia 2007b, p. 59; 2007a, p. 52; Kemenkopolhukam 2006a, pp. 29, 34–35; Marin 2005, p. 35; Suristiyono 2005, p. 49; Dewan Maritim Indonesia 2007c, pp. 4-8–4-9).[1] The use of *preman* organizations for port security is part of an institutionalized habit that predates the introduction of containerization in Indonesian ports in the 1980s and has continued to the present (Sciascia 2013; Febrica 2017a).[2] This epiphenomenon occurs alongside Indonesia's everyday politics, is widely discussed in the media and is acknowledged by government officials, legislators and members of *preman* organizations (*Kompas*, 16 May 2002; *Viva*, 31 December 2012; *Tribun Manado*, 5 February 2015a, 5 February 2015b; *Berita Manado*, 8 March 2013; *Jakarta Post*, 16 November 2013; *Manado Post*, 11 April 2015).[3] Despite international pressure following the 9/11 attacks for the Indonesian government to improve its counterterrorism measures, the practice of using *preman* organizations for port security has been sustained by a combination of precarious and heterogenous political coalitions that have led the government to focus on low-key approaches to dealing with terrorism and by a lack of resources, manpower and equipment to advance the country's maritime security.

Second, the key *preman* organizations involved in port and coastal security have varied across time and location. In the past, Pemuda Pancasila (PP) played an instrumental role in securing ports in Jakarta and North Sulawesi. PP had significant power over port security during the New Order era because of its control over port labour. The introduction of containerization in the 1980s at Indonesia's major ports led to the displacement of many labourers responsible for handling break-bulk cargo. This contributed to diminishing the role of PP in port security in Indonesia. The end of Indonesia's authoritarian regime was also marked by the rise of ethnic-based *preman* organizations in many parts of the country. Some of these organizations have become important players in local security. In Jakarta, one of the largest Betawi-based organizations, FBR, has been used for port security purposes. In Manado and Bitung, the key *preman* organizations involved in port and coastal security are Minahasan ethnic-based organizations such as Brigade Manguni and Milisi Waraney. The emergence of ethnic-based *preman* organizations does not suggest, however, that the hyper-nationalist CSOs that existed since the New Order era have been completely weakened. In Batam, for instance, *preman* organizations such as PP and PPM continue to participate in port and coastal security.

Third, the focus of cooperation between government authorities and *preman* organizations shows variations from one place to another. In Jakarta, Manado and Bitung, the main impulse that prompts cooperation between *preman* organizations and government authorities, especially intelligence units, is counterterrorism. But in contrast to Jakarta and North Sulawesi, the matter of terrorism is not seen as a pressing security concern in the Riau Islands. In Batam and Tanjung Pinang, human trafficking and smuggling are the most immediate concerns that create opportunities for government and *preman* organizations to cooperate.

Fourth, there is no single standard for the degree of training given by Indonesian security authorities to members of *preman* organizations across the provinces. Interviews, documents and media reports show that neither members of FBR in Jakarta nor those of Brigade Manguni and Milisi Waraney in North Sulawesi have received basic military training from the government security authorities.[4] In comparison, members of *preman* organizations in the Riau Islands, such as PP and PPM, receive regular basic military training.[5] These two organizations have historic links with the Indonesian military, and, according to their leaders, some of their members are used to help guard border areas and outlying islands.

Fifth, as shown in several incidents in Jakarta, North Sulawesi and the Riau Islands, *preman* organizations could be a source of insecurity rather than security. In Jakarta, violent clashes leading to deaths, destruction of public property and the closures of ports are common (Oke Zone, 15 April 2010; Detik, 21 August 2013; Polda Metro Jaya, 21 January 2015). Clashes have also taken place between different *preman* organizations, between *preman* organizations and private security companies, and between these organizations and the government. During the gubernatorial election involving Basuki Tjahja Purnama, perceptions of the use of *preman* organizations were deeply divisive. For instance, a couple of senators representing Jakarta were in favour of the role of *preman* organizations in security.[6] In contrast, the Jakarta provincial government under Purnama strongly opposed the presence of *preman* organizations (CNN Indonesia, 11 April 2016).[7] The Riau Islands sits at the middle of the insecurity spectrum in terms of the frequency of conflicts of interest generated by the use of *preman* organizations in the security sector. In Batam and Tanjung Pinang, security authorities and the local government displayed mixed feelings about the involvement of *preman* organizations in security. They have used *preman* organizations to fill the gap between the supply and demand of security in their territory. But low-scale clashes are sometimes unavoidable because of the involvement of *preman* organizations in supporting illicit activities in the Riau Islands. In contrast to Jakarta and Batam, officials in North Sulawesi share a positive perception of the assistance of *preman* organizations in providing security (*Tribun Manado*, 5 February 2015a; 5 February 2015b; *Manado Post*, 28 March 2015; 11 April 2015).[8] This does not mean, however, that the use of *preman* organizations for security purposes has been trouble free. There have been several incidents where *preman* organizations have backed businesses that violated laws. In one of these incidents, members of the largest *preman* organization in North Sulawesi had come into conflict with the local communities that they claimed to protect.

Sixth, the use of *preman* organizations for port and coastal security in Jakarta, North Sulawesi and the Riau Islands raises questions of government control over these organizations. On the one hand, the Indonesian government has used *preman* organizations for security purposes and tried to exercise control over these organizations. The *preman* organizations that are discussed in this book are also fully registered with the Agency for National Unity and Politics (Kantor Kesatuan Bangsa dan Politik) at the city/provincial level and with the Ministry of Home Affairs at the national level. But incidents such as the Koja riot in Jakarta demonstrate a lack of government control over *preman* organizations. *Preman* organizations in North Sulawesi, including Milisi Waraney and Brigade Manguni, have much better relations with government officials and the security authorities compared with their counterparts in Jakarta. It is unclear, however, to what extent the government is aware of the anti-illegal-fishing operations carried out by members of one of these organizations in the Sulawesi Sea. Such activities can be very dangerous if carried out by unarmed and underequipped civilians and could potentially create diplomatic tensions with the flag states of the ships targeted in these operations if injuries to crew or destruction of the targeted ships occurs. In a similar vein, although the government security authorities have trained several *preman* organizations in Batam and Tanjung Pinang, the placement of members of these CSOs to guard border areas or to carry out "ceremonial shows of force" such as *apel siaga* in outlying islands—including Natuna Regency, bordering the South China Sea, and Nipah Island, which borders the Strait of Malacca—could be problematic. Given rising anxiety over territorial disputes in the South China Sea, continuous acts of illegal, unreported and unregulated fishing by the Chinese fishing militias in the North Natuna Sea, and the presence of unsettled maritime boundaries between Indonesia and Malaysia in the southernmost part of the Strait of Malacca, any provocation or mistakes by members of the *preman* organizations could escalate tension in these areas.

Contributions to Literature on Indonesian Politics

This book offers three major contributions to the literature on Indonesian politics. First, by providing an explanation of the use of *preman* organizations for port security in Indonesia, it sheds light on the dynamics and tensions between state and non-state actors in securing the country's ports and outlying islands. It contributes to filling a significant gap in the literature, as there is currently no book-length treatment that systematically explains the involvement of *preman* organizations in Indonesia's maritime security. The existing literature on Indonesia's *preman* organizations is largely descriptive, it focuses on the political constellation of the country during and after the New Order era, and it does not explicitly examine the role of *preman* organizations in maritime security. Those titles that do focus on the outsourcing of border control to *preman* organizations are fragmented, and they consider only one case of the involvement of non-governmental actors at a time (notably, the area adjacent to the Strait of Malacca). This book covers a much broader set of cases of the participation of *preman* organizations in maritime border security, and it has explained the involvement of non-governmental actors in securing Indonesian ports that are situated in three key sea lanes of communication in

Southeast Asia: the Strait of Malacca, the Sunda Strait and the Sulu-Sulawesi Sea.

Second, this book shows the extent of problems posed by terrorism in Indonesia, and Southeast Asia in general, and how a developing country like Indonesia copes with this threat. It offers an account of some of the measures being taken by the Indonesian government to prevent terrorist attacks and improve port security across the country. In particular, the book discusses unconventional measures such as collecting information, conducting joint operations, and training *preman* organizations to help detect terrorist movements across the country.

Third, drawing not only from the official narrative but also contemporary documents, this book provides insight into the decision-making for Indonesia's security policy since 1998. From 1998 until the present day, Indonesia's security policies have continued to be guided by the doctrine of the Total People's Defence and Security System, which places a major emphasis on the responsibilities of civilians in national defence. Government documents and speeches made by key decision-makers—including the president and senior officials from the military and such civil institutions as the Ministry of Defence and the Coordinating Ministry for Political, Legal and Security Affairs—continue to echo the role of the Total People's Defence and Security System as guiding Indonesia's maritime security policies (Kemenkopolhukam 2005; 2006, pp. 29, 34–35; Dewan Maritim Indonesia 2007b, pp. 60–61; Indonesian Ministry of Defence 2008, p. 86; 19 January 2022). After the 9/11 attacks, the combination of pressure from the United States for Indonesia to improve its maritime security and the need to secure vast maritime areas with only limited resources have contributed to sustaining the practice of using *preman* organizations to secure ports and coastlines in various parts of the country. And because of the twin processes of democratization and decentralization in post-authoritarian Indonesia, the use and degree of acceptance of *preman* organizations in each region are informed by the dynamics of local politics. After 1998, *preman* organizations have become valuable sources of political support for politicians seeking election or re-election. Despite claiming neutrality, *preman* organizations have provided support to their members who run for public office and for politicians who are affiliated with their organizations. As shown in this book, *preman* organizations in some cases also challenge democratically elected leaders and local government decisions.

Contributions to Literature beyond Indonesian Studies

This book concentrates on the use of *preman* organizations for port security in Indonesia. By doing so, it provides two contributions to literature beyond Indonesian studies. First, it offers valuable insights on the use of non-state security providers by a developing non-Western democracy. The international relations literature on non-state security providers tends to focus on the use of private military companies by developed countries or multinational companies in combat and non-combat operations in countries such as Sierra Leone, Iraq and Afghanistan (Adams 2003; Shearer 1998; Davis 2000; Sullivan 2002). Those that specifically examine the use of non-state security providers in maritime security tend to focus on counter-piracy operations in East Africa and the Indian Ocean. Whether, why and how a non-Western and developing country decides to use non-state security providers to improve its national security has been overlooked.

Second, this book makes a valuable theoretical contribution to the wider debate on the concept of civil society. It focuses on the uncivil traits of civil society that have been overlooked by both the international relations and policy analysis literature. The theoretical aspect of this book is important, because the existing literature on civil society and the specific scholarly works on Indonesia's civil society organizations are largely descriptive and focus only on those that display the key characteristics of voluntary, not-for-profit, non-political and non-violent organizations. This book argues that in post-authoritarian Indonesia a large number of *preman* organizations have sought and gained legal status as "legitimate" CSOs. In practice, however, their mode of operation does not echo the principles of Western civil society, that they be voluntary, self-generating, self-supporting, autonomous from the state and bound by a legal order or set of shared rules. Rather, a large number of *preman* organizations are ready to use violence and intimidation to achieve their economic, social and political goals.

Third, this book provides useful insights on the measures taken by non-Western democratic countries to address terrorism in the aftermath of the 9/11 attacks. Security studies scholars have dedicated their overwhelming attention to various exceptional security practices associated with the US-led war on terror, including the curtailment of individual freedom, detention camps, extraordinary rendition, and aerial targeted killings (see Mabee and Vucetic 2018, p. 101). Very little attention has been given to studying how the implications of the global war on terror by the United States manifests outside the Western liberal democratic sphere. This book has demonstrated that, in responding to the war on terror, the Indonesian government has incorporated a combination of measures, such as the introduction of anti-terrorism legislation in 2002 enabling security personnel to detain suspected terrorists for twenty days, which can be extended for a further six months based on preliminary evidence reported by intelligence services; an array of new maritime trade security measures, such as the establishment of the Priority Line and MITA risk-profiling systems; and continued use of *preman* organization to monitor port security (see Tan and Ramakrishna 2004, p. 96; Febrica 2017b).

Future Work

This book has addressed the key question as to whether the use of *preman* organizations for port security represents a change or a continuation in Indonesia's security practices. It has also identified the tensions between the Indonesian government and *preman* organizations in securing ports and coastal areas. In doing so, this book has revealed several further questions that warrant attention and would thus provide fruitful lines for further inquiry.

First, how do media and the government portray ethnic *preman* organizations and their role in enacting violence in Indonesia? Since 1998, there has been a surge of ethnic-based *preman* and youth organizations in Indonesia. These include FBR in Jakarta, Brigade Manguni in North Sulawesi and Persatuan Pemuda Tempatan in Batam. However, the rise of ethnic *preman* organizations has been overlooked, because, since the 9/11 attacks and the 2002 Bali bombings, the media and scholarly works have tended to focus on radical or militarized Islamic organizations. This line of inquiry will provide a fresh perspective to understand the current state of non-state organized violence in Indonesia and its connections to and effects on the tribal aspect of society. Existing literature that touches on the connection between tribalism and organized violence tends to focus on Middle-Eastern and African countries, with only a few exceptions (see Cohen and Middleton 1970; Mikell 1996; Rowland 2009). Little attention has been paid to tribalism within a democratic Asian country.

Second, it is worthwhile asking to what extent *preman* organizations contribute to escalating electoral violence. Analysis of interviews, documents and media reports show that, although *preman* organizations tend to claim neutrality during elections, most of them in fact have actually lent support to local and national politicians in elections. Since Indonesia began its democratic transition in 1998, the level of electoral violence has been deemed low. But since the introduction of direct local elections in 2005, the refusal by the losing parties to accept the results led to outbreaks of violence in different parts of Indonesia, such as Aceh and Papua (IPAC 2013). In several of these incidents, groups and clans associated with the electoral candidates were involved in instigating violence (ibid.). The involvement of *preman* organizations in rallying political support or escalating electoral violence is beyond the scope of this book, but this line of enquiry can certainly be developed further.

Third, in this book, it is explained that members of *preman* organizations have been used to help secure ports, coastal areas and outlying islands in several provinces, including North Sulawesi and the Riau Islands. Some of these places are close to areas affected by maritime disputes. The involvement of *preman* organizations for maritime security opens another line of enquiry regarding the use of non-governmental actors in disputed maritime areas. One question to pose is what are the implications of the use of *preman* organizations in maritime disputes in Southeast Asia? In disputed waters such as the South China Sea, for example, claimant states such as China, Vietnam and the Philippines have used fishing militia to defend their claims in the region (Zhang and Bateman 2017, pp. 290–92). Future inquiries, therefore, can focus on assessing the use of non-governmental actors and its implications in disputed waters such as the South China Sea.

Having explained the use of *preman* organizations in securing Indonesia's ports and coastal areas, it is clear that the role of *preman* organizations in the development of Indonesia is an area of continued significance to scholars and policymakers in Indonesia and Southeast Asia. It is important that scholars and policymakers understand that security dynamics in ports and coastal areas in Indonesia are often influenced by the activities of both state and non-state security providers.

Notes

1. Interviews with a senator from the Riau Islands, 18 August 2015, Jakarta; and a senator from Jakarta, 18 August 2015, Jakarta.
2. Interviews with the head of the National Leadership Assembly of Pemuda Pancasila, 19 September 2016, Jakarta; staff of the Port

Directorate, Indonesian Ministry of Transportation, 6 August 2015, Jakarta; the chairman, vice chairman and secretary of Pemuda Pancasila Batam, 17 February 2016, Batam.

3. Interviews with staff of the Port Directorate, Indonesian Ministry of Transportation, 6 August 2015, Jakarta; an official from the Indonesian National Defence Council, 7 August 2015; an official from the Indonesian Coordinating Ministry for Political, Legal and Security Affairs, 21 August 2015; the head of the Agency for National Unity and Politics, Bitung government, 14 November 2016, Bitung; the head of Security Facilitation, Arts, Culture, Economics, Religion and Society Section, North Sulawesi provincial government Agency for National Unity and Politics, 17 November 2016, Manado; a retired senior police official, 12 February 2016, Manado; a police officer, 8 February 2015, Manado; a senior official from Batam Police, 18 February 2016, Batam; a senator from the Riau Islands, 18 August 2015, Jakarta; a senator from Jakarta, 18 August 2015, Jakarta; a senior government official from Bitung, 9 February 2016, Bitung; a member of the Minahasa Utara parliament, 13 February 2016, Manado; the head of the Agency for National Unity and Politics, Manado city government, 10 November 2016, Manado; the vice-head of the Tanjung Pinang parliament, February 2016, Tanjung Pinang; the head of the National Leadership Assembly of Pemuda Pancasila, 19 September 2016, Jakarta; the chairman, vice chairman and secretary of Pemuda Pancasila Batam, 17 February 2016, Batam; the vice-head of Ikatan Pemuda Karya Tanjung Pinang, February 2016, Tanjung; a senior representative of Pemuda Panca Marga Batam/the head of the Komite Nasional Pemuda Indonesia Batam, 15 February 2016, Batam; and the chairman of Forum Betawi Rempug, 31 March 2016, Jakarta.

4. Interviews with the vice-chairman of Milisi Waraney, 5 February 2016, Manado; one of the leaders of the Milisi Waraney youth organization, 5 February 2015, Manado; and a member of Milisi Waraney, 5 February 2016, Manado.

5. Interviews with the secretary of Pemuda Pancasila Batam, 17 February 2016, Batam; and a senior representative of Pemuda Panca Marga Batam/ the head of Komite Nasional Pemuda Indonesia Batam, 15 February 2016, Batam.

6. Interviews with a senator from Jakarta (Dewan Perwakilan Daerah, DKI Jakarta), 18 August 2015, Jakarta; and a senator from Jakarta, 21 August 2015.

7. Interview with a senior official of the Agency for National Unity and Politics, Jakarta provincial government, 30 September 2016, Jakarta.

8. Interviews with the head of the Agency for National Unity and Politics, Manado city government, 10 November 2016, Manado; the head of the Security Facilitation, Arts, Culture, Economics, Religion and Society Section, North Sulawesi provincial government Agency for National Unity and Politics, 17 November 2016, Manado; a retired senior police officer, 12 February 2016, Manado; and a police officer, 8 February 2015, Manado.

Bibliography

This bibliography is divided into two sections. General sources are listed first, followed by news sources.

General Sources

Acharya, Amitav. 2003. "Democratisation and the Prospects for Participatory Regionalism in Southeast Asia". *Third World Quarterly* 24, no. 2: 375–90.

Adams, Thomas K. 1999. "The New Mercenaries and the Privatization of Conflict". *US Army War College Quarterly: Parameters* 29, no. 2: 103–16.

Ahram, Ariel I. 2011. "Origins and Persistence of State-Sponsored Militias: Path Dependent Processes in Third World Military Development". *Journal of Strategic Studies* 34, no. 4: 531–56.

Airriess, Christopher A. 1989. "The Spatial Spread of Container Transport in a Developing Regional Economy: North Sumatra, Indonesia". *Transportation Research Part A* 23, no. 6: 453–61.

Allison, Laura, and Monique Taylor. 2017. "ASEAN's 'People-Oriented' Aspirations: Civil Society Influences on Non-traditional Security Governance". *Australian Journal of International Affairs* 71, no. 1: 1–18.

Anderson, Benedict. 2001. *Violence and the State in Suharto's Indonesia*. New York: SEAP Publications.

Antlöv, Hans, Derick W. Brinkerhoff, and Elke Rapp. 2010. "Civil Society Capacity Building for Democratic Reform: Experience and Lessons from Indonesia". *Voluntas* 21, no. 3: 417–39.

APEC Desk of the Republic of Indonesia Customs. 2011. *Collective Action Plan*. Jakarta: APEC Desk of the Republic of Indonesia Customs.

Arksey, Hilary, and Peter Knight. 1999. *Interviewing for Social Scientists*. London: Sage.
ASEAN. 2009. *ASEAN Statistical Yearbook 2008*. Jakarta: ASEAN Secretariat.
Aspinall, Edward. 2013. "A Nation in Fragments". *Critical Asian Studies* 45, no. 1: 27–54.
Avant, Deborah D. 2005. *The Market for Forces: Consequences of Privatizing Security*. Cambridge: Cambridge University Press.
Ayoob, Mohammed. 1984. "Security in the Third World: The Worm About to Turn?" *International Affairs* 60, no. 1: 41–51.
Badan Informasi Geospasial. 2018. "Pentingnya Informasi Geospasial untuk Menata Laut Indonesia". 16 September 2018. http://big.go.id/berita-surta/show/pentingnya-informasi-geospasial-untuk-menata-laut-indonesia.
Badan Koordinasi Keamanan Laut (Bakorkamla). 2004. "Workshop Selat Malaka: Pola Pengamanan Selat Malaka dan Permasalahannya". Bakorkamla: Jakarta.
———. 2010. *Buku Putih Bakorkamla 2009*. Jakarta: Pustaka Cakra.
Badan Perencanaan Pembangunan Nasional (Bappenas). 2011. *Sandingan Alokasi Pagu Definitif APBN Tahun 2005–2010 Berdasarkan Program Per Kementerian/Lembaga (Juta Rupiah): Kementerian Koordinator Bidang Politik dan Keamanan*. Jakarta: Direktorat Pertahanan dan Keamanan.
Badan Pusat Statistik. 2020a. *Statistik Perdagangan Luar Negeri Indonesia Impor 2020*, vol. 3. https://bps.go.id/publication/2021/06/10/d07497dba7c9de331a23bb0a/statistik-perdagangan-luar-negeri-indonesia-impor-2020-jilid-iii.html (accessed 31 July 2022).
———. 2020b. *Statistik Perdagangan Luar Negeri Indonesia Ekspor 2020*, vol. 1. https://bps.go.id/publication/2021/07/06/bdae29cceed062aef4a6d148/statistik-perdagangan-luar-negeri-indonesia-ekspor-2020-jilid-i.html (accessed 31 July 2022.
Bakker, Laurens. 2016. "Organized Violence and the State: Evolving Vigilantism in Indonesia". *Bijdragen Tot De Taal, Land-En Volkenkunde* 172, pp. 249–77.
Baldor, Lolita, C. 2004. "Coast Guard Issuing More Fines as Port Security Deadline Nears". 25 March 2004. https://homeport.uscg.mil/cgi-bin/st/portal/uscg_docs/MyCG/Editorial/20061206/CGfines.pdf?id=866396f80278fd7b62ae4aa2622c9ac5bff8d406&user_id=2a47d4dbfd24ce2da39438e736cab2d6 (accessed 17 October 2012).
Bantuan Hukum. 2018. "Menyikapi Perpres Pelibatan TNI dalam Penanganan Terorisme".

3 August 2018. https://bantuanhukum.or.id/menyikapi-perpres-pelibatan-tni-dalam-penanganan-terorisme/.

Barker, Joshua. 1998. "State of Fear: Controlling the Criminal Contagion in Suharto's New Order". *Indonesia* 66: 7–42.

Barter, Shane J. 2013. "State Proxy or Security Dilemma? Understanding Anti-rebel Militias in Civil War". *Asian Security* 9, no. 2: 75–92.

Baylis, John. 2008. "International and Global Security". In *The Globalization of World Politics*, edited by J. Baylis, S. Smith, and P. Owne. New York: Oxford University Press.

Bea Cukai. 2022. "Selama Tahun 2021, Bea Cukai Batam Berhasil Melakukan Penindakan Dengan Total Estimasi Nilai Barang Sebanyak Rp156,92 Miliar". 10 January 2022. https://www.beacukai.go.id/berita/selama-tahun-2021–bea-cukai-batam-berhasil-melakukan-penindakan-dengan-total-estimasi-nilai-barang-sebanyak-rp156–92–miliar.html.

Beittinger-Lee, Verena. 2009. *(Un)Civil Society and Political Change in Indonesia: A Contested Arena*. Abingdon: Routledge.

Bellamy, Chris. 2011. "Maritime Piracy: Return of the World's Second-Oldest Security Problem". *RUSI Journal* 156, no. 6: 78–83.

Bertrand, Romain. 2004. "Behave Like Enraged Lions: Civil Militias, the Army and the Criminalisation of Politics in Indonesia". *Global Crime* 6, no. 3: 325–44.

Bhakti, Ikrar Nusa. 2009. *Reformasi Sektor Keamanan: Sebuah Pengantar*. Jakarta: Institute for Defense, Security and Peace Studies.

Brown, David, and Ian Douglas Wilson. 2007. "Ethnicized Violence in Indonesia: Where Criminals and Fanatics Meet". *Nationalism and Ethnic Politics* 13, no. 3: 367–403.

Brown, David, and Ian Wilson. 2007. "Ethnicized Violence in Indonesia: The Betawi Brotherhood Forum in Jakarta". Murdoch University Asia Research Centre Working Paper no. 145. http://wwwarc.murdoch.edu.au/publications/wp/wp145.pdf (accessed 25 October 2018).

Brown, James. 2012. "Pirates and Privateers: Managing the Indian Ocean's Private Security Boom". Lowy Institute for International Policy Analysis. http://www.lowyinstitute.org/files/brown_pirates_and_privateers_web.pdf (accessed 14 July 2015).

Bryman, Alan. 2004. *Social Research Methods*, 2nd ed. Oxford: Oxford University Press.

Bueger, Christian, Jan Stockbruegger, and Sascha Werthes. 2011. "Pirates, Fishermen and Peacebuilding: Options for Counter-piracy Strategy in Somalia". *Contemporary Security Policy* 32, no. 2: 356–81.

Buzatu, Anne-Marie, and Benjamin S. Buckland. 2015. "Private

Military & Security Companies: Future Challenges in Security Governance". Geneva Centre for the Democratic Control of Armed Forces Working Paper no. 3. http://www.foresightfordevelopment.org/sobipro/55/1183–private-military-and-security-companies-future-challenges-in-security-governance (accessed 22 January 2018).

Carana. 2004. *Impact of Transport and Logistics on Indonesia's Trade Competitiveness*. http://www.carana.com/images/PDF_car/Indonesia%20Transport%20and%20Logistics%20Report.pdf (accessed 20 January 2011).

Chachavalpongpun, Pavin. 2012. "Responsibility to Protect in Southeast Asia: Enlarging Space for Civil Society". NTS Working Paper no. 7. http://www.rsis.edu.sg/NTS/resources/research_papers/NTS_Working_Paper7.pdf (accessed 24 January 2018).

Chalk, Peter. 1998. "Political Terrorism in South-East Asia". *Terrorism and Political Violence* 10, no. 2: 118–34.

———. 2012. "Private Maritime Security Companies and Maritime Security". Paper presented at the United Arab Emirates Conference, "A Regional Response to Maritime Piracy: Enhancing Public-Private Partnerships and Strengthening Global Engagement", Dubai, 2012, the Institute for Near East and Gulf Military Analysis. http://www.counterpiracy.ae/upload/Briefing/Peter%20Chalk-Essay-Eng.pdf (accessed 5 November 2014).

Chapsos, Ioannis, and Paul Holtom. 2015. "Floating Armouries in the Indian Ocean". *Small Arms Survey* 52: 1–4. http://psm.du.edu/media/documents/reports_and_stats/think_tanks/sas_floating-armories-indian-ocean.pdf (accessed 14 July 2015).

Chong, Terence. 2012. "Civil Society Engagement in ASEAN". In *Regional Outlook: Southeast Asia 2012/2013*, edited by Michael J. Montesano and Lee Poh Onn, pp. 35–44. Singapore: Institute of Southeast Asian Studies.

Chow, Jonathan T. 2005. "ASEAN Counterterrorism Cooperation since 9/11". *Asian Survey* 45, no. 2: 302–21.

Cohen, Ronald, and John Middleton. 1970. *From Tribe to Nation in Africa: Studies in Incorporative Process*. Scranton: Chandler.

Collier, Kit. 1999. "The Armed Forces and Internal Security in Asia: Preventing the Abuse of Power". East West Center Occasional Papers Politics and Security Series no. 2. http://www.eastwestcenter.org/fileadmin/stored/pdfs/PSop002.pdf (accessed 17 July 2015).

Collins, Elizabeth Fuller. 2002. "Indonesia: A Violent Culture?" *Asian Survey* 42, no. 4: 582–604.

Colombijn, Freek, and J. Thomas Lindblad. 2002. *Roots of Violence in*

Indonesia: Contemporary Violence in Historical Perspective. Leiden: Institute of Southeast Asian Studies.

Coutrier, P.L. 1988. "Living on an Oil Highway". *Ambio* 17, no. 3: 186–88.

Cribb, Robert. 2000. "From Petrus to Ninja: Death Squads in Indonesia". In *Death Squads in Global Perspective: Murder with Deniability*, edited by Bruce B. Campbell and Arthur D. Brenner, pp. 183–202. New York: St. Martin's Press.

Cribb, Robert, and Michele Ford. 2009. "Indonesia as an Archipelago: Managing Islands, Managing the Seas". In *Indonesia beyond the Water's Edge*, edited by Robert Cribb and Michele Ford. Singapore: Institute of Southeast Asian Studies.

Davis, James R. 2000. "Fortune's Warrior: Private Armies and the New World Order". Vancouver: Douglas & McIntyre.

Dewan Maritim Indonesia. 2007a. *Analisis Potensi Ekonomi Maritim Dalam Rangka Perumusan Kebijakan Ekonomi Maritim Indonesia*. Jakarta: Sekretariat Jenderal Departemen Kelautan dan Perikanan.

———. 2007a. *Perumusan Kebijakan Strategi Pengamanan Wilayah Nasional*. Jakarta: Departemen Kelauatan dan Perikanan.

———. 2007b. *Laporan Perumusan Kebijakan Kelembagaan Tata Pemerintahan di Laut*. Jakarta: Departemen Kelautan dan Perikanan.

———. 2007c. *Perumusan Kebijakan Grand Strategi Pembangunan Kelautan*. Jakarta: Departemen Kelautan dan Perikanan.

Dewan Perwakilan Rakyat Republik Indonesia. 2002. Law No. 3/2002 on State Defence (UU No. 3/2002 Tentang Pertahanan Negara). https://www.dpr.go.id/dokjdih/document/uu/300.pdf (accessed 11 August 2022).

Dexter, Lewis Anthony. 1970. *Elite and Specialized Interviewing*. Evanston: Northwestern University Press.

Dinas Komunikasi, Informatika dan Statistik Pemprov DKI Jakarta. 2017. "Geografis Jakarta". http://www.jakarta.go.id/v2/news/category/geografis-jakarta (accessed 10 April 2017).

Direktorat Jenderal Perhubungan Laut. 2010. *Kronologis Kunjungan United States Coast Guard di Indonesia*. Jakarta: Direktorat Kesatuan Penjagaan Laut dan Pantai.

Djalal, Hasjim. 2009. "Indonesia's Archipelagic Sea Lanes". In *Indonesia beyond the Water's Edge*, edited by Robert Cribb and Michele Ford. Singapore: Institute of Southeast Asian Studies.

Elman, Colin. 1996. "Horses for Courses: Why Not Neorealist Theories of Foreign Policy?" *Security Studies* 6, no. 1: 7–53.

Embassy of the Kingdom of the Netherlands in Indonesia. 2007. "Power and Change Analysis (PCA)". 13 November 2007. Jakarta: Embassy of the Kingdom of the Netherlands.

Emmers, Ralf. 2003. "ASEAN and the Securitization of Transnational Crime in Southeast Asia". *Pacific Review* 16, no. 3: 419–38.

Febrica, Senia. 2010. "Securitizing Terrorism in Southeast Asia: Accounting for the Varying Responses of Indonesia and Singapore". *Asian Survey* 50, no. 3: 569–90.

———. 2014. "Securing the Sulu-Sulawesi Seas from Maritime Terrorism: A Troublesome Cooperation?" *Perspectives on Terrorism* 8, no. 3: 64–83.

———. 2015. "Why Cooperate? Indonesia and Anti-maritime Terrorism Cooperation". *Asian Politics & Policy* 7, no. 1: 105–30.

———. 2017a. "Port Security and Militarized NGOs in Indonesia". 5 April 2017. https://lisa.gerda-henkel-stiftung.de/port_security_and_militarized_ngos_in_indonesia?nav_id=6947&language=en (accessed 12 August 2022).

———. 2017b. *Maritime Security and Indonesia*. London: Routledge.

———. 2017c. "Southeast Asian Countries' Fight against Terrorism: Refining the Importance of Audience in Securitization". In *The Palgrave Handbook of Global Counterterrorism Policy*, edited by S.N. Romaniuk, S. Webb, D. Irrera, and F. Grice. London: Palgrave MacMillan.

———. 2020. "ASEAN Counterterrorism Cooperation and Human Rights Protection". In *International Human Rights and Counter-terrorism*, edited by Eran Shor and Stephen Hoadley. New York: Springer.

———. 2021. "Two Sides of the Same Coin: The Emergence and Role of Civil and Un-civil Society in Indonesia". In *Counter-terrorism and Civil Society: International Challenges since 9/11*, edited by Scott N. Romaniuk and Emeka Thaddues Njoku. Manchester: Manchester University Press.

Ford, Michele, and Lenore Lyons. 2013. "Outsourcing Border Security: NGO Involvement in the Monitoring, Processing and Assistance of Indonesian Nationals Returning Illegally by Sea". *Contemporary Southeast Asia* 35, no. 2: 215–34.

Friedman, Thomas, and Robert Kaplan. 2002. "The State of Discord". *Foreign Policy* 129: 64–70.

Gerard, Kelly. 2013. "From the ASEAN People's Assembly to the ASEAN Civil Society Conference: The Boundaries of Civil Society Advocacy". *Contemporary Politics* 19, no. 4: 1–16.

———. 2014. "ASEAN and Civil Society Activities in 'Created Spaces': The Limits of Liberty". *Pacific Review* 71, no. 1: 1–23.

Gilson, Julie. 2011. "Governance and Non-governmental Organizations in East Asia: Building Region-Wide Coalitions". In *Civil Society and*

International Governance, edited by Armstrong, Bello, Gilson, and Spini. London: Routledge.

Gomez, James, and Robin Ramcharan. 2012. "The Protection of Human Rights in Southeast Asia: Improving the Effectiveness of Civil Society". *Asia-Pacific Journal on Human Rights and the Law* 2: 27–43.

Gourevitch, Peter. 1978. "The Second Image Reversed: The International Sources of Domestic Politics". *International Organization* 32, no. 4: 881–912.

———. 2002. "Domestic Politics and International Relations". In *Handbook of International Relation*, edited by Walter Carlsnaes, Thomas Risse, and Beth A. Simmons. London: Sage.

Grieco, Joseph M. 1988. "Anarchy and the Limits of Cooperation: A Realist Critique of the Newest Liberal Institutionalism". *International Organization* 42, no. 3: 487–88.

Hadiz, Vedi. 2003. "Reorganizing Political Power in Indonesia: A Reconsideration of So-Called Democratic Transitions". *Pacific Review* 16, no. 4: 591–611.

———. 2004. "Indonesian Local Party Politics". *Critical Asian Studies* 36, no. 4: 615–36.

———. 2008. "Indonesia a Decade after Reformasi: Continuity or Change?" http://web.iaincirebon.ac.id/ebook/moon/Indonesia/s4_vedi.pdf (accessed 17 July 2015).

Hall, Rodney Bruce, and Thomas J. Biersteker. 2002. *The Emergence of Private Authority in Global Governance*. Cambridge: Cambridge University Press.

Hansen, Stig Jarle. 2008. "Private Security & Local Politics in Somalia". *Review of African Political Economy* 35, no. 118: 585–98.

Hargono, Slamet, Sugiono Sutomo, and Joesron Alisyahbana. 2013. "The Influence of the Port to the Economical Growth of the Batam Island". *Procedia Environmental Sciences* 17: 795–804.

Headman, Eva-Lotta. E. 2008. *Conflict, Violence and Displacement*. New York: SEAP Publications.

Hefner, Robert W. 1993. "Islam, State, and Civil Society: ICMI and the Struggle for the Indonesian Middle Class". *Indonesia* 56: 1–35

Hendrickson, Dylan, and Andrzej Karkoszka. 2002. "The Challenges of Security Sector Reform". In *SIPRI Yearbook 2002: Armaments, Disarmament and International Security*, pp. 175–201. http://www.sipri.org/yearbook/2002 (accessed 17 July 2015).

Heryanto, Ariel, and Vedi Hadiz. 2005. "Post-authoritarian Indonesia". *Critical Asian Studies* 37, no. 2: 251–75.

Howell, Jude, and Jeremy Lind. 2009. "Changing Donor Policy and

Practice in Civil Society in the Post-9/11 Aid Context". *Third World Quarterly* 30, no. 7, pp. 1279–96.

Ibrahim, Rustam. 2011. "Civil Society in Indonesia". In *An ASEAN Community for All: Exploring the Scope for Civil Society Engagement*, edited by Terence Chong and Stefani Elies. Singapore: Friedrich Ebert Stiftung.

Indonesian Ministry of Defence. 2008. *Defence White Paper*. Jakarta: Ministry of Defence.

———. 2022. "Wamenhan Herindra Soroti Pentingnya Kolaborasi dalam Upaya Mengupdate Kebijakan Pertahanan Negara". 19 January 2022. https://www.kemhan.go.id/2022/01/19/wamenhan-herindra-soroti-pentingnya-kolaborasi-dalam-upaya-mengupdate-kebijakan-pertahanan-negara.html.

Indonesian Ministry of Foreign Affairs. 2005. *Diskusi Panel tentang Studi Kebijakan Kelautan Indonesia dalam Rangka Mendukung pembangunan dan Integritas Nasional, Surabaya, 7–8 April 2005*. Jakarta: Departemen Luar Negeri.

Indonesian Ministry of Transportation. 2016. *Statistik Perhubungan 2015*. Jakarta: Indonesian Ministry of Transportation.

Indonesian National Human Rights Commission. 2014. *No. 3.094/K/PMT/XII/2013 Recommendation on the Follow up Monitoring and Investigation of PT Mikgro Metal Perdana' Licence and Iron Ore Mining in Bangka Island, North Minahasa to the Head of North Sulawesi Police Force, 17 February 2014*.

Institute for Defense, Security and Peace Studies, Aliansi Jurnalis Independent and Friedrich Ebert Stiftung. 2008. "Perjalanan Sihankamrata Sejak Awal Kemerdekaan RI". *Newsletter Media dan Reformasi Sektor Keamanan*, no. VI/09/2008.

Institute for Policy Analysis of Conflict (IPAC). 2013. "Electoral Violence". http://www.understandingconflict.org/en/conflict/index/6/Electoral-Violence (accessed 1 January 2019).

Jayasuriya, Kanishka, and Garry Rodan. 2007. "Beyond Hybrid Regimes: More Participation, Less Contestation in Southeast Asia". *Democratization* 14, no. 5: 773–94.

Kaldor, Mary. 2007. *New & Old Wars*. Stanford: California Press.

Kemenkopolhukam. 2005. *Hasil Survey Bidang Politik, Pertahanan dan Keamanan*. Jakarta: Kemenkopolhukam.

———. 2006a. *Laporan Akuntabilitas Kinerja (LAKIP) Tahun 2005*. Jakarta: Kemenkopolhukam.

———. 2006b. *Penetapan Rencana Kinerja Tahun 2006*. Jakarta: Kemenkopolhukam.

———. 2008a. *Catatan Desk Koordinasi Pemberantasan Terorisme (DKPT)*.

Jakarta: Kementerian Koordinator Bidang Politik, Hukum dan Keamanan.

———. 2008b. *Evaluasi Pengelolaan Bidang politik, Hukum dan Keamanan Tahun 2007*. Jakarta: Kemenkopolhukam.

Kementerian Kelautan dan Perikanan. 2013. "Daftar Pelabuhan". http://pipp.djpt.kkp.go.id/profil_pelabuhan/kategori_pelabuhan (accessed 19 April 2017).

Kementerian Komunikasi dan Informasi. 2022. "Anggaran pendidikan terus bertambah". https://indonesiabaik.id/infografis/anggaran-pendidikan-terus-bertambah (accessed 11 August 2022).

Khanh, Huynh Kim, and Hans H. Indorf. 1982. "Southeast Asia 1981: Two Currents Running". *Southeast Asian Affairs 1982*, edited by Huynh Kim Khanh. Singapore: Institute of Southeast Asian Studies.

Komisi Pemilihan Umum. 2019. "Hasil hitung suara pemilu presiden & wakil presiden RI 2019". https://pemilu2019.kpu.go.id/#/ppwp/hitung-suara/ (accessed 8 August 2022).

Kristiansen, Stein, and Lambang Trijono. 2005. "Authority and Law Enforcement: Local Government Reforms and Security Systems in Indonesia". *Contemporary Southeast Asia* 27, no. 2: 236–54.

Laksmana, Evan. 2019. "Indonesia as 'Global Maritime Fulcrum': A Post-mortem Analysis". Asia Maritime Transparency Initiative. 8 November 2019. https://amti.csis.org/indonesia-as-global-maritime-fulcrum-a-post-mortem-analysis/.

Lee, S.W., D.W. Song, and Cesar Ducruet. 2008. "A Tale of Asia's World Ports: The Spatial Evolution in Global Hub Port Cities". *Geoforum* 39, no. 1: 372–85.

Lee, Terence. 2000. "The Nature and Future of Civil-Military Relations in Indonesia". *Asian Survey* 40, no. 4: 692–706.

Leksana, Grace Tjandra. 2008. Urban Youth, Marginalization and Mass Organization: Involvement in the Betawi Brotherhood Forum in Jakarta. https://thesis.eur.nl/pub/6700/Grace%20Tjandra%20Leksana%20CYS.pdf (accessed 24 October 2018).

Lembaga Ketahanan Nasional. 2021. "Gubernur Lemhannas RI Hadiri FGD Rancangan Perpres Tugas TNI dalam Mengatasi Aksi Terorisme". Lemhannas. 15 December 2021. http://www.lemhannas.go.id/index.php/berita/berita-utama/1359-gubernur-lemhannas-ri-hadiri-fgd-rancangan-perpres-tugas-tni-dalam-mengatasi-aksi-terorisme (accessed 31 July 2022).

Liddle, R. William. (1999). "Regime: The New Order". In *Indonesia beyond Suharto: Polity, Economy, Society Transition*, edited by Donald K. Emmerson. New York: Sharpe.

Liss, Carolin. 2008. *Privatising the Fight against Somali Pirates*. Murdoch

University Asia Research Centre Working Paper no. 152. https://www.murdoch.edu.au/Research-capabilities/Asia-Research-Centre/_document/working-papers/wp152.pdf (accessed 5 November 2014).

Mabee, Bryan, and Srdjan Vucetic. 2018. "Varieties of Militarism: Towards a Typology". *Security Dialogue* 49, nos. 1–2: 96–108.

Majelis Pimpinan Nasional Pemuda Pancasila. 2017. *Sejarah Pemuda Pancasila*. http://pemudapancasila.or.id/sejarah/ (accessed 21 October 2018).

Marin, Djasri. 2005. "Kondisi Keamanan dan Hukum Menghadapi Tantangan Keutuhan NKRI". In *Catatan Forum Dialog dan Konsultasi: Peningkatan Keamanan, Ketertiban dan Penegakan Hukum*. Jakarta: Kemenkopolhukam.

Mietzner, Marcus. 2012. "Indonesia's Democratic Stagnation: Anti-reformist Elites and Resilient Civil Society". *Democratization* 19, no. 2, pp. 209–29.

Mikell, Gwendolyn. 1996. "Ethnic Particularism and the Creation of State Legitimacy in West Africa". *Tulsa Journal of Comparative and International Law* 4, no. 1: 99–115.

Møller, Bjorn. 2009. *Piracy, Maritime Terrorism and Naval Strategy*. Danish Institute for International Studies Report no. 2. http://pure.diis.dk/ws/files/73101/DIIS_Report_2009_02_Piracy_maritime_terrorism_and_naval_strategy.pdf (accessed 22 January 2018).

Mudayat, Aris Arif, Pitra Narendra, and Budi Irawanto. 2009. *Power and Conflict Relations Journal* 1, no. 1: 75–96. http://pcd.ugm.ac.id/wp-content/uploads/PCD-Journal-Vol.I-2009_Aris-Arif-Mudayatdkk-State-and-Civil-Society-Rela-onships-in-Indonesia.pdf (accessed 26 April 2017).

Nik, R.H., and S. Permal. 2008. "Security Threats in the Straits of Malacca". In *Profile of the Straits of Malacca: Malaysia's Perspective*, edited by H.M. Ibrahim and Hairil Anuar Husin. Kuala Lumpur: Maritime Institute of Malaysia.

Noor, Farish A. 2012. "The Forum Betawi Rempug (FBR) of Jakarta: An Ethnic-Cultural Solidarity Movement in a Globalising Indonesia". RSIS Working Paper no. 242. Singapore: Nanyang Technological University. https://www.rsis.edu.sg/rsis-publication/idss/242–wp242–the-forum-betawi-rempu/#.W8ydA9QrKt8 (accessed 21 October 2018).

NU (Nahdlatul Ulama) Online. 2021. "Jumlah Besar Nahdliyin Punya Bobot Politik Strategis". 17 December 2021. https://www.nu.or.id/nasional/survei-jumlah-besar-nahdliyin-punya-bobot-politik-strategis-WyiQO.

Nugroho, Yanuar, and Sofie Shinta Syarief. 2012. *Beyond Click-Activism?*

New Media and Political Processes in Contemporary Indonesia. Berlin: Friedrich Ebert Stiftung. http://www.library.fes.de/pdf-files/bueros/asia-media/09240.pdf (accessed 26 April 2017).

Nyman, Mikaela. 2006. *Democratising Indonesia: The Challenges of Civil Society in the Era of Reformasi*. Copenhagen: NIAS.

Ono, Keishi. 2013. "Piracy off the Coast of the Somalia and Indian Ocean, and Anti-piracy Operation by Private Military and Security Companies". National Institute for Defense Studies Briefing Memo. http://www.nids.go.jp/english/publication/briefing/pdf/2013/briefing_e175.pdf (accessed 14 July 2015).

Parlan, Hening. 2014. "Policy and Advocacy: Role of Civil Society in Disaster Management Bill Processes in Indonesia". In *Civil Society Organization and Disaster Risk Reduction: The Asian Dilemma*, edited by Takako Izumi and Rajib Shaw. Tokyo: Springer.

Paul, T.V., G. John Ikenberry, and John A. Hall. 2003. *The Nation State in Question*. New Jersey: Princeton University.

Perhimpunan Bantuan Hukum dan Hak Asasi Manusia Indonesia. 2020. "Siaran Pers Koalisi untuk Reformasi Sektor Keamanan: 75 Tahun TNI – Kemunduran Reformasi TNI". 5 October 2020. https://pbhi.or.id/75–tahun-tni-kemunduran-reformasi-tni/.

Permana, Yogi Setya. 2016. "Informal Security Groups as Social Non-movement in Indonesia: Case of Buru Jejak in Central Lombok". *Makara Hubs-Asia* 20, no. 2: 77–87.

Pohl, Florian. 2006. "Islamic Education and Civil Society: Reflections on the *Pesantren* Tradition in Contemporary Indonesia". *Comparative Education Review* 50, no. 3: 389–409.

Polda Metro Jaya. 2015. "Rekonsiliasi Pasca Bentrokan Antara Kelompok Ambon Dengan Kelompok FBR". 21 January 2015. http://www.poldametrojaya.info/info-satwil/restro-jakut/rekonsiliasi-pasca-bentrokan-antara-kelompok-ambon-dengan-kelompok-fbr.html.

Polner, Mariya. 2010. "Compendium of Authorized Economic Operator (AEO) Programmes". WCO Research Paper no. 8. http://www.wcoomd.org/files/1.%20Public%20files/PDFandDocuments/research/aeo_compendium.pdf (accessed 11 August 2011).

Quayle, Linda. 2012. "Bridging the Gap: An 'English School' Perspective on ASEAN and Regional Civil Society". *Pacific Review* 25, no. 2: 199–222.

Rahim, Lily Zubaidah, and Juliet Pietsch. 2015. "Introduction: States, Critical Citizens, and the Challenge of Democratization in Southeast Asia". *Japanese Journal of Political Science* 16, no. 2: 139–42.

Richard, Theodore T. 2010. "Reconsidering the Letter of Marque: Utilizing

Private Security Providers against Piracy". *Public Contract Law Journal* 39, no. 3: 411–64.

Richardson, Michael. "Securing Choke Points at Sea against Terrorists". *Straits Times*, 19 January 2004.

Riyono, Tio. 2022. "Perkembangan Terorisme dan Anggaran Penanganan Terorisme di Indonesia". *Buletin APBN* 7, no. 2: 7–10. Pusat Kajian Anggaran Sekretariat Jenderal DPR RI, Jakarta. https://puskajianggaran.dpr.go.id/produk/detail-buletin-apbn/id/142 (accessed 9 August 2022).

Robinson, Geoffrey. 2001. "People's War: Militias in East Timor and Indonesia". *South East Asia Research* 9, no. 3: 271–318.

Rodrigue, Jean-Paul, and Theo Notteboom. 2009. "The Geography of Containerization: Half a Century of Revolution, Adaptation and Diffusion". *GeoJournal* 74, no. 1: 1–6.

Roosa, John. 2003. "Violence and the Suharto Regime's Wonderland". *Critical Asian Studies* 35, no. 2: 315–23.

Ross, Shani, and Joshua Ben-David. 2009. "Somali Piracy: An Escalating Security Dilemma". *Harvard Africa Policy Journal* 5: 55–70.

Rowland, Jennifer. 2009. "Democracy and the Tribal System in Jordan: Tribalism as a Vehicle for Social Change". Independent Study Project Collection Paper no. 749.

Ruland, Jurgen. 2009. "Deepening ASEAN Cooperation through Democratization? The Indonesian Legislature and Foreign Policymaking". *International Relations of the Asia-Pacific* 9, no. 3: 373–402.

Ryter, Loren. 1998. "Pemuda Pancasila: The Last Loyalist Free Men of Suharto's Order?" *Indonesia* 66: 45–73.

Scheffler, Alessandro. 2010. "*Piracy-Threat or Nuisance?*" NATO Defense College Research Division. https://www.files.ethz.ch/isn/113596/rp_56en.pdf (accessed 22 January 2018).

Sciascia, Alban. 2013. "Monitoring the Border: Indonesian Port Security and the Role of Private Actors". *Contemporary Southeast Asia* 35, no. 2: 163–87.

Sebastian, Leonard C. 2003. "Indonesian State Responses to September 11, the Bali Bombings and the War in Iraq: Sowing the Seeds for an Accommodationist Islamic Framework?" *Cambridge Review of International Affairs* 16, no. 3: 429–46.

Sekretariat Jenderal Departemen Kelautan dan Perikanan. 2006. *Sosialisasi Nilai-Nilai Kemaritiman*. Jakarta: Departemen Kelautan dan Perikanan.

Shearer, David. 1998. *Private Armies and Military Intervention*. New York: Oxford University Press.

Sidel, John. 2004. "Bossism and Democracy in the Philippines, Thailand, and Indonesia: Towards an Alternative Framework for the Study of 'Local Strongmen'". In *Politicising Democracy: The New Local Politics of Democratisation*, edited by John Harriss, Kristin Stokke, and Olle Tornquist, pp. 51–74. Basingstoke: Palgrave Macmillan.

Singer, Peter W. 2007. *Corporate Warriors: The Rise of Privatized Military Industry*. Ithaca: Cornell University Press.

Silverstein, Josef. 1982. "The Military and Foreign Policy in Burma and Indonesia". *Asian Survey* 22, no. 3: 278–91.

Simpson, Brad. 2013. "The Act of Killing and the Dilemmas of History". *Film Quarterly* 67, no. 2: 10–13.

Sindre, Gyda Marås. 2005. *Violence and Democracy: Indonesia's Paramilitary Puzzle*. PhD dissertation, University of Oslo. https://www.duo.uio.no/handle/10852/13765 (accessed 1 October 2015).

Singh, Bilveer. 2004. "The Challenge of Militant Islam and Terrorism in Indonesia". *Australian Journal of International Affairs* 58, no. 1: 47–68.

Sittnick, Tammy M. 2005. "State Responsibility and Maritime Terrorism in the Strait of Malacca: Persuading Indonesia and Malaysia to Take Additional Steps to Secure the Strait". *Pacific Rim Law and Policy Journal* 14: 743–69.

Smith, Chris. 2001. "Security-Sector Reform: Development Breakthrough or Institutional Engineering?" *Conflict, Security and Development* 1, no. 1: 5–20.

Solingen, Etel. 2005. "ASEAN Cooperation: The Legacy of the Economic Crisis". *International Relations of the Asia Pacific* 5, no. 1: 30–53.

Sondakh, Bernard Kent. 2004. "Pengamanan Wilayah Laut Indonesia". *Indonesian Journal of International Law* (special edition), pp. 1–26.

Spearin, Christopher. 2010. "A Private Security Solution to Somali Piracy". *Naval War College Review* 63, no. 4: 56–71.

Stevenson, Jonathan. 2010. "Jihad and Piracy in Somalia". *Survival* 52, no. 1: 27–38.

Sullivan, John P. 2002. "Terrorism, Crime and Private Armies". *Low Intensity Conflict and Law Enforcement* 11, no. 2: 239–53.

Supriyadi. 2010. "DJBC Ikut Serta dalam Latihan Bersama TNI-Polri untuk Penanggulangan Teroris". *Warta Bea Cukai*. Jakarta: Direktorat Jenderal Bea dan Cukai.

Suristiyono (Komisaris Besar Polisi dan Wakil Direktur Polair Babinkam Polri). 2005. "Penyelenggaraan Keamanan dan Ketertiban di Kawasan Perairan Selat Malaka". In *Pertemuan Kelompok Ahli Kebijakan Terpadu Pengelolaan Keamanan Selat Malaka, Medan, 19–20 Juli 2005*. Jakarta: Departemen Luar Negeri.

Tan, See Seng, and Kumar Ramakrishna. 2004. "Interstate and Intrastate Dynamics in Southeast Asia's War on Terror". *School of Advanced International Studies* (SAIS) *Review* 24, no. 1: 91–105

US Coast Guard. 2005. "Navigation and Vessel Inspection Circular (NVIC) No. 02–05". 15 February 2005. https://homeport.uscg.mil/cgi-bin/st/portal/uscg_docs/MyCG/Editorial/20061012/NVIC2-05_2.pdf?id=9f75e3fedc14830306cc2ce463770be203bec5cd&user_id=-f3e0323a048c9c4431fa1032dc4787d5.

———. 2004. "Press Release: Coast Guard to Begin International Port Security Visits". 15 April 2004. https://homeport.uscg.mil/mycg/portal/ep/contentView.do?contentTypeId=2&channelId=-18389&contentId=55243&programId=50389&programPage=%2Fep%2Fprogram%2Feditorial.jsp&pageTypeId=0&BV_SessionID=@@@@0102172244.1350476151@@@@&BV_EngineID=ccceadfidgdflkdcfngcfkmdfhfdfgo.0.

US Department of Defense. 2003. "Deputy Secretary Wolfowitz (Interview with Southeast Asian Journalists) 28 January 2003". http://www.defenselink.mil/transcripts/transcript.aspx?transcriptid=1356.

US Department of Homeland Security. 2005. "The National Strategy for Maritime Security". 20 September 2005. http://georgewbush-whitehouse.archives.gov/homeland/maritime-security.html (accessed 13 March 2011).

US Embassy in Jakarta. 2008. "U.S. Coast Guard Issues Advisory to Indonesia on Port Security". 26 February 2008. http://jakarta.usembassy.gov/pr_02262008.html.

US Energy Information Administration. 2012. "World Oil Transit Chokepoints: Malacca". 22 August 2012. http://www.eia.doe.gov/cabs/world_oil_transit_chokepoints/malacca.html.

Ufen, Andreas. 2006. "Political Parties in Post-Suharto Indonesia: Between politik aliran and 'Philippinisation'". GIGA Working Papers no. 37. http://repec.giga-hamburg.de/pdf/giga_06_wp37_ufen.pdf (accessed 17 July 2015).

Valencia, Mark J. 2006. "Security Issues in the Malacca Straits: Whose Security and Why It Matters?" In *Building a Comprehensive Security Environment in the Straits of Malacca: Proceedings of the MIMA International Conference on the Straits of Malacca, 11–13 October, 2004*. Kuala Lumpur: Maritime Institute of Malaysia.

Van Klinken, Gerry, and Joshua Barker. 2009. *State of Authority: The State in Society in Indonesia*. New York: SEAP Publications.

Waltz, Kenneth N. 1979. *Theory of International Politics*. New York: McGraw-Hill.

———. 1986. "Anarchic Order and Balance of Power". In *Neorealism and*

Its Critics, edited by Robert O. Keohane. New York: Columbia University Press.

———. 2000. "Globalization and American Power". *The National Interest* 59: 46–56.

Weatherbee, Donald E. 2004. "Governance in Southeast Asia: The Good, the Bad and the Ugly". In *Growth and Governance in Asia*, edited by Y. Sato, pp. 179–91. Hawaii: Asia-Pacific Center for Security Studies. http://www.apcss.org/Publications/Edited%20Volumes/GrowthGovernance_files/Pub_Growth%20Governance/Pub_GrowthGovernance%20book.pdf (accessed 17 July 2015).

Weiss, Meredith L. 2008. "Civil Society and Close Approximations Thereof". In *Southeast Asia in Political Science: Theory, Region and Qualitative Analysis*, edited by Erik Martinez Kuhonta, Dan Slater, and Tuong Vu. California: Stanford University Press.

Wilson, Ian Douglas. 2006. "Continuity and Change: The Changing Contours of Organized Violence in Post–New Order Indonesia". *Critical Asian Studies* 38, no. 2: 265–66.

Zhang, Hangzhou, and Sam Bateman. 2017. "Fishing Militia, the Securitization of Fishery and the South China Sea Dispute". *Contemporary Southeast Asia* 39, no. 2: 288–314.

News Sources

Antara. 2016. "Ormas Islam tuntut Ahok dihukum mati". 14 October 2016. https://www.antaranews.com/berita/590179/ormas-islam-tuntut-ahok-dihukum-mati.

Batam Pos. 2005. "Pemuda Pancasila Bakti Sosial Tiap Bulan". 18 May 2005.

———. 2012. "PPM Tanam 200 Pohon di Pulau Nipah: H. Lulung Dilantik Panglima TNI". 3 March 2012.

———. 2012. "Pelabuhan Tanjung Ayun Sakti Diklaim Milik Pribadi Rawan Konflik dengan Masyarakat". 30 April 2012.

———. 2012. "Kantor BC Dijaga Ketat". 25 June 2012.

———. 2016. "DPRD Desak Pemkab Cari Solusi Secepatnya: Pasokan Sembako Tergantung dari Malaysia". 16 September 2016.

———. 2016. "Ditengah Kepungan Penyeludup". 26 September 2016.

BBC. 2013. "BNPT bangun pusat deradikalisasi teroris". 27 August 2013. http://www.bbc.co.uk/indonesia/berita_indonesia/2013/08/130827_lapas_khusus_terorisme.

———. "Ahok: Police Name Jakarta Governor as Blasphemy Suspect". 16 November 2016. https://www.bbc.co.uk/news/world-asia-37996350.

Berita Manado. 2011. "BMI Promosikan Wisata Bitung

di Bali". 28 May 2011. http://beritamanado.com/bmi-promosikan-wisata-bitung-di-bali/.

———. 2013. "Berita Sulut Temui Sondakh". 25 February 2013. http://beritamanado.com/bmi-sulut-temui-sondakh/.

———. 2013. "Brigade Manguni Diminta Bentuk Divisi Intelijen". 8 March 2013. http://beritamanado.com/brigade-manguni-diminta-bentuk-divisi-intelejen/.

———. 2013. "BMI Diminta Mantapkan Semangat Identitas Diri". 9 March 2013. http://beritamanado.com/bmi-diminta-mantapkan-semangat-identitas-diri/.

———. 2013. "Maengkom Akui Pendiri Gerindra Tetapi Manguni Tetap Netral". 10 March 2013. http://beritamanado.com/maengkom-akui-pendiri-gerindra-tapi-bmi-tetap-netral/.

———. 2013. "Kaloh Masih Dipercayakan Pimpin BMI Bitung". 25 June 2013. http://beritamanado.com/kaloh-masih-dipercayakan-pimpin-bmi-bitung/.

———. 2013. "Berita Foto: Atraksi Kebal Divisi Bela Negara". 10 November 2013. http://beritamanado.com/berita-foto-atraksi-kebal-divisi-bela-negara/.

———. 2014. "Keluarga Prabowo Terluka, Rhamdhani Terancam Digugat". 12 June 2014. http://beritamanado.com/keluarga-prabowo-terluka-rhamdani-terancam-digugat/.

———. 2015. "BMI Sambangi Polda Sulut". 4 February 2015. http://beritamanado.com/bmi-sambangi-polda-sulut/.

———. 2015. "Berita Foto: HUT Brigade Manguni Indonesia ke-13". 9 March 2015. http://beritamanado.com/berita-foto-hut-brigade-manguni-indonesia-ke-13/.

Berita Sore. 2011. "Konflik Dua OKP Medan Utara Minta Segera Dituntaskan". 12 August 2011. http://beritasore.com/2011/08/12/konflik-dua-okp-medan-utara-minta-segera-dituntaskan/ (1 November 2014).

CNBC Indonesia. 2019. "Inilah Peta Partai Pengusung Capres-Cawapres Pemilu 2019". 10 August 2018. https://www.cnbcindonesia.com/news/20180810195720-16-28087/inilah-peta-partai-pengusung-capres-cawapres-pemilu-2019.

CNN Indonesia. 2014. "Ahok Bukan Gubernur DKI Nonmuslim Pertama". 19 November 2014. https://www.cnnindonesia.com/nasional/20141119094501-20-12427/ahok-bukan-gubernur-dki-nonmuslim-pertama.

———. 2016. "Ahok: Oknum Ormas Seperti Preman yang Jual Lapak di Ciliwung". 11 April 2016. http://www.cnnindonesia.com/nasional/20150823175400-20-73928/ahok-oknum-ormas-seperti-preman-yang-jual-lapak-di-ciliwung/.

———. 2016. "Korban Tewas Kapal TKI Tenggelam di Batam 18 Orang". 2 November 2016. https://www.cnnindonesia.com/nasional/20161102205537-20-169813/korban-tewas-kapal-tki-tenggelam-di-batam-18-orang.

———. 2019. "Ahok sang Pemicu Rentetan Aksi Bela Islam dan Nama Besar 212". 22 January 2019. https://www.cnnindonesia.com/nasional/20190115135955-32-360979/ahok-sang-pemicu-rentetan-aksi-bela-islam-dan-nama-besar-212.

———. 2019. Masih Banyak Mobil 'Tak Penting' Pakai Sirene dan Strobo, 18 June 2019. https://www.cnnindonesia.com/teknologi/20190618140127-384-404241/masih-banyak-mobil-tak-penting-pakai-sirene-dan-strobo.

Detik. 2013. "Beda Satpol PP Dulu dan Kini: Kisah Satpol PP Yang Selamat Dari Insiden Tanjung Priok". 21 August 2013. http://news.detik.com/berita/2336478/kisah-satpol-pp-yang-selamat-dari-insiden-tanjung-priok.

———. 2014. "3 Aksi FPI Meminta Ahok Mundur Sebagai Gubenur". 12 February 2014. http://news.detik.com/berita/2764699/3-aksi-fpi-meminta-ahok-mundur-sebagai-gubernur.

———. 2015. "Ini Penampakan Ormas yang Hadang dan Intimidasi Petugas Bea Cukai di Cilincing". 8 October 2015. http://news.detik.com/berita/3039236/ini-penampakan-ormas-yang-hadang-dan-intimidasi-petugas-bea-cukai-di-cilincing.

———. 2019. "Begini Peta Kekuatan DPR 2019-2024, Koalisi Jokowi Dominan". 1 October 2019. https://news.detik.com/berita/d-4728867/begini-peta-kekuatan-dpr-2019-2024-koalisi-jokowi-dominan.

———. 2020. "4 Alasan Pemerintah Tetapkan FPI Ormas Terlarang di RI". 30 December 2020. https://news.detik.com/berita/d-5315789/4-alasan-pemerintah-tetapkan-fpi-ormas-terlarang-di-ri/3.

The Economist. 2014. "Indonesia's Presidential Election: Jokowi's Day Though His Opponent Attempts to Spoil It". 26 July 2014. http://www.economist.com/news/asia/21608800-though-his-opponent-attempts-spoil-it-jokowis-day.

———. 2014. "Consolidating Counter Terrorism Efforts". 2 October 2014. http://country.eiu.com/article.aspx?articleid=222348606&Country=Indonesia&topic=Politics.

Harian Jaya Pos. 2016. "Pengukuhan Tonaas Brigade Manguni Wangko". 7 February 2016. http://www.harianjayapos.com/detail-11634-pengukuhan-tonaas-brigade-manguni-wangko.html.

Jakarta Post. 2003. "Paddy's Pub Is Back More Secure than Ever". 7 August 2003.

———. 2006. "Civilian Forces Planned to Help Patrol Islands". 29 June 2006.

———. 2008. "Reward Offered for Wanted Gunman". 24 June 2008.

———. 2008. "Gunman in Monas Ambush Not Provocateur, Says Police". 26 June 2008.

———. 2008. "Gang Rule North Jakarta as Local Govt Fails". 3 July 2008.

———. 2008. "FBR Demands Land Rights to Mall". 6 August 2008.

———. 2011. "Osama's Death Will Not Stop Local Radicals: Experts". 3 May 2011.

———. 2013. "Fishermen Demand an End to Land Reclamation Project". 16 November 2013. http://www.thejakartapost.com/news/2013/11/16/fishermen-demand-end-land-reclamation-project.html.

———. 2016. "Protestors Reject Communism, to Take Law in Own Hands". 11 May 2016.

———. 2016. "Ahok to Cease Funding for Opposing Organizations". 8 September 2016.

———. 2017. "Ahok Guilty of Blasphemy, Sentenced to Two Years". 9 May 2017. http://www.thejakartapost.com/news/2017/05/09/ahok-guilty-of-blasphemy-sentenced-to-two-years.html.

Kompas. 1999. "BBM Pertamina Diselundupkan ke Kapal Asing". 17 December 1999.

———. 2002. "Menarik Mengaitkan FBR dengan Sutiyoso". 30 March 2002.

———. 2002. "Hari Marwah Rakyat Kepri Pelabuhan Laut Tanjung Pinang Diblokir". 16 May 2002.

———. 2002. "Calon Anggota Komnas HAM Diuji DPR: Prinsip Universalisme HAM Jadi Fokus Pertanyaan". 27 June 2002.

———. 2002. "Tipar Cakung Mulai Normal: Ketua Umum FBR Minta Maaf". 19 July 2002.

———. 2002. "Kalah Menang Semua Jadi Arang". 22 July 2002.

———. 2002. "Aksi-aksi Massa ke MPR Makin Marak". 9 August 2002.

———. 2002. "FBR Menyerang Kelompok Wardah Hafidz di Komnas HAM". 13 September 2002.

———. 2003. "FBR Bentrok dengan Petugas Tramtib, Dua Luka". 2 October 2003.

———. 2005. "Presiden Tinjau Perbatasan RI-Malaysia". 8 March 2005.

———. 2005. "TNI Tetap Bersiaga di Kawasan Ambalat". 16 March 2005.

———. 2014. "Lapor ke Wapres, Kapolri Sebut Indonesia Rawan Terorisme". 30 October 2014. http://nasional.kompas.com/

read/2014/10/30/18574331/Lapor.ke.Wapres.Kapolri.Sebut. Indonesia.Rawan.Terorisme.

———. 2016. "Buktikan Klaim sebagai Ormas Terbesar, NU Terbitkan Kartu Anggota Nasional". 7 April 2016. https://regional.kompas.com/read/2016/04/07/14013651/Buktikan.Klaim.sebagai.Ormas.Terbesar.NU.Terbitkan.Kartu.Anggota.Nasional.

———. 2017. "Ini Transkrip Lengkap Pernyataan SBY soal Telepon ke Ma'ruf Amin…". 2 February 2017. https://nasional.kompas.com/read/2017/02/02/06060071/ini.transkrip.lengkap.pernyataan.sby.soal.telepon.ke.ma.ruf.amin.?page=all.

———. 2017. "Pelabuhan Ikan Jalur Narkoba". 4 February 2017.

———. 2018. "MoU Perbantuan TNI dalam Penanganan Unjuk Rasa dan Kerusuhan Diperpanjang". 2 February 2018. https://nasional.kompas.com/read/2018/02/02/16072341/mou-perbantuan-tni-dalam-penanganan-unjuk-rasa-dan-kerusuhan-diperpanjang.

———. 2020. "Muncul Permintaan Soal UU Perbantuan TNI, DPR: Agak Susah". 13 May 2020. https://nasional.kompas.com/read/2020/05/13/23143181/muncul-permintaan-soal-uu-perbantuan-tni-dpr-agak-susah?page=all.

———. 2012. "552 Aksi Teror Terjadi Sejak Tahun 2000, Terbanyak Ada di Era SBY Kompas". 30 March 2021. https://nasional.kompas.com/read/2021/03/30/15460211/552-aksi-teror-terjadi-sejak-tahun-2000-terbanyak-ada-di-era-sby?page=all.

———. 2021. "Prabowo sebut anggaran pertahanan RI tetap 0.8 persen dari GDP". 9 August 2021. https://nasional.kompas.com/read/2021/07/09/21465031/prabowo-sebut-anggaran-pertahanan-ri-tetap-08-persen-dari-gdp.

Liputan6. 2014. "Diduga Diserang Ormas, Posko Pemuda Pancasila Mampang Rusak". 10 August 2014. http://news.liputan6.com/read/2089091/diduga-diserang-ormas-posko-pemuda-pancasila-mampang-rusak.

Manado Post. 2015. "BMI Siap Bantu Polisi Perangi ISIS". 28 March 2015. http://manadopostonline.com/read/2015/03/28/BMI-Siap-Bantu-Polisi-Perangi-ISIS/8294.

———. 2015. "Sulut Bulat Perangi Teroris-ISIS". 11 April 2015. http://manadopostonline.com/read/2015/04/11/Sulut-Bulat-Perangi-Teroris-ISIS/8574.

Media Indonesia. 2017. "Dandim Lebak Akhirnya Dicopot Karena Latih FPI". 8 January 2017. http://mediaindonesia.com/news/read/86586/dandim-lebak-akhirnya-dicopot-karena-latih-fpi/2017-01-08.

Merdeka. 2013. "FBR dan Forkabi minta Ahok mundur karena arogan".

29 July 2013. http://www.merdeka.com/jakarta/fbr-dan-forkabi-minta-ahok-mundur-karena-arogan.html.

———. 2022. "Profil: FX Hadi Rudyatmo". 30 July 2022. https://m.merdeka.com/fx-hadi-rudyatmo/profil.

Metro. 2014. "Kader Partai Demokrat Dilarang Jadi Menteri Jokowi-JK". 26 August 2014. http://news.metrotvnews.com/read/2014/08/26/282967/kader-partai-demokrat-dilarang-jadi-menteri-jokowi-jk.

Oke Zone. 2010. "FBR Siap Kerahkan Massa ke Koja". 15 April 2010. http://news.okezone.com/read/2010/04/15/338/322837/fbr-siap-kerahkan-massa-ke-koja.

———. 2016. "Desak Ahok Mundur, FPI Datangi DPRD DKI". 4 April 2016. http://news.okezone.com/read/2016/04/04/338/1353381/desak-ahok-mundur-fpi-datangi-dprd-dki.

Sindo. 2015. "Sekelompok Ormas Serang Petugas Bea Cukai Pelabuhan". 8 October 2015. http://metro.sindonews.com/read/1051334/170/sekelompok-ormas-serang-petugas-bea-cukai-pelabuhan-1444274917.

Singapore Window. 2002. "Lee Kuan Yew Interview with Talk Asia on CNN". 9 February 2002. http://www.singapore-window.org/sw02/020209c1.html.

Sumut Pos. 2013. "Desak Pembebasan 18 Tersangka Pembunuh 8 WN Myanmar Ormas-Polisi Bentrok, 10 Cedera". 13 April 2013. http://sumutpos.co/2013/04/55969/ormas-polisi-bentrok-10-cedera.

Tempo. 2015. "FBR dan Ormas Lain Kembali Tuntut Ahok". 26 February 2015. https://foto.tempo.co/read/beritafoto/26853/FBR-dan-Ormas-Lain-Kembali-Tuntut-Ahok-Mundur/1.

———. 2015. "Ricuh Pasar Gembrong, 7 Anggota FBR Jadi Tersangka". 11 August 2015. https://metro.tempo.co/read/news/2015/08/11/064690896/ricuh-pasar-gembrong-7-anggota-fbr-jadi-tersangka.

———. 2016. "Soal TNI & Terorisme, DPR Disarankan Buat RUU Perbantuan TNI". 25 July 2016. https://nasional.tempo.co/read/790219/soal-tni.

———. 2017. "TNI Akui Latih FPI Bela Negara". 7 January 2017. https://m.tempo.co/read/news/2017/01/07/078833694/tni-akui-latih-fpi-bela-negara.

———. 2017. "Penjelasan TNI Soal Latihan Bela Negara dengan Anggota FPI". 8 January 2017. https://m.tempo.co/read/news/2017/01/08/078833700/penjelasan-tni-soal-latihan-bela-negara-dengan-anggota-fpi.

Tribun Batam. 2010. "Ganggu Tambang Bauksit,

———. 2010. "Ganggu Tambang Bauksit, 13 Anggota PP Diamankan Polisi". 13 December 2010. http://batam.tribunnews.com/2010/12/13/ganggu-tambang-bauksit-13-anggota-pp-diamankan-polisi.

———. 2011. "Supriatna Alami Empat Luka Tusukan". 1 April 2011a. http://batam.tribunnews.com/2011/04/01/supriatna-alami-empat-luka-tusukan.

———. 2011. "Polisi dan PP Buru Edi si Pelaku Penusukan". 1 April 2011b. http://batam.tribunnews.com/2011/04/01/polisi-dan-pp-buru-edi-si-pelaku-penusukan.

———. 2011. "Oknum OKP Ancam Kasat Reskrim: Pimpinan Marudut Sayangkan Tindakan Penembakan Anggotanya". 1 May 2011. http://batam.tribunnews.com/2011/05/01/pimpinan-marudut-sayangkan-tindakan-penembakan-anggotanya.

———. 2011. "Peringati Sumpah Pemuda dengan Baksos". 30 October 2011. http://batam.tribunnews.com/2011/10/30/peringati-sumpah-pemuda-dengan-baksos.

———. 2012. "PP Batam Bantah Anggotanya Dalangi Kerusuhan". 19 June 2012. http://batam.tribunnews.com/2012/06/19/pp-batam-bantah-anggotanya-dalangi-kerusuhan.

———. 2013. "Kantor Sekuriti Industrial Park Hancur". 31 October 2013a. http://batam.tribunnews.com/2013/10/31/kantor-sekuriti-industrial-park-hancur.

———. 2013. "Demonstrasi Buruh Mulai Tidak Terkendali". 31 October 2013b. http://batam.tribunnews.com/2013/10/31/demonstrasi-buruh-mulai-tidak-terkendali.

———. 2014. "Ratusan Anak Yatim Piatu Buka Bersama Srikandi Pemuda Pancasila". 21 July 2014. http://batam.tribunnews.com/2014/07/21/ratusan-anak-yatim-piatu-buka-bersama-srikandi-pemuda-pancasila.

———. 2014. "Anggota Pemuda Pancasila Tanjungpinang Diminta Membantu Pemerintah". 23 December 2014. http://batam.tribunnews.com/2014/12/23/anggota-pemuda-pancasila-tanjungpinang-diminta-membantu-pemerintah.

———. 2015. "Pelabuhan Beton Sekupang Rawan Penyelundupan Narkoba dan Barang? Ini Penjelasannya". 24 December 2015. http://batam.tribunnews.com/2015/12/24/pelabuhan-beton-sekupang-rawan-penyelundupan-narkoba-dan-barang-ini-penjelasannya.

———. 2016. "Di Pelabuhan Internasional Batam Centre Ditemukan Sabu tak Bertuan Seberat 517 Gram". 11 January 2016. http://batam.tribunnews.com/2016/01/11/di-pelabuhan-internasional-batam-centre-ditemukan-sabu-tak-bertuan-seberat-517-gram.

———. 2016. "Menimalisir Penyakit yang Disebabkan Sampah,

PAC PP Bengkong Lakukan Goro Massal". 10 February 2016. http://batam.tribunnews.com/2016/02/10/newsvideo-menimalisir-penyakit-yang-disebabkan-sampah-pac-pp-bengkong-lakukan-goro-massal.

———. 2016. "PAC Pemuda Pancasila Kecamatan Bengkong Gelar Gotong Royong di Empat Kelurahan". 10 February 2016. http://batam.tribunnews.com/2016/02/10/pac-pemuda-pancasila-kecamatan-bengkong-gelar-gotong-royong-di-empat-kelurahan.

———. 2016. "Oknum Ormas Ini Hancurkan Kios Warga di Tanjunguma". 6 March 2016. http://batam.tribunnews.com/2016/03/06/newsvideo-oknum-pemuda-pancasila-hancurkan-kios-warga.

———. 2016. "Narkoba di Batam: Pembawa 2.500 Butir Pil Ekstasi dari Malaysia ke Batam Ini Ternyata Suami-Istri". 11 March 2016. http://batam.tribunnews.com/2016/03/11/pembawa-2500-butir-pil-ekstasi-dari-malaysia-ke-batam-ini-ternyata-suami-istri.

———. 2016. "Puluhan Anggota LSM dan Ormas Demonstrasi Minta Kepala BP Batam Angkat Kaki". 11 April 2016.

———. 2016. "Pemuda Pancasila Anambas Rangkul OKP dan LSM Lakukan 'Bersih-bersih' Laut". 18 April 2016. http://batam.tribunnews.com/2016/04/18/pemuda-pancasila-anambas-rangkul-okp-dan-lsm-lakukan-bersih-bersih-laut.

———. 2016. "Begini Modus Pungli yang Diduga Dilakukan Oknum Ditpam BP Batam di Pelabuhan Batam Centre". 28 April 2016. http://batam.tribunnews.com/2016/04/28/begini-modus-pungli-yang-diduga-dilakukan-oknum-ditpam-bp-batam-di-pelabuhan-batam-centre.

———. 2016. "Tiga Calon TKI Ilegal dan Satu Tekong Diperiksa Polda Kepri karena Hendak ke Malaysia". 19 July 2016. http://batam.tribunnews.com/2016/07/19/tiga-calon-tki-ilegal-dan-satu-tekong-diperiksa-polda-kepri-karena-hendak-ke-malaysia.

———. 2016. "Tiga Tekong TKI Illegal Ditangkap Saat Hendak Berangkatkan Puluhan TKI". 29 July 2016. http://batam.tribunnews.com/2016/07/29/newsvideo-tiga-tekong-tki-illegal-ditangkap-saat-hendak-berangkatkan-puluhan-tki.

———. 2016. "Ini Jurus Pemuda Pancasila Anambas Perangi Narkoba". 7 August 2016. http://batam.tribunnews.com/2016/08/07/ini-jurus-pemuda-pancasila-anambas-perangi-narkoba.

———. 2016. "Antisipasi Mudik Natal-Tahun Baru, Gubernur Inspeksi Pelabuhan Kijang". 16 December 2016. http://batam.tribunnews.com/2016/12/16/antisipasi-mudik-natal-tahun-baru-gubernur-inspeksi-pelabuhan-kijang.

———. 2017. "Polresta Barelang Buka Posko Korban Kapal TKI Tenggelam di Pelabuhan Batam Centre". 24 January 2017.

http://batam.tribunnews.com/2017/01/24/polresta-barelang-buka-posko-korban-kapal-tki-tenggelam-di-pelabuhan-batam-centre.

———. 2017. "BNN Kepri Tangkap Kurir Sabu di Pelabuhan Karimun, Diduga Sabu Sekilo dari Malaysia". 14 February 2017. http://batam.tribunnews.com/2017/02/14/bnn-kepri-tangkap-kurir-sabu-di-pelabuhan-karimun-diduga-sabu-sekilo-dari-malaysia.

———. 2017. "Sabu Asal Malaysia Lagi, Lewat Pelabuhan Tikus Lagi. BNN: Kerja Keras Terus Kita!" 17 February 2017. http://batam.tribunnews.com/2017/02/17/sabu-asal-malaysia-lagi-lewat-pelabuhan-tikus-lagi-bnn-kerja-keras-kita.

Tribun Manado. 2011. "BM Minsel Kecam Bom Solo". 25 September 2011. http://manado.tribunnews.com/2011/09/25/bm-minsel-kecam-bom-solo.

———. 2011. "LSM di Minut Desak Polisi Usut Proyek Bermasalah". 21 December 2011. http://manado.tribunnews.com/2011/12/21/lsm-di-minut-desak-polisi-usut-proyek-bermasalah.

———. 2012. "Jeffry Tak Gentar dengan Nama Besar". 8 August 2012. http://manado.tribunnews.com/2012/08/08/jefry-tak-gentar-dengan-nama-besar.

———. 2012. "Waraney Esa Bitung Angkut Puluhan Karung Berisi Sampah". 11 August 2012. http://manado.tribunnews.com/2012/08/11/waraney-esa-bitung-angkut-puluhan-karung-berisi-sampah.

———. 2012. "BM Sinyalir Sulut Diincar Teroris". 7 November 2012. http://manado.tribunnews.com/2012/11/07/bm-sinyalir-sulut-diincar-teroris.

———. 2013. "HUT ke-11 BMI, Tonaas Wangku: Jangan Masuk Ranah Politik". 9 March 2013. http://manado.tribunnews.com/2013/03/09/hut-ke-11-bmi-tonaas-wangku-jangan-masuk-ranah-politik.

———. 2013. "Waraney Minta Pemko 'Basmi' LSM tak Terdaftar". 7 June 2013. http://manado.tribunnews.com/2013/06/07/waraney-minta-pemko-basmi-lsm-tak-terdaftar.

———. 2014. "Milisi Waraney: Cegah Paham Radikal Masuk". 8 August 2014. http://manado.tribunnews.com/2014/08/08/milisi-waraney-cegah-paham-radikal-masuk.

———. 2014. "Waraney Puser Intana Tolak Paham ISIS". 15 August 2014. http://manado.tribunnews.com/2014/08/15/waraney-puser-intana-tolak-paham-isis.

———. 2014. "Pelantikan Pdt Batara Rocky Ronoko sebagai Tonaas Brigade Manguni Manado". 27 August 2014. http://manado.tribunnews.com/2014/08/27/pelantikan-pdt-batara-rocky-ronoko-sebagai-tonaas-brigade-manguni-manado.

———. 2015. "Wakapolda Sulut Harapkan Brigade Manguni Contohi Pecalang di Bali". 5 February 2015a.

———. 2015. "Jangan Sampai Masyarakat Takut Lihat Seragam BM". 5 February 2015b.

———. 2015. "Bupati Minahasa Minta Polisi Tegas Soal Perkelahian Karena Miras". 5 May 2015. http://manado.tribunnews.com/2015/05/05/bupati-minahasa-minta-polisi-tegas-soal-perkelahian-karena-miras.

———. 2015. "Waraney Selenggarakan Turnamen Futsal Sekaligus Ajarkan Budaya". 5 September 2015. http://manado.tribunnews.com/2015/09/05/waraney-selenggarakan-turnamen-futsal-sekaligus-ajarkan-budaya.

Viva. 2010. "Politisi DPR Setuju Anggaran Densus 88 Naik". 28 September 2010. http://politik.news.viva.co.id/news/read/180064-anggaran-densus-88-naik-dengan-catatan.

———. 2012. "Kemeriahan Tahun Baru di Berbagai Kota Indonesia". 31 December 2012.

Index

"411" protest movement, 70
9/11 attacks
   aftermath, 33, 135, 140
   international pressure, and, 22–30
   Islamic organizations, and, 141
   security improvement, and, 1–2, 8, 18, 21–22, 34, 45–46, 139

A
Abdul Haris Nasution, 52
"Action to Defend Islam (Aksi Bela Islam)", 71
Agency for National Unity and Politics (Badan Kesatuan Bangsa dan Politik)
   Bitung Township, branch of, 98
   early awareness forum, and establishment of, 61, 87–88
   funds allocation, and, 82–83
   North Sulawesi, branch of, 96
   organizations registered with the, 49, 137
Agus Harimurti Yudhoyono, 69
Ahmadiyah, 57
Ahmad Yani, 52
AIDS awareness, 119
"Alert Meeting" (Apel Siaga), 117
Aliansi Masyarakat Jakarta (AMJ), 57
Al Qaeda, 23
Ambalat block, dispute in, 54
American Studies Center, 16
Amurang Port, 4
Andi Anzhar Cakrawijaya, 57

Angkatan Muda Pembaharuan, 4
Anies Baswedan, 69, 70–71
anti-terrorism agency (BNPT), 37–38
anti-terrorism legislation, 24, 141
ASEAN, 51
Assistance of the Indonesian National Armed Forces Law, 13
Association of the Indonesian Independence Supporters (Ikatan Pendukung Kemerdekaan Indonesia), 52
Australian Embassy, bomb attack, 24
authoritarian regime, 4, 11, 35, 41, 46, 134, 136
authority, source of, 5–6
Automatic Identification System (AIS), 20

B
Badan Keamanan Rakyat, 32
Bali bombings, 1, 8, 18, 21, 24–25, 135, 141
Bamus Betawi (Badan Musyawarah Masyarakat Betawi), 45, 55, 60, 63
Banjarmasin Port, 28
Basuki Tjahja Purnama (Ahok), 45, 58, 60, 137
   protests against, 69–71, 74
Batak, ethnic group, 56
Batam
   illicit activities in, 121–29, 136
   ports in, 107

preman and youth organizations in, 109, 119
see also Riau Islands; Tanjung Pinang
Batam Centre Port, 113, 123
Batam Concession Agency (BP Batam), 120–21, 127
Batam International Ferry Terminal, 5
Batam Naval Base, 113
Batam Post, 18, 117
Batu Ampar Ferry Terminal, 5
Belawan International Container Port, 120
Belawan Multi-Purpose Terminal, 28
Berita Manado, 92
Betawi culture consultative body, *see* Bamus Betawi
Betawi, ethnic group, 55–56, 60–61
BIN (Badan Intelijen Negara), 61, 87
Bitung Port, 4–5, 30, 82, 89, 93, 98
border security, 15–17, 44, 117–18, 138
Brigade Manguni
    counterterrorism, support for, 84
    ethnic-based organization, as, 136, 141
    funding of, 82–83
    government officials, and relations with, 137
    members, 80
    North Sulawesi, in, 80–100
    paramilitary wing, 81, 87, 97
    police, cooperation with, 30, 89–100
political candidate, and support for, 45
Brunei-Indonesia-Malaysia-Philippines East ASEAN Growth Area (BIMP-EAGA), 5
Buhias port, 5
Bukide port, 5
Bumbung Pramiadi, 123
Bush, President, 24

C

Caltex Oil Terminal Dumai, 28
Charles Ngili, 92
Civil Defence (Pertahanan Sipil), 32
civilians, and defence role, 41–43, 118
civil society
    agents for change, as, 11
    concept of, 140
    data collection, and, 17
    establishment of, 3
    military organizations, and relations with, 9
    principles of, 14
    state defence, and, 34, 40
    study of, 12–15
    uncivil elements of, 30–31
Civil Society Network for Security Sector Reform, 13
civil society organizations (CSOs)
    definition, 31–32
    formation of, 30–31
    funding allocation to, 18
    grants and social assistance to, 62, 64–65
    organizations registered as, 108
    port security, and involvement with, 19, 30, 50
    preman organizations, as, 31, 50, 54, 90–91
    radical, 85
    study of, 12–15
    see also un-civil organizations
CNN, 23
coalition pattern, and political system, 7
community-based monitoring system (Siswasmas), 43
containerization policy, 51–53, 135
Coordination Forum for Terrorism Prevention (Forum Koordinasi Pencegahan Terorisme), 29, 61
Coordinating Ministry for Political, Legal and Security Affairs, 15, 18, 34, 39, 42, 44, 70, 139
Core Command (Koti), 52, 118
counterterrorism
    Brigade Manguni support for, 84
    Forum Betawi Rempug support for, 29–30
    government approach to, 22, 36, 45, 135–36
    intelligence, 96
    measures adopted, 8, 13, 24–25, 27, 38
    military participation in, 14
    policies, 34
    programmes, 29–30
    spending on, 17, 38
    see also terrorism
COVID-19 pandemic, 38
customs clearance system, 26

D

Daecky Maengkom, 97
decentralization, 139
Directorate General of Customs, 72
Directorate General of Sea Transportation, 15, 59, 63, 91, 112
Directorate General of Transportation, 89

Djasri Marin, 42
Dompak port, 5
drug smuggling, 72
Dutch colonial authority, 9–10, 32, 55

E

Early Awareness Forum (Forum Kewaspadaan Dini), 29, 61–62, 88, 94
East Asia Summit, 36
Edy Waleleng, 79
electoral violence, 141–42
electronic cargo information, 26
Elsam, 13
Embun Pelangi, 127
ethnic-based gangs, 52
extortion, 120–21

F

Facebook, 89
Fadloli El Muhir, 55, 57
Fauzi Bowo (Foke), 58, 60
Forum Betawi Rempug (FBR)
  command centres, 58–59
  conflicts, and, 51, 66–69
  counterterrorism programmes, engagement with, 29–30
  election campaign, involvement in, 45
  establishment, 55–56
  ethnic-based, 12, 50, 61, 73, 141
  members, 56–60
  operation, 59
  parent organization, 63
  political protests, and, 69–71
  security services, and, 59–62, 73–74, 135
  support for, 44
  undercover tasks, and, 61
  vigilantism, and, 57
Forum Komunikasi Anak Betawi (Forkabi), 45, 50, 66, 71
Forum Komunikasi Putra Putri Purnawirawan dan Putra Putri TNI Polri (FKPPI), 62, 118
Forum Pembela Islam, 50
Forum Umat Islam, 71
Fransiskus Xaverius Hadi Rudyatmo, 69
Free Aceh Movement, 22
Fretelin/Falintil, 22
Front Pembela Islam (FPI), 57, 69–71, 85, 120

G

gamma ray scanner, 27

Garda Nusantara, 118
Garuda Indonesian Airways, hijacking of, 22
Gatot Subroto, 52
Gerakan Anti-Trafficking, 127
Gerakan Pemuda Ansor, 4, 108
Gerakan Pemuda Kabah, 3, 50
globalization, 5–7
global maritime fulcrum (GMF), 36–37
Golkar, 35, 79
gubernatorial election, 58, 63, 69, 71, 74, 112, 137

H

Habib Rizieq Shihab, 70
Haji Lulung, 117
Hang Nadim Airport, 113
Hanny Pantouw, 82, 96–97
Hanura, 35
Harbour Bay Ferry Terminal, 5
Hendrik Hermanus Joel Ngantung, 69
Hi-Co scan device, 27
House of Representatives, 13
human rights, 14, 56
human trafficking, 19, 94, 97–98, 106, 120, 122
  countering, 125–27

I

Ikatan Pemuda Karya (IPK), 3, 12, 108, 110, 115–16, 118
  police, cooperation with, 125
Ikatan Pemuda Nahdatul Ulama, 4
illegal, unreported and unregulated (IUU) fishing, 99, 138
IMO regulations, 20
Indonesia
  exports, 4
  independence, 32, 46
  maritime territory, 1–2, 36
  national defence, 32
  non-oil exports, and, 51
  population, 4
  terrorist attacks in, 22–24
"Indonesia Awesome Coalition" (Koalisi Indonesia Hebat), 35
Indonesian Armed Forces (TNI), 13, 33, 39, 116
Indonesian Communist Party, 10
Indonesian Customs, 27
Indonesian Maritime Board, 33, 39, 41–42
Indonesian National Defence Institute (Lemhanas), 42

Indonesian Navy, 37–39
Indonesian Ports Cooperation, 28
Indonesian Red Cross, 119
Indonesian special forces (Kopassus), 118
Indonesian Ulema Council, 70
Indonesian waters, vessels plying, 20
Indonesia Onward Coalition (Koalisi Indonesia Maju), 35
Intelkam, 61
Intel Kramat Tujuh, 61
Internal Security Act, Singapore, 24
International Maritime Organization, 112
International Port Security Program, 28
International Ship and Port Facility Security Code (ISPS), 2, 29, 71, 89, 112–13
Islamic groups, 3, 31
Islamic State of Iraq and Syria (ISIS), 38, 70, 85, 94
Islamic terrorism, 85

J
Jakarta
  indigenous people of, 55
  ports in, 49
  territory of, 49
Jakarta International Container Terminal, 28, 59
Jakarta Post, 18, 73, 80, 93
Jakarta Supreme Advisory Council, 57
Jamaah Ansharut Daulah, 23
Jamaah Ansharut Tauhid, 23
Jamaah Islamiyah, 23, 94
Japanese occupation, 9–10
Jaringan Penyelamat Umat Islam, 120
Jeffry Mentu, 45
Joint Betawi Forum (Forum Betawi Bersatu), 69
Joko Widodo (Jokowi)
  presidential election, and, 35, 45
  gubernatorial campaign, and, 58, 69
  maritime security spending, under, 36–39
  preman organizations under, 34
Jusuf Kalla, 35
Juwono Sudarsono, 34

K
Kabil Marine and Oil Base Port, 5
Kahakitang port, 5
Kalama port, 5
Kawaluso port, 5
Kawio port, 5
Ken Arok, robber king, 9
Ketupat Operation, 114
Koja port, 29
Komando Bela Negara, 87
Komando Inti, 111
Kompas, 18, 63, 80, 112
Kontras, 13
Koperasi Abadi, 124
Krisno Siregar, 92

L
LAB 45, 23
land disputes, 66
Laskar Bali, 30
Laskar Merah Putih, 73–74
Law No. 2/2002 on the Indonesian Police, 13, 40
Law No. 3/2002 on State Defence, 13, 40–41
Law No. 17/2013, 73
Law No. 34/2004 on the Indonesian Armed Forces, 13
Lee Kuan Yew, 23
Lembaga Studi Pertahanan dan Studi Strategis Indonesia, 13
Lilin Operation, 114
Lipang port, 5
Local Intelligence Committee (Komite Intelijen Daerah), 29, 61
Lutfi Hakim, 45, 55–56, 61

M
Madurese, ethnic group, 56, 61
Majelis Mujahidin Indonesia, 120
Makobar Port, 115
Manado Port, 4, 91, 98
Manado Post, 18, 83–84, 86, 91, 93, 97
maritime security
  challenges to, 46, 135, 139
  exercises, 28
  expert, 110
  governance, 39
  policy, 24
  preman organizations for, use of, 10, 98, 142
  research on, 15
  responsibility for, 33
  spending for, 25–26, 36–37
  threats, 40, 42
Maritime Security Agency (Bakamla), 24–25, 29, 38
Maritime Security Coordinating Board (Bakorkamla), 24

maritime security directive, 28
maritime security spending, 37–38
maritime trade, 27, 46, 141
maritime traffic, 2, 4
Marriott Hotel, bomb attack, 24
Ma'ruf Amin, 35, 70
Marunda Port, 72
Matutuang port, 5
Mbah Priok, sacred tomb of, 67–68, 74
Megawati Soekarno Putri, 33, 39, 57, 89
Milisi Waraney
  electoral support, and, 45
  ethnic-based organization, as, 136
  funding of, 82–83
  members, 80
  North Sulawesi, in, 80–100
  security authorities, cooperation with, 30, 89–92, 95, 97–100, 137
Minahasan, ethnic group, 80
Ministry of Defence, 25–26, 37, 116, 139
Ministry of Home Affairs, 13, 31, 32, 52, 62, 137
Ministry of Law and Human Rights, 62
Ministry of Maritime and Fisheries Affairs, 41
Ministry of Transportation, 25, 54, 90
MITA risk-profiling system, 27, 141
Mohammad Iqbal, 68
monitoring, controlling, and surveillance (MCS) system, 43
Muara Angke fishing port, 72
Mujahidin Indonesia Barat, 23
Mujahidin Indonesia Timur, 23
Musyawarah Kekeluargaan Gotong Royong (MKGR), 44

N
Nachrowi Ramli, 57–58
Nahdlatul Ulama, 3, 35, 80
NasDem, 35
national anti-terrorism board, 96
National Defence Board, 15
National Defence Council (Dewan Ketahanan Nasional), 43, 116
national defence system, 40–41
National Human Rights Commission of Indonesia, 57, 93–94
national intelligence body, *see* BIN
nationalism, 41–42
national legislative election, 4
national logistics agency (Bulog), 124–25
National Narcotics Bureau, 72, 123
National Search and Rescue Agency (Basarnas), 118
neorealism, 6
New Order, 3, 9–10, 52, 55, 78–79, 135–36, 138
"new war", 6
NGOs (non-governmental organizations), 15, 17, 53, 57, 127
Nicholas Undap, 82, 86
Nongsa Pura Ferry Port, 5
North Sulawesi
  Agency for National Unity and Politics, branch of, 96
  Brigade Manguni in, 80–100
  container ports in, 4–5
  geographical landscape, 19
  Milisi Waraney in, 80–100
  Pemuda Pancasila (PP) in, 78–79
  preman organizations in, 80–81, 88
  territory of, 77

O
Organisasi Papua Merdeka (OPM), 22

P
Padang, ethnic group, 56
Pam Swakarsa (voluntary security forces), 43
paramilitary group
  Brigade Manguni, 81, 87, 97
  civilian, 34
  developing world, in, 10
  martial arts training, and, 52
  membership of, 2–3
  Pemuda Pancasila (PP), 111, 118
  political parties, association with, 11
  state authority, and, 6
  state-sponsored, 31
Partai Amanah Rakyat, 57
Partai Demokrasi Indonesia Perjuangan (PDIP), 35
Partai Keadilan dan Persatuan Indonesia, 35
Partai Kebangkitan Bangsa (PKB), 35
Partai Persatuan Pembangunan (United Development Party), 3, 35
Pelantar Dua port, 5, 110
Pelindo II Conventional Terminal Jakarta, 28
Pemuda Alawiyah, 4
Pemuda Ansor, 3, 12
Pemuda Muhammadiyah, 4
Pemuda Muslimin, 4

Pemuda Panca Marga (PPM)
  funding of, 62–63
  ideology, 50
  military training, 118, 136
  members, 108, 116
  security contracts, and, 113
  state-sponsored, 31
Pemuda Pancasila (PP)
  conflicts, 66–68, 119–20
  gangster organization, as, 3, 63
  government authorities, cooperation with, 90, 95, 112–19, 124
  government-registered, 52
  ideology, 50
  influence, 54
  members, 12, 108
  nationalist outlook, 4
  National Leadership Council, 124–25
  North Sulawesi, in, 78–79
  paramilitary wing, 111, 118
  ports, and control of, 18
  reduction of role, and, 53, 73
  state-sponsored, 31
  support for, 44
Peoples' Security Organization (Organisasi Keamanan Rakyat), 32
Persatuan Pemuda Tempatan, 141
Persaudaraan Muslimin Indonesia, 71
Pertamina Unit Pengolahan II Dumai, 28
Pertamina Unit Pengolahan V Balikpapan, 28
Pesantren Ziyadatul Mukhtadi'ien, 55
Petta port, 5
Police Partners' Communication Centre (Sentra Komunikasi Mitra Polisi), 126
politics of exclusion, 55
Port Authority, 15
port labour, 52–54, 79, 129, 135
Port of Belawan, 12
port security advisories (PSAs), 2, 18, 21, 28, 29, 45–46, 67
ports management, 28
Portuguese colonial authority, 9–10
Prabowo Subianto, 45, 69, 83
preman organizations
  areas of work, 22
  conflicts among, 3, 49, 66, 67, 74, 119–21
  CSOs, as, 31, 50, 54, 90–91
  funding of, 15, 81–83
  government authorities, assisting, 29, 46, 94–100, 114, 119, 126
  government-registered, 52
  government, tensions with, 63, 66, 74, 107, 136–37
  illicit activities, and, 50–51, 63, 71–73, 107, 120–21, 127–29, 134, 137
  Joko Widodo, role under, 34
  labour associations, control over, 114–15, 129
  maritime security, and, 10, 98, 142
  members, 2–3, 44
  military training, and, 89, 118, 136
  North Sulawesi, in, 80–81, 88
  political support, as source of, 44–45
  politics, involvement in, 69, 142
  representatives of, 16–18
  state instrument of violence, as, 10
  Tanjung Pinang, in, 108, 110, 119
  terrorism, and combating, 19, 62, 100
Presidential Decree, 13
presidential election, 4, 35, 38, 45, 69, 83
Presidential Emergency Decree on the Prevention of Terrorism, 24
Presidential Instruction, 51, 53
Priority Line risk-profiling system, 27, 141
private military companies (PMCs), 8
ProPatria, 13
PT Badak Bontang, 28
PT Dua Karya Abadi, 120–21
PT Gerbang Nusa Perkasa, 93
PT Indominco Mandiri Bontang, 28
PT Kembang Utara, 93
PT Mikgro Metal Perdana, 93
PT Multimas Nabati Asahan, 28
PT Pelabuhan Indonesia, 59
PT Pelabuhan Indonesia I Cabang Dumai, 28
PT Pelindo II, 67, 87
PT Pertamina Plant, 67
PT Pertamina Unit Pemasaran III, 28
PT Philia Citra Sejahtera, 68
PT Pupuk Kaltim Bontang, 28
PT Terminal Peti Kemas Surabaya, 28

R

Raja Ali Haji, 110
"rat ports", 115–16, 122–26
Regional Financial and Property Management Agency, 82
regional intelligence community (Kominda), 88
Riau Islands

illicit activities in, 121–29
territory of, 106
trafficking transit points, as, 121–22
see also Batam; Tanjung Pinang
Riau Islands Chamber of Commerce, 115, 125
risk-profiling system, 27, 46
Ritz Carlton Hotel, bomb attack, 24
Rohingya refugees, 120
Rumah Faye, 127

S
Samudera port, 72, 74
Sanur Bersatu, 30
Satpol Pamong Praja, 67–68, 87, 120
Sawang port, 5
sea lanes of communications (SLOC), 3
sea robbery, 23
sectarian violence, 80
security, privatization of, 6–7, 10
Sekupang Ferry Terminal, 5
Sekupang Port, 115
Semarang International Container Terminal, 28
Senipah Terminal Total E&P Indonesia Balikpapan, 28
September 11 attacks, *see* 9/11 attacks
shipping trade, 4
Singapore-Johor-Riau (SIJORI) growth triangle, 5
Societe Generale de Surveilance, 52
Sonny Sariowan, 85
Sony Sumarsono, 86
South China Sea, disputed areas of, 118, 142
Sri Bintan port, 5
Sripayung Batu port, 5
state defence programme (Bela Negara), 61
state intelligence agency, *see* BIN
State Intelligence Law, 13
Stefy Yance Mamuya, 68
Strait of Lombok, 2–4
Strait of Malacca, 2–5, 138–39
smuggling, and, 122
vessels plying, 24
Strait of Singapore, 2–3, 5
vessels plying, 24
Student Army (Tentara Pelajar), 32
Suharto, 3, 9–11, 35, 40–41, 46, 78, 134, 139
resignation of, 12, 22, 30–31, 50, 55
Suhartono, 117
Suka Duka Baladika Bali, 30

"Sunda Kelapa declaration", 33–34
Sunda Strait, 2–4, 139
Sungai Jang port, 5
Supreme Court, 93
Suristiyono, 43
surveillance team (Tim Wara Wiri), 61
Susilo Bambang Yudhoyono, 34, 40, 69
Sutarman, 38
Sutiyoso, 57

T
Tahuna port, 5
Tanjung Emas port, 28
Tanjung Merbau port, 5
Tanjung Perak port, 27–28
Tanjung Pinang, 5, 20
illicit activities in, 121–29, 136
ports in, 107
preman organizations in, 108, 110, 119
see also Batam; Riau Islands
Tanjung Priok Port, 4, 27–28, 50, 74, 123
busiest container port, as, 49
conflicts in, 67–68
employment opportunities, 52–54
largest port, as, 51
Tanjung Unggat Port, 110
Telaga Punggur Domestic Port, 5
terrorism
combating, 84–85, 89, 94, 139
funding to deal with, 25
global, 7, 47
government approach to, 135–36
measures adopted against, 8, 13, 27
preman organizations, and role combating, 19, 62, 100
prevention of, 61, 96, 97
reported acts of, 22–24
threats, 36, 40
war against, 29–30, 46
see also counterterrorism
"terrorist nest, a", 23
Tim Manguni Polda Resort, 89
Tjahjo Kumolo, 94
Total People's Defence and Security System (Sistem Pertahanan Keamanan Rakyat Semesta), 32, 41–43, 46, 139
doctrine, 33, 40
tribalism, 141
Tribun Batam, 18, 111, 112, 119–20, 123
Tribun Manado, 18, 83–86, 91–93, 96

U

Ucok Cantik, 119
un-civil organizations, 14, 31, 140
    see also civil society organizations (CSOs)
Universitas Indonesia, 16
Universitas Maritim, 110
Urban Poor Community (KMK), 57, 63
US Coast Guard, 2, 18, 21, 28–29, 67
US ports, 2

V

Village Guerrilla and Security Forces (Pasukan Gerilya Desa and Organisasi Keamanan Desa), 32

W

Wardah Hafidz, 57
war on terror, 24, 29, 35, 140–41
"war zone", 118
Waterfront City Teluk Senimba Ferry Terminal, 5
Wilmar Marpaung, 84, 95, 97
Wolfowitz, Paul, 23
World Customs Organization Data Model, 26
World War II, 10

X

X-ray scanners, 27

Y

Yapto, 79
youth organizations (OKP), 114

About the Author

Senia Febrica is the Knowledge Exchange Associate and an early career researcher at the One Ocean Hub, the University of Strathclyde, Scotland. She is also an honorary senior researcher at the American Studies Center, Universitas Indonesia, and the Indonesian Institute of Advanced International Studies (INADIS), Jakarta, Indonesia. Her research sits at the intersection between international relations, security studies, and the study of international organizations. Specifically, it focuses on maritime security cooperation and the particular challenges it poses in Southeast Asia (paying special attention to Indonesia, Malaysia, Singapore and the Philippines). She has conducted research on international cooperation to tackle a range of non-traditional maritime security issues—such as piracy and armed robbery against ships; marine pollution; and illegal, unreported and unregulated (IUU) fishing in Southeast Asia—and the role of traditional authorities in resolving conflict over natural resources in Indonesia.

Febrica received her doctorate from the University of Glasgow. Prior to joining the One Ocean Hub, she worked as a researcher for the American Studies Center at Universitas Indonesia. Febrica was a United Nations–Nippon Foundation Fellow (2012–13) and a Gerda Henkel Stiftung postdoctoral fellow (2015–17). This book is based on her postdoctoral research titled "The Securitization of Indonesia's Maritime Borders: Outsourcing of Border Security to Militarized Non-governmental Organizations", which was funded by Gerda Henkel Stiftung. The findings and opinions expressed in this publication are not those of the One Ocean Hub, Gerda Henkel Stiftung, the American Studies Center, Universitas Indonesia, or INADIS.

Dr Febrica's first book, *Maritime Security and Indonesia: Cooperation, Interests, and Strategies*, was published in 2017, and her second manuscript, *Indonesia and the Indo-Pacific*, was published in 2023.

www.ingramcontent.com/pod-product-compliance
Lightning Source LLC
Chambersburg PA
CBHW070640300426
44111CB00013B/2183